AF328714

Book Yourself Solid

for CREATIVES

The Fastest, Easiest, Most Reliable System *for* Getting More Clients Than You Can Handle, Even if You Hate Marketing *and* Selling

Michael Port
New York Times Bestselling Author

with **Joana Galvão**

WILEY

Library of Congress Cataloging-in-Publication Data is Available:

ISBN: 9781394236275 (cloth)
ISBN: 9781394236282 (ePub)
ISBN: 9781394236299 (ePDF)

COVER DESIGN: WILEY

Printed and bound in Great Britain by Bell & Bain Ltd, Glasgow

This book is a love story disguised as a business book. It's a love story between you and all the inspiring clients you will serve.

Contents

Joana's Note   *vii*

Preface   *xi*

Acknowledgments   *xv*

MODULE ONE   Your Foundation   **1**

CHAPTER 1   The Red Velvet Rope Policy   3

CHAPTER 2   Why People Buy What You're Selling   17

CHAPTER 3   Develop a Personal Brand   34

CHAPTER 4   How to Talk About What You Do   49

MODULE TWO   Building Trust and Credibility   **61**

CHAPTER 5   Becoming a Likable Expert in Your Field   63

CHAPTER 6   The Book Yourself Solid Sales Cycle Process   75

CHAPTER 7   The Book Yourself Solid Keep-in-Touch Strategy   92

MODULE THREE   Simple Selling and Perfect Pricing   **105**

CHAPTER 8   Perfect Pricing   107

CHAPTER 9   Super Simple Selling   120

**MODULE FOUR   The Book Yourself Solid Six
Core Self-Promotion Strategies**   **129**

CHAPTER 10   The Book Yourself Solid Networking Strategy   133

CHAPTER 11   The Book Yourself Solid Direct Outreach Strategy   155

CHAPTER 12   The Book Yourself Solid Referral Strategy   177

CHAPTER 13   The Book Yourself Solid Speaking Strategy   188

CHAPTER 14   The Book Yourself Solid Writing Strategy   213

CHAPTER 15   The Book Yourself Solid Web Strategy   230

Part 1   Designing Your Website   232

Part 2   Getting Visitors to Your Website   242

Part 3   Building Your Social Media Platform   254

Final Thoughts   269

References   273

Ready to Be Fully Booked?   275

About the Authors   277

Index   279

Joana's Note

> *You can't connect the dots looking forward; you can*
> *only connect them looking back.*
> —Steve Jobs

Early into my first job as a graphic designer for an award-winning London-based design agency, I found myself increasingly dissatisfied with my job and career prospects. The notion of a 9-to-5 job for the rest of my life felt like a prison – long hours, limited holidays, and a lack of creative freedom that stifled my passion and ambition. Sound familiar? I decided to embark on a new path and take the leap into freelancing, where I could fully express my creativity and build my career on my own terms. I secretly spent my hour-long commute and lunch times reading, researching, studying, and honing my skills. That's where I came across the original *Book Yourself Solid* by Michael Port, first released in 2006 (Wiley).

In the original author's note, Michael shared the challenges he faced when starting his own business and how these difficulties propelled him to develop the *Book Yourself Solid* system, a comprehensive marketing and business system designed specifically for service professionals. Michael detailed how he meticulously researched, tested, and refined the system, transforming his own business in the process. He then went on to share this system with his clients, helping countless other service professionals attract more clients, increase their income, and build fulfilling careers. Inspired by his success and the proven effectiveness of the system, I thought, "If it worked for all those people, it could certainly work for me as long as I put in the effort."

There was too much at stake for me, and failing wasn't an option. I was going against everyone's advice. My mum said, "You have no clue how to serve a client; quitting so early in your career is just silly." My senior designer warned, "You have no clients. Going out on your own is career suicide." Some of my peers added, "You need at least another decade if you're going to make it work." But after reading all the reviews and researching the success of the book up to that day, I knew I was in good company. Armed with book in hand, I handed in my resignation letter and got to work.

The promise of the book was delivered. I not only fell in love with marketing and selling by turning it into a meaningful pursuit, but I quickly was booked solid with more clients than I could handle. Ten months into implementing the system, and at age 22, I had a six-figure creative business that quickly turned into a 10-person design agency.

When the book was released in April 2006, *Book Yourself Solid* was the number-two best-selling book on Amazon – not just in the business category but number two in *all* books. It has since become an evergreen resource for professional service providers all over the United States, the United Kingdom, and Canada. It's been translated into Spanish, Vietnamese, Bulgarian, Polish, Bahasa Indonesian, Orthodox Chinese, Korean, and others. It's included in the curriculums at graduate-level business schools and is touted as recommended reading by professional associations like the National Association of Realtors, which called *Book Yourself Solid* a "must read."

Combining all the revised and complementary editions, *Book Yourself Solid* has sold more than a million copies. While Michael shared in the original note that he was surprised by the book's success, those who read it and implement the system aren't.

Later in my career, in 2021, I was considering launching a coaching business alongside my agency to help other creative service professionals grow their businesses. I discovered that I could get certified in teaching the *Book Yourself Solid* system. Having experienced firsthand the effectiveness of the system and being able to stand wholeheartedly behind it, it was a no-brainer for me. I jumped at the chance.

Since getting certified, I have coached more than 200 students in more than 40 countries and led them through the *Book Yourself Solid* system. Similar to Michael's experience, I watched their success unfold before my eyes.

I could hear confidence, pride, and accomplishment in their voices. Their businesses took off. My students, who were creative service providers of all kinds – graphic designers, illustrators, copywriters, photographers, video editors, web designers – started to get booked solid (well, most of them – the ones who did the work).

Every now and then, I'd email Michael about some of their success stories, sharing gratitude for making this available for certification so more of us could share the system and with it, help more service providers. But I wasn't expecting what came next.

In the spring of 2023, I received an email that had me dancing across my whole house with joy. Michael was inviting me to cowrite with him this very book you're holding in your hands: an updated version of the original *Book Yourself Solid* book but specific to creative service professionals like yourself.

Together, we want you to know it is realistic for you to become a successful creative service provider. But you need to learn the skills necessary to promote your work and become the go-to creative in your area before it's too late. There is no question that the *Book Yourself Solid* system can change your business and your life.

You love what you do. You're great at what you do. You stand in the service of others, you change lives, and you are a remarkable human being for doing so – now it's time to get booked solid.

This book offers a way toward a profitable, meaningful, and absolutely booked-solid creative business, overflowing with as many clients as your heart desires – clients who energize and inspire you, clients with whom you do your best work, clients who will pay you handsomely.

We hope you feel the same exhilaration in building your creative business as I did along with the thousands of other service professionals that have been supported and propelled by the *Book Yourself Solid* system every day. We expect that this system will not only inspire you but will keep you keenly focused on learning and relearning, experimenting, and honing all that is within you. We are certain the secret to your success isn't just in the work that we do together. It lies within you. *Book Yourself Solid for Creatives* will simply help facilitate your greatness.

We are all on this path together, learning from one another. We are all seeking joy, love, success, and happiness. Continue to trust that you are making a huge difference in the lives of your clients, yourself, and society as a whole.

Here's to you – to focusing on getting as many clients as your heart desires. Please come to the *Book Yourself Solid* system with an open heart and mind. Completely remove, or at least set aside, any preconceived ideas fluttering in your head. Let the process be revealed to you step-by-step.

The *Book Yourself Solid* way is one of abundance, joy, and meaning. It's our deep honor to serve you. As any silly, serious, significant, strategic, personal, or professional questions come up, please give me a shout. I'm always delighted to hear from you. Fire off any and all questions to me at joana@gifdesignstudios.com. If there is anything we can do to serve you, please just ask.

Warmly,
Joana Galvão

Preface

The Book Yourself Solid system is supported by both practical and philosophical principles.

From a practical perspective, there may be two simple reasons why you don't serve as many clients as you'd like to today. Either you don't know what to do to attract and secure more clients or you know what to do but you're not actually doing it. The Book Yourself Solid system is designed to help you solve both of these problems, including the information you need to book more clients. If you already know what to do but aren't doing it, we hope to inspire you into action and help you stay accountable so you build the business of your dreams. Moreover, you may be surprised to learn that marketing isn't really what gets you clients. It's what you do once someone becomes aware of you that books you the business. The Book Yourself Solid system is designed to show you how to create the awareness you need for the services you offer and then exactly what to do to book the business once someone becomes aware of you.

From a philosophical perspective, we believe that if you have something to say, if you have a message to deliver, and if there are people you want to serve, then there are people in this world whom you are *meant* to serve. Not kinda, sorta, because they're in your target market . . . but *meant* to. If this doesn't resonate for you now, we believe it will when you have read this book and begun to follow the Book Yourself Solid way.

The system is organized into four modules:

Your Foundation
Building Trust and Credibility
Simple Selling and Perfect Pricing
The Book Yourself Solid Six Core Self-Promotion Strategies

We will begin by building a foundation for your creative business that is unshakable. If you are truly serious about becoming a successful creative service provider, you must have a steadfast foundation on which to stand. You will then be ready to create and implement a strategy for building trust and credibility. You'll be considered a credible expert in your field, and you'll start to earn the trust of the people you'd like to serve. You'll price your offerings in the sweet spot of the client's desires, and you'll know how to have sales conversations of the highest integrity that work. Then, and only then, will you execute the six core self-promotion strategies, thereby creating awareness for the valuable services you offer by using promotional strategies that are based on your talents – strategies that feel authentic and honest.

To help you design a service business overflowing with clients who inspire and energize you, this book includes written exercises and Booked Solid Action Steps that will support you in thinking bigger about your business. We walk you through the steps on the path to serving as many clients as your heart desires.

You will want to retain your responses to the written exercises for regular review. We have prepared a complimentary downloadable workbook that includes all of the written exercises and Booked Solid Action Steps contained in this book. Simply visit the Book Yourself Solid website and download the workbook so that you may begin today to take the necessary steps to get more clients than you can handle.

Go to https://www.bookyourselfsolid.com/creativesworkbook and download your free copy of the workbook so you have it in your hands before you turn another page. So, your first Action Step is to get your workbook. While you'll no doubt get great value just from reading this book, the true value – and your success – lies in your decision to take an active role and to participate fully by doing the exercises and taking the Booked Solid Action Steps we've outlined.

Please work through Book Yourself Solid in sequential order. No skipping, jumping, or moving ahead – the Book Yourself Solid Six Core Self-Promotion Strategies are effectively implemented only after your foundation, credibility-building, pricing, and sales strategies are in place. One of the main reasons that creative service providers say they hate marketing and selling is that they're trying to market without these essential elements, which is like eating an egg before it's cooked – of course, you'll hate it. So, no matter how compelled you are to skip ahead, we urge you to *please* follow the system and watch the process unfold. Remember, self-promotion just creates awareness for the products and services you sell. It's what you do once someone becomes aware of you that earns you the business. All the marketing in the world won't do you much good if you have a weak foundation (or none at all), can't demonstrate credibility, and don't know how to earn trust, price your offers, or have an effective sales conversation.

So many talented and inspired creative service providers like you run from marketing and sales because they have come to believe that the marketing and selling process is pushy and self-centered and borders on sleazy. This old-school paradigm is not the Book Yourself Solid way. It is the typical client-snagging mentality. And you must *never* fall into this way of thinking and being. If you do, you'll operate in a mentality of scarcity and shame as opposed to one of abundance and integrity.

Ask yourself these questions:

- How can I be fully self-expressed in my work to create meaning for me and those whom I serve?
- How can I work only in the areas of my greatest strengths and talents so that I can shine?
- How many relationships with people of purpose did I make and deepen?
- How can I better listen to and serve my ideal clients?
- How can I wow people with substance?
- How can I over-deliver on my promises to my clients?
- How can I cooperate with other professionals to create more abundance?

If you keep asking yourself these questions, set a solid foundation for your business, build trust and credibility within your marketplace, learn how to price and sell your offerings, and use the Six Core Self-Promotion Strategies, you'll be booked solid in no time.

Acknowledgments

The first line of the acknowledgments section in virtually every book goes something like this: to list everyone we want to thank for their contributions to this book would be a book in itself. You really don't know how true that is until you write your own book. It seems like books are written by one person in solitary confinement in a cabin in the Berkshires or the French Alps. But rarely is that the case. This book is better because of the people around us. Family, friends, colleagues, and clients offer their ideas, relentlessly, at times. So, if you determine that what we've put on paper has merit, you can thank the people around us. They're the ones who deserve the credit. We just form the sentences.

Your Foundation

Being booked solid as a creative service provider requires that you have a solid foundation. That foundation begins like this:

- Choose your ideal clients so you work only with people who inspire and energize you.
- Understand why people buy what you are selling.
- Develop a personal brand to make you memorable and unique.
- Talk about what you do without sounding confusing or bland.

Over the course of Module One, we'll step you through the process of building your foundation so that you have a platform on which to stand, a perfectly engineered structure that will support all of your business development and marketing, and – dare we add – personal growth. That's because being in business for yourself, especially as someone who stands in the service of others, requires constant personal reflection and growth.

Over the years, we've found that many people want to hurry through the foundation and just get to the marketing. Please resist this temptation. Remember, marketing rarely gets you clients. What you do once someone becomes aware of you is what actually books you the business. We're aware that we've said this three times now. We'll say it again later. It bears repeating. You need a solid foundation on which to stand first.

Building your foundation may seem like a lot of work. Maybe it is. That all depends on your definition of work, we suppose. But having a solid foundation that feels secure to your potential clients is the first key to business success.

Building your foundation is a bit like putting a puzzle together. We're going to take it one piece at a time, and when we're done, you'll have laid the foundation for booking yourself solid.

The Red Velvet Rope Policy

He who trims himself to suit everyone will soon whittle himself away.
—Raymond Hull

Imagine that a friend has invited you to accompany her to an invitation-only special event. You arrive and approach the door, surprised to find a red velvet rope stretched between two shiny brass poles. A nicely dressed man asks your name, checking his invitation list. Finding your name there, he flashes a wide grin and drops one end of the rope, allowing you to pass through and enter the party. You feel like a star.

Do you have your own Red Velvet Rope Policy that allows in only the most ideal clients, the ones who energize and inspire you? If you don't, you will shortly. Why?

First, because when you work with clients you love, you'll truly enjoy the work you're doing; you'll love every minute of it. (Well, almost every minute of it. It is work, after all.) And when you love the work you do, you'll do your *best* work, which is essential to booking yourself solid.

Second, because you *are* your clients. They are an expression and an extension of you. Do you remember when you were a teenager and your mother or father would give you a hard time about someone you were hanging out with? Your parents may have said that a particular kid was a bad influence. As a teen, you may have thought about how unfair that felt, but the truth is that you are the company you keep. The people you spend time with make a significant impact on your state of mind and how you feel about yourself. Let this be the imperative of your business: choose your clients as carefully as you choose your friends.

The first step in building your foundation is to choose your ideal clients – the individuals or businesses with whom you do your best work or the people or environments that energize and inspire you. We're going to help you identify specific characteristics of individuals or organizations that would make them ideal to work with. You will then develop a rigorous screening process to find more of them. We're also going to help you prune your current client list of less-than-ideal clients.

When Joana began her career as a freelance graphic designer, she found herself lucky. Most of the clients that came her way seemed to all fit the description of "ideal client." That was until a particular sales call where the potential client raised a handful of red flags. In an attempt to scare the client away, Joana asked for double what she normally would for the project, and to her surprise, the client said yes.

As she dove into the project, she started to dread working on it, not because of the creative challenge itself but because of the client's behavior. This particular client didn't seem to value her creative input, would delay payments, and was overly critical of her work. They asked for more rounds of revisions than were included in the scope of the project, and they pushed back when asked to pay extra for it. The experience was nothing short of draining, with many days ending in Joana questioning her decision to freelance at all.

She no longer looked forward to jumping into her work alongside her morning coffee. The snooze button got hit more often, and she'd find herself procrastinating, dreading her inbox. Each "just one more tiny revision" felt like it could be the final push that sent her over the edge.

It didn't take long for Joana to quickly realize that even for double her rate, it wasn't worth it to work with nonideal clients, and she started to implement her own Red Velvet Rope Policy. It was a game changer, creating a positive ripple effect. She soon started to leap out of bed again, excited to dive into new projects. This excitement was palpable, and it helped deepen the relationship between her and her clients. In fact, she even started flying out to meet some of them face-to-face. This not only made her relationships with her clients stronger but created opportunities for her to be introduced to new ones, just as ideal.

Joana also discovered that when she worked only with ideal clients, her designs got even better. Feeling pumped and into her work meant she could give it her all, leading to doing her best work.

Live by the Red Velvet Rope Policy of ideal clients. Doing so will increase your productivity and happiness. Plus, it allows you to do your best work, which means your clients get the best results possible, which in turn leads to more clients and referrals than you can handle by yourself.

For maximum joy, prosperity, and abundance, think about the person you are when you are performing optimally, when you are with all the people who inspire and energize you. Now think about all of the frustration, tension, and anxiety you feel when you work with clients who are less than ideal – not so good, right?

Wouldn't it be great to spend every day working with clients who are ideal for you, clients whom you can hardly believe you get paid to work with? This ideal is completely possible once you identify who you want to work with and determine with certainty that you will settle for nothing less. Once you do that, it's just a matter of knowing which of your existing clients qualify and how to acquire more just like them.

> **1.1.1 Written Exercise:** To begin to identify the types of clients you don't want, consider which characteristics or behaviors you refuse to tolerate. What turns you off or shuts you down? What kinds of people should *not* be getting past the red velvet rope that protects you and your business?

Dump the Duds

Let's take this a step further. It's time to dump your dud clients. We can just hear your shocked protestations and exclamations. "I thought this was a book about getting clients, not dumping them!" We're referring to the *dud* clients – not all of your clients. It sounds harsh, but think about it. Your dud clients are those you dread collaborating with. They sap your creativity, bore you to tears, or leave you endlessly frustrated with the project, even after giving it your all.

Most creatives choose their career out of passion for their craft. They choose this path to express their creativity and connect with others through their work. However, along the way, many of these talented individuals find themselves burned out and experiencing creative blocks regularly because of working with too many dud clients.

When Joana faced this problem with a retainer client who represented 30% of her agency's revenue, she was terrified at the thought of letting them go. She thought that if she got rid of them, her reputation would crumble and so in turn would her business. But guess what? Dumping this client brought about only positive outcomes, and the team thanked her for it.

There are likely many reasons you *think* you can't dump your dud clients, and we know this can seem really scary early on, but hang in there with. Embrace the concept and trust that this is sound advice from loving teachers and a necessary step on the path to booking yourself solid.

Why have clients, or anyone for that matter, in your life who zap your energy and leave you feeling empty? You might decide to dump five dud clients in one week, or you may decide to dump one per month over the next year. The Red Velvet Rope Policy may be provocative. It might not feel like an easy thing to do. It requires a leap of faith (faith in yourself), but the emotional and financial rewards will be transformational. Within a few weeks of dumping your duds, you may add a dozen or more delightful clients. Sure, you'll increase your revenue if you add more ideal clients to your roster, but you'll also feel at peace and at ease as a business owner and creative. You'll enjoy your work more. Maybe not straightaway, but that Red Velvet Rope Policy? It's your ticket to a more positive workday. It'll keep the duds away and ensure you choose your ideal clients – people who inspire and energize you and, more important, allow you to do your best work.

Ask yourself: "Would I rather spend my days working with incredibly amazing, exciting, supercool, awesome people who are both clients and friends, or spend one more agonizing, excruciating minute working with barely tolerable clients who suck the life out of me?" Any initial discomfort or loss you may feel when dumping your duds will pay off in the long run.

Using the phrase "dump your dud clients," suggests that there is something wrong with them. But that's not necessarily the case. Well, in some cases you may have a real nut job on your hands, but most of the time, they're just not right for *you*. A client who doesn't resonate with your style, for example, could be a dream for another creative who creates work in the style that client is after. Keep in mind that you don't need to create conflict and fire clients. You just need to stop signing on to their projects. You can be tactful, diplomatic, and loving. You can even attempt, when appropriate, to refer them to a colleague who might be a better fit. Whenever possible, keep it simple. Try, "I'm not the best person to serve you." Or "I don't think we'd be a good fit."

Are you always going to get a positive response when dumping your dud clients? Maybe not. If the first thing that comes to mind is "I don't want anyone out there thinking badly of me," we're with you. We love helping people, and we want people to think well of us. But living life fully can require difficult conversations, and you can't please everyone. To even try is an exercise in futility, as the following Aesop fable demonstrates.

The Old Man, the Little Boy, and the Donkey

An old man, a little boy, and a donkey were going to town. The little boy rode on the donkey, and the old man walked beside him. As they went along, they passed some people who remarked it was a shame the old man was walking and the little boy was riding. The man and boy thought maybe the critics were right, so they changed positions.

Later, they passed some people who remarked, "What a shame! He makes that little boy walk." They then decided they both would walk.

Soon they passed some more people who thought they were stupid to walk when they had a decent donkey to ride. So they both rode the donkey. Later, they passed some people who shamed them by saying how awful to put such a load on a poor donkey. The boy and man said they were probably right, so they decided to carry the donkey. As they crossed the bridge, they lost their grip on the animal. He fell into the river and drowned.

The moral of the story? *If you try to please everyone, you might as well kiss your ass goodbye.*

When considering who you want to work with, look for qualities in a person who you resonate with, so you don't limit yourself to just thinking about the clients you don't yet have. Your Red Velvet Rope Policy is a filtration system that lets in ideal clients. However, you can choose to loosen or tighten the rope at will. We're not (necessarily) asking you to turn away your very first clients. We understand what you're up against. When you start your business, if you feel that you'd like to keep your red velvet rope a little looser so you can work with more clients, go right ahead.

For example, a recent graduate who is just venturing into freelancing for the first time should have some non-negotiable traits built into their Red Velvet Rope Policy, but it could make sense for them to keep their red velvet rope closer to the ground so they can build a client roster and, critically, generate the revenue necessary to ensure the revenue they need.

Just make sure you know what is ideal and what isn't ideal about the people you're letting into the VIP room. As you become booked solid, you'll tighten your red velvet rope and become even more exclusive so as to work only with those who energize and inspire you and – most important – allow you to do your best work.

1.1.2 Written Exercise: Now take a good, hard look at your current clients. Be absolutely honest with yourself. Who among your current clients fits the profile you've just created of people who should *not* have gotten past the red velvet rope that protects you and your business?

1.1.3 Booked Solid Action Step: Dump the dud clients you've just listed in the preceding exercise. It may be just one client, or you may need another two pages to write them all down. Is your heart pounding? Is your stomach churning at just the thought? Have you broken out in a cold sweat? Or are you jumping up and down with excitement now that you've been given permission to dump your duds? Maybe you're experiencing both sensations at the same time; that's totally normal. Do it and you'll feel better.

Taking a Booked Solid Action Step is a bold action and requires courage. And courage is not about being fearless – it's about owning your fear and using it to move you forward, to give you strength. There is no more rewarding feeling than the pride you'll feel once you've moved past the fear to do what you set out to do. Maybe you'll find it easier to take it one step at a time. Start by dismissing just one of those dud clients.

The feeling of empowerment you'll have once you've done it will motivate you to continue pruning your list of clients until the duds have all been removed.

What to Do When You Don't (Yet) Have Clients

But Michael and Joana, what if I just started my business and don't yet have clients, let alone dud clients? Ah, yes, excellent point. Consider yourself lucky. You'll never have to worry about dud clients because you'll put your Red Velvet Rope Policy in place on day one.

In just a moment, you'll begin to create your Red Velvet Rope Policy. If you're starting a new business and don't yet have many, or any, clients to speak of at this point, as you're working through the exercises, think about current or former co-workers, friends, or even service providers that you've hired in the past. To create your future Red Velvet Rope Policy, you'll be able to draw on your past experiences – who inspired you and who made you want to do them bodily harm. Refrain. Rewind. Remember: love and kindness. Love and kindness.

Pruning Your Client List

If you're struggling with the idea of pruning your client list, keep in mind that it's for your client's benefit as much as it is for yours. If you're feeling empty and drained, or frustrated and dreading the interaction with the client, then you're giving that client far less than your best, and it's both of you who are suffering for it. You owe it to these clients to refer them to someone who can, and will, do their best work with them. If you are working with people with whom you do not do your best work, you are out of integrity. And as we discussed earlier, you *are* your clients. When your clients go out into the world and speak of you to others, they are representing you.

With whom do you want to be associated – the duds or the ideal clients? It's also the ideal clients, those who are wildly happy with you and your services, who are most likely to go out and talk about you to others, to refer other clients like themselves, more ideal clients. The fewer duds you allow to hang around, the more ideal clients you have room for, the more referrals you'll get, and so on.

Clients are like family, so we know this can be hard and can cause a period of intense and painful negative energy worrying about those challenging client relationships. It's exhausting and takes away from providing the best creative services for your clients. It is impossible to be your most effective, most attentive, and most precise self when working with less than ideal clients.

Joana's agency had been working with a client for more than three years — let's call her Sophie. Wanting to serve Sophie as best as she could, over time, Joana started to expand her offerings beyond her agency's usual capabilities, handling everything from brand identity design to web design and development to editorial design and social media graphics. However, the quick turnaround needed for the latter began to stress the team. This, coupled with the reduced creativity social media design required for this brand, started making the work feel monotonous. The team started to dread working on Sophie's account, and Joana started to find it harder to keep them motivated.

It wasn't that Sophie was demanding or difficult; it was just that this particular task didn't align with the team's passion or expertise. Moreover, the process for quick turnaround social media graphics was so distinct from their other projects that it disrupted their day-to-day operations, making everything feel more challenging than it should.

Recognizing this mismatch, Joana decided to do something about it. She approached Sophie, explaining that while they cherished handling her branding and web needs, both areas for which Joana's agency was known, they believed she would benefit from someone with a keen passion for social media design to take over that role.

To ensure Sophie was well taken care of, Joana introduced her to a freelancer starting out, who she knew and trusted, proficient in social media design and already an admirer of Sophie's brand. This move was a win–win. Sophie gained an expert who was enthusiastic about her social media needs and at a more budget-friendly rate. Meanwhile, Joana's team was free to channel their energy back into their true strengths: branding and web design.

The decision not only re-energized Joana's team but also ensured that Sophie received phenomenal service in every domain. It was a clear demonstration of the benefits of aligning client relationships with one's strengths and passions.

Imagine if Joana hadn't taken this action. From experience, this is how we know the story would have played out instead: Joana and her team would have grown increasingly resentful of the work they were doing and therefore of the client. They would have started to diminish the quality of their service or, even worse, find themselves snapping back at yet another urgent social media request. This would have in turn led to a poor experience for the client and eventually a termination of the contract. Not to mention, it would have ended all the referrals this client had been sending Joana their way.

This is what can happen when you work with clients who are not ideal for you. At some point, you're going to create a conflict, whether intentionally or not, because you're going to be frustrated with those clients. Those clients will think you're not providing them with good service – and they'll be right. It doesn't serve you or the client when you stay in a less than ideal situation. If you do, you'll have former clients going out into the world telling anyone who will listen that you're the worst person to work with. And while navigating nonideal client relationships can be challenging, remember that parting ways, or redefining the project parameters, doesn't have to be painful. Done with care and integrity it can result in a win–win experience for all parties involved, setting the stage for more ideal clients to come your way.

Creating Your Red Velvet Rope Policy

The benefits of working with ideal clients are many and meaningful:

- You'll get to do your best work.
- You'll feel invigorated and inspired.
- You'll connect with clients on a deeper level.
- You'll feel successful and confident.
- You'll know your work matters and is changing lives.
- You'll feel fully self-expressed.

Joana knows her ideal client's traits so well she even created a framework for them:

Here's her DREAM client framework:

- **D**ecisive (can make decisions in a timely manner)
- **R**espectful (of Joana's time, her team's time, and their process)
- **E**ngaged (communicative and responsive throughout the project, giving honest feedback in a timely and constructive manner to help move the project forward)
- **A**daptable (open to new ideas out of their comfort zone and new tools to facilitate the process)
- **M**otivated (committed to the vision of their company and the end goal of the project)

Your list might look completely different.

Take heed: how much money a client has or doesn't have is not what this is about. Your Red Velvet Rope Policy considers *what kind of person* you're dealing with, not how much this person has or doesn't have. People with fat wallets are often the primary consideration for many creatives who wind up working with clients who are less than ideal. Notice that my list considers the *qualities* of my ideal clients first – who they *are* rather than what they *have* or the circumstances they're in.

1.1.4 Written Exercise: Define your ideal client. What type of people do you love being around? What do they like to do? What do they talk about? With whom do they associate? What ethical standards do they follow? How do they learn? How do they contribute to society? Are they smiling, outgoing, or creative? What kind of environment do you want to create in your life? And who will get past the Red Velvet Rope Policy that protects you? List the *qualities, values,* or *personal characteristics* you'd like your ideal clients to possess.

1.1.5 Written Exercise: Now let's look at your current client base. Who do you love interacting with the most? Who do you look forward to seeing? Who are the clients who don't feel like work to you? *Who is it you sometimes just can't believe you get paid to work with?* Write down the names of clients, or people you've worked with, who you love to be around.

> **1.1.6 Written Exercise:** Get a clear picture of these people in your head. Write down the top five reasons you love working with them. What about working with them turns you on?

> **1.1.7 Written Exercise:** Now go deeper. If you were working only with ideal clients, what qualities would they absolutely *need* to possess for you to do your *best* work with them? Be honest and don't worry about excluding people. Be selfish. Think about yourself. For this exercise, assume you will work only with the best of the best. Be brave and bold and write without thinking or filtering your thoughts.

How different were the last two lists? You may have nailed it the first time. Maybe you're right on track, or maybe you have some perfect client opportunities to uncover.

By knowing who your ideal clients are and selecting only those who have at least 75% of the qualities you identified, you will have more fun, accomplish greater results, and experience incredible joy and fulfillment in your business.

This is beneficial because you'll be able to identify other ideal clients you'd love to work with. People enjoy knowing how important they are to you, and if they know you do your best work with, and for, people like them, they are much more inclined to work with you. It raises the stakes for them.

Look at these requirements and think about how you can start to turn them into filters. Joana takes this as seriously as she takes preparing formula for her baby's bottles. Just as she won't compromise on the quality of the water to ensure her baby's well-being by filtering and boiling it, she is equally conscious when it comes to accepting projects for her agency. Just as contaminated water could be harmful for her newborn, the wrong client can disrupt the well-being of her team. Just like every mother will only give the best to her child, Joana is careful about only bringing in the best-fit clients and projects so that she and the team can perform at optimal level, enjoy collaborations, and produce their best work.

Joana's client filters include these:

- She feels more energized and excited after working with her clients.
- Her clients seek out her and her team's expertise and trust in their creative guidance.
- Her clients are committed to the project and honor their part of the contract such as giving feedback in a timely manner.
- Her clients get along well with her team.
- Her clients are naturally optimistic and do not complain (much).

1.1.8 Written Exercise: What filters do you want to run your perfect clients through?

Ideal Clients, the Duds, and Everyone Else

As you eliminate the duds, you'll open up room for ideal clients. As you use the Book Yourself Solid system to attract more and more ideal clients, you'll discover that you're happier, more vibrant, more energetic, and more productive. You'll be on fire. You'll be giving your clients the best of yourself and your services, and you'll love every minute of it.

1.1.9 Written Exercise: Draw a simple table with three columns. Label the first column "Ideal Clients," the second "Duds," and the third "Everyone Else." Now divide your clients into these three groups. Don't hold back or leave anyone out.

As if that weren't enough, you may begin to notice that many of your midrange clients, those who made neither the ideal client nor the dud list, are undergoing a transformation. Why? While you were working with dud clients, you weren't performing at your best. If you think that that wasn't affecting your other clients, think again. The renewed energy and the more positive environment you'll create as a result of letting go of the duds will most likely rejuvenate the relationships between you and some of your mid-range clients, turning many of them into ideal clients.

1.1.10 Written Exercise: Brainstorm your own ideas for reigniting these midrange clients. Contemplate the ways in which you may, even inadvertently, have contributed to some of your clients being less than ideal clients. Are there ways in which you can light a new fire or elicit greater passion for the work you do together? Do you need to set and manage expectations more clearly right from the beginning? Can you enrich the dynamics between you by challenging or inspiring your clients in new ways? Go ahead – turn off your left-brain logical mind for a moment and let your right-brain creativity go wild.

Carefully observe the ways in which your relationships with your clients begin to shift as you embrace the Book Yourself Solid way. Some of your midrange clients may fall away. Others may step up their game and slide into the ideal client category.

When you're fully self-expressed, fully demonstrating your values and your views, you'll naturally attract and draw to yourself those you're best suited to work with, and you'll push away those you're not meant to work with.

A Perpetual Process

The process we've just worked through is one that you must do on a regular basis. Pruning your client list is a perpetual process because all relationships naturally cycle. The positive and dynamic relationships you have now with your ideal clients may at some point reach a plateau, and the time may come to go your separate ways. You'll get more comfortable with the process over time. It's one that has so many rewards that it's well worth the effort.

Let author Tom Peters sum it up for us: "This is your life. You *are* your clients. It is fair, sensible, and imperative to make these judgments. To dodge doing so shows a lack of integrity."

We'll go one step further and say that doing so is one of the best and smartest business and life decisions you can make. It's crucial to your success and your happiness. Prune regularly, and before you know it, you'll be booked solid with clients you love working with.

2

Why People Buy What You're Selling

Before everything else, getting ready is the secret of success.
—Henry Ford

The next few steps we take down the Book Yourself Solid path will feel either like you're skipping over stepping stones or like you're taking giant leaps of faith. Either way, these few steps will be well worth the time spent. Stay by our side as we walk and work together on getting you booked solid.

Taking the following four steps will help you keenly understand why people buy what you're selling, an essential component in creating demand for your services:

Step 1: Identify your target market.
Step 2: Understand the urgent needs and compelling desires of your target market.
Step 3: Determine the number-one biggest result your clients get.
Step 4: Uncover and demonstrate the benefits of your offers.

Step 1: Identify Your Target Market

If you're a bit like Joana, the fresh spark you get from diving into a new project, particularly in a completely new industry, captivates you. And if you're nodding along, our guess is that you'll be tempted to skip this chapter, thinking picking a target market is not for you. Please don't. Our promise, if you'll stick with us, is to show you that this is not only a key part of the solution to getting booked solid, but that it can also be even more creatively fulfilling than taking on a new project in a new industry each time.

Now that you've looked at the qualities of the people you want to work with, it's time to identify your target market, that is, the specific group of people or businesses you serve. For example, your target market might be e-commerce business owners, software-as-a-service (SaaS) companies, or fashion brands. Your ideal clients are a small subset of the target market you choose to serve. Remember, your ideal clients are those individuals who energize and inspire you. Your target market is the demographics of the group you're most passionate about serving. Your ideal clients are a small subset of your target market. Not all people in your target market are ideal clients for you. Nonetheless, it is just as important to identify the right target market as it is to identify the ideal clients.

It's also important to understand the difference between your target market and your niche. If you've done other research or reading on the subject of building your business, you may have heard both of these terms before, and you may have heard them used interchangeably. However, in the Book Yourself Solid system, they are *not* synonymous. There's an important distinction between the two: your target market is the group of people you serve, and your niche is the service you specialize in offering to your target market. For example, you and Joana may both serve the same target market, say, e-commerce businesses, but offer them different services. Joana might specialize in brand identity and packaging design, and you might specialize in conversion copywriting. We'll get to your niche in Chapter 3. Before we can talk more about the services you offer, you've got to identify your target market.

Even if you believe you have identified and chosen a target market, please don't skip this section. We often see creative service professionals struggle with a few common missteps when it comes to choosing a target market. Some make the mistake of being too broad in their choice, lacking the necessary focus. Others pick a market because it seems like the smart, most profitable choice, not because it sparks their passion. Then there are those who swing the other way: they choose a target market in an industry they love but forget to check if it's a viable and profitable option. For the sake of your own success, read through this section, even if you don't think you need to. If your target market isn't specific enough or the right one for you, the rest of the book won't be as effective. Besides, you just might be surprised at what you discover.

There are four primary reasons to choose a target market:

1. It helps you pinpoint where your potential clients are. By having a well-defined target market; you can more effectively identify the right communities, podcast, and publications for exposure; and know the key influential people to network with. It's about being in the right places and becoming known where your potential clients are.

2. Virtually every target market is already active in specific communication channels. For your marketing to work, your clients need to spread your messages for you. If they're already interacting in established channels, they can easily share their experiences with your services, allowing your marketing messages to travel that much faster. What are these channels? Environments that are set up to help a group communicate – as we mentioned earlier: communities, social media groups, clubs, various publications, events, and more.

3. You get to develop a deep understanding of your client's needs. This insight will then inform how you structure your services, present your offerings, and create your marketing to ensure you address their primary concerns and desires. You're also able to refine your processes to best serve them.

4. Finally, choosing a target market lets the people in that target market know that you're dedicated to them and are exclusively concerned with solving their problems and fulfilling their needs. This dedicated focus strengthens your brand's trustworthiness in your client's eyes, creating a loyal client base that appreciates your specialized attention.

Marketing and sales isn't about trying to persuade, coerce, or manipulate people into buying your services. It's about putting yourself out in front of, and offering your services to, those whom you are meant to serve – people who already need and are looking for your services.

To reach the people you're meant to serve, you've got to know where to find them. That's why an essential step is for you to identify a very specific target market to serve.

No matter how much you might like to be everything to everyone, it's just not possible. Attempting to do so would not only be overwhelming but could also dilute the very essence of your work and its impact. Think about it: if you're diving into a new target market with each project, you're essentially starting from scratch every time. This involves crafting a proposal that suits their specific needs, doing fresh research, and potentially adapting a new working format. All these initial steps can significantly eat up a lot of the time you would be using for ideation and creation, the two most critical phases in the work of a creative service provider. Consequently, with less time spent in these areas, the quality of your work could suffer, doing a disservice to both you and your clients.

If you're just starting out in your business or if you've been working in your business for a while but are not yet booked solid, you may be tempted to market to anyone and everyone with the assumption that the more people you market to, the more clients you'll get. While narrowing your market to gain more clients may seem counterintuitive, that's exactly what you need to do to successfully book yourself solid.

Think of narrowing your market this way: which would you rather be – a small fish in a big pond or a big fish in a small pond? It's much easier to carve out a very lucrative domain for yourself once you've identified a specific target market. And once you're a big fish in a small pond, you'll get more invitations than you can handle to swim in other ponds. Remember that, as a consumer, especially when the stakes are high, you go narrow. All things being equal, you seek out the specialist, the provider who most narrowly focuses on your particular need.

There are two primary ways to grow a creative service business. You can choose a target market and, over time, continue to add new services to this same target market. For example, if your target market is e-commerce brands and you're currently offering them brand identity design, as you grow, you might start offering them packaging design and e-commerce websites. Alternatively, once you get booked solid in one target market, you can begin to market and sell the same services in additional vertical target markets. So, if you currently serve e-commerce skin care brands, you might offer the same services to e-commerce make-up brands. Once you get a foothold in that market, you might then begin to focus on e-commerce brands in other industries.

You might be thinking "If I specialize and work only with a specific group of people, or specific types of companies within a specific industry, won't that limit my opportunities? And what if I get bored?" Let us answer the second question first. It's natural for creatives to worry about getting creatively stuck — we thrive on variety and the thrill of fresh new challenges. But consider this: Is the issue that you're worried about monotony, or have you perhaps picked a market that doesn't truly light up your creativity? One that doesn't give you the space to explore and innovate as you'd hoped?

Now as for the notion of feeling restricted by opportunities, we believe honing in on a target market can actually have the opposite effect. Here's why: it streamlines your marketing efforts, your processes, leaving you with more time to hone your skills more precisely and increase the speed at which you get better at your work. All things that will help you grow your business and reputation faster. This in turn can also lead to deeper satisfaction as you might find more time for passion projects or exciting opportunities that come from being a notable player in a focused target market. Plus, becoming known in a market doesn't mean you're trapped. There's always room to expand later.

Take Joana, for example. When she launched her agency, Gif Design Studios, she doubled down on helping coaches and consultants grow their personal brands through conversion-driven websites. This focus didn't limit her; it established her reputation. Once she was fortunate enough to start becoming known in that field and being recommended to the top industry experts in the field, she later moved into e-commerce companies too. This happened because she was working with a coach to e-commerce business owners who invited her to speak at his conference, and suddenly Gif Design Studios was starting to gain traction in a brand-new target market — e-commerce brands.

Expertise breeds opportunity. You might start with a specific market, but as you grow and evolve, diversifying — whether by diving into new markets or new services — is a natural progression. It's not about putting limits on your business; it's about giving it a strong foundation from which to grow from.

Your Passions, Natural Talents, and Knowledge Are Key

If you haven't yet chosen a target market, let's do it now. Let's start with some questions: What are you most passionate about? What excites you? What do you enjoy doing so much that it feels more like play than work and that will allow you to make the most of your natural talents and your knowledge?

Why start by thinking of your own needs, desires, and passions rather than those of your clients? For one very simple reason: if you are not passionate about what you're doing, if your heart isn't in it, if it doesn't have meaning to you, then you are not going to devote the time and energy required to be successful, and as a result you'll never, in a million years, be able to convince people in your target market that you're the best person to help them.

We've often found, when working with clients, that they've chosen a target market based on what they think makes sense or will earn them the most money. The end result is that they're bored, frustrated, and struggling to book themselves solid. Don't make that mistake. It is imperative that you work with a target market that excites you and that you can feel passionate about serving. If you don't, growing your business will quickly feel like drudgery, and you'll be miserable. When you choose a target market you're passionate about, growing your business will feel like passionate play and will bring you joy.

That's not to say you shouldn't also consider your clients. If you've been in business for a while, even if you may not have as many clients as you'd like, the clients you do have can help with this process. Look at the projects you've worked on. Identify common threads — for instance, a recurring industry, a particular style, certain project types, or the personalities of the brands you're working with. If a pattern emerges, it could signify that these elements naturally resonate with you or that your style and skills particularly appeal to this segment. Perhaps your target market has already chosen you and you just haven't stopped to think about it long enough to realize it, and then focus your marketing there.

1.2.1 Written Exercise: Take a few moments to think about the following questions and then jot down whatever comes to you. Doing so will provide you with clues to the target market you're best suited to serve. Your passion, your natural talents, and what you already know and want to learn more about are key.

- What are the different types of companies or industries that often require your creative services?
- Among these, which do you feel a strong connection with or find excitement about working with?
- In which industries do you know people in or already have clients in?
- Which areas do you have the most knowledge about or, on the flip side, would you find fascinating to learn more about through your creative work?
- What elements of your creative process are you most passionate about?
- What natural talents and strengths do you bring to your work?
- What unique skills or styles do you bring to your projects?
- Within your field of expertise, what themes or aspects are you most informed about?

1.2.2 Written Exercise: Consider your life experience and interests. You'll be able to more sincerely identify and empathize with your target market if you share common life situations or interests.

- What life situations or roles do you identify with that might enhance your understanding in relation to certain types of projects of target market?
- Do you have any interests or hobbies that might align with certain themes, industries, or client types, potentially making you an ideal creative partner for them?

Now that you've given some thought to these questions, are some new possibilities beginning to emerge? Let's take a look at a few examples that might help you see how you can incorporate some of your answers into serving a target market:

- Imagine you're an avid gamer outside of your professional life as a motion designer. There's a whole community there in need of your expertise – game developers, streamers, or gaming events might greatly benefit from your motion design skills and deep understanding of the industry.
- Say you're a copywriter and you took a career break to raise a family; this personal journey might resonate deeply with parenting bloggers and children's brands. Your genuine understanding of this life stage could translate into authentic, relatable content for their newsletters.
- Imagine you're a lettering artist who can't get enough of playing with typography. Your projects could be perfect for children's book publishers, toy companies, or brands with a youthful, energetic vibe seeking to infuse more fun into their visual identity.
- Imagine you're a graphic designer with a passion for sustainability and the environment. You could carve out a niche for yourself working with eco-friendly e-commerce brands, green startups, or conservation initiatives, using your visual skills to help them make an impact.

Let's take this last example and examine it more closely. This graphic designer, fueled by personal values, decides to lend their talent to causes they believe in. Starting locally, they assist green projects with striking visuals and meaningful campaigns. Their portfolio expands, telling a narrative of their commitment to the cause.

Their reputation grows, not just as a skilled designer but as a genuine advocate for environmental responsibility. This unique stance attracts like-minded clients, creating a career for this designer that is both professionally rewarding and personally significant.

Are you beginning to see the ways in which your values, passions, natural talents, knowledge, life experience, and even interests and hobbies might help you choose a more specific target market? Play, explore, and have fun with this process.

> **1.2.3 Written Exercise:** For now, we just want you to answer this question: who is your target market? If you're not ready to make this choice, list the possibilities that appeal to you. Sit with them for a while (but not for too long) and then choose one. Even if you're not sure at this point, it will become clearer to you as you work through the next few chapters.

We've worked with many creatives who *knew* on some level the target market they most wanted to serve and for one reason or another discounted it. Turn off your inner censor when doing this exercise and allow yourself to at least explore every possibility, no matter how wild, silly, or unrealistic it may seem on the surface.

If You Feel Stuck

For some, choosing a target market doesn't come easily. It can feel very challenging, and when you've been told how important it is to identify a target market and it doesn't come quickly and easily, the pressure to choose can feel overwhelming and uncomfortable.

Part of what keeps us stuck is that we take ourselves, and the process, too seriously. We turn it into a big deal and wind up getting increasingly frustrated with the whole thing, and with ourselves. Suddenly the process has become another thing to beat ourselves up about. Needless to say, the frustration and self-criticism just further block our creativity and intuition, and the next thing we know, we're in this awful cycle, like a hamster on an exercise wheel, spinning around and around and getting nowhere.

Take a few deep breaths. Let yourself off the hook. See if you can approach the process with an attitude of play. Think of it as a jigsaw puzzle – challenging but fun. The point isn't to finish as quickly as possible. The point is to enjoy the journey and to find the target market that is right for you.

Another approach we've seen be effective for many is getting clarity through action. Instead of pressuring yourself to pick the perfect target market that you'll stick with for the rest of your career, which we get can make the task feel very daunting, is to allow yourself to experiment. Choose a market to focus on for a couple of months first. Direct your marketing efforts there and engage with that audience. See how it feels. Does this market excite you? Can you see the potential projects it will bring? After this period, reassess. If it still doesn't feel quite right, allow yourself the freedom to shift focus to another market. This *clarity through action* process can be incredibly enlightening and is often a quicker path to discovering where your passion and profitable market intersect.

And a word of caution: resist the urge to overhaul your website with each market shift. Keeping your online presence neutral and adaptable during this phase prevents the website revisions from becoming a form of procrastination or getting in the way of you achieving results.

As with any jigsaw puzzle, first you sort through all the pieces to find the edges, the pieces easiest to identify and put together. Then you take your time sorting through the rest. You pick one piece up, you compare it to the bigger picture on the box, and you try to figure out where it might go. One piece at a time, the picture comes together. When you get tired or bored or frustrated or you just feel drawn to do something else, get up and walk away, and as you go about the rest of your day, don't stress out about whether you'll ever get the puzzle finished.

Some days you might spend an hour or two with it; other times only minutes. Maybe every once in a while you stop for mere seconds, pick up a piece or two, and pop them right in where they fit as you pass by. Maybe a friend or family member stops by for a visit, picks up that piece that's been making you crazy for days, and pops it right into place for you.

Choosing a target market you can feel passionate about serving can be enjoyable and immensely rewarding if you approach the process with an open mind and an attitude of play, reaching out for help from family, friends, or a professional business coach to guide you.

Revisit the written exercises in step 1 and approach them with a spirit of play. Don't analyze; just jot down whatever answers come to you. Make it a game, listing as many ideas and possibilities as you can think of. If you're still having difficulty, ask someone to play with you. Someone outside your process can offer ideas and suggestions that occur to them, which you may not have the objectivity to consider. Remember to turn your inner censor off for this process. If you need to, let go of the process altogether for a while and move on. Releasing the pressure of having to choose sometimes allows ideas that were blocked to come racing through.

Step 2: Identify the Urgent Needs and Compelling Desires of Your Target Market

Your target market's urgent needs and compelling desires prompt them to go in search of you and your services, so it's critical to be able to identify and address them when they come looking or you'll miss your window of opportunity.

> **You must offer what your potential clients want to buy, not what you want to sell or think they should want to buy. You must be able to look at your services from your client's perspective — their urgent needs and compelling desires.**

Your clients' urgent needs are the things they must have right away, usually pressing problems, and often the things they would like to move away from. Here are a few examples of urgent needs your clients may have:

- A captivating logo or website that aligns with their brand identity, enticing visitors to become clients or customers
- A book landing page to promote an upcoming release
- An email nurture sequence optimized for conversion, for their upcoming launch
- Innovative packaging design that will make their product stand out on the shelf following a deal with a retailer
- A promotional video/trailer for their product idea, to help them land their Kickstarter funding goal

Their compelling desires are the things that they want in the future. Here are a few examples:

- Building a strong brand that stands out in the market
- Growing their business through high-quality and unique branding and marketing materials
- Cultivating a wide-reaching online presence that translates into a loyal growing audience and global sales

- Transitioning from a hands-on, bootstrapping entrepreneur to one who delegates creative tasks, thereby focusing more on their primary business strengths

---

1.2.4 Written Exercise: What are five of your clients' *urgent* needs? (What problems must they solve right away?)

Example: The urgent need that may have prompted you to buy this book might be a feeling of stress because you know you need more clients (and more money) but don't know where or how to begin marketing your business. Maybe the bills are really starting to pile up and you're afraid. Or maybe you know what to do to market your services but just aren't doing it. You're procrastinating, and your business is suffering as a result.

1.2.5 Written Exercise: What are five of your clients' *compelling desires*? (What would they like to move toward?)

Example: Let's use you as an example again. Your compelling desire might be to feel confident and in control as you get as many clients as you would like. Maybe you want financial freedom. Maybe you just want to be able to take a real vacation every year. Or maybe it's all about having a thriving business that includes doing what you love and making great money doing it.

Step 3: Determine the Biggest Result Your Clients Get

This simple step might be the most important step in understanding why people buy what you're selling. What is the number-one result you help your clients achieve or get? And when we say "number-one result," we mean one big one. Of course, we know there are lots of things that you help your clients achieve, experience, or get. But, generally, when a client comes looking for you, they're looking to solve one big problem or achieve one big result. Think about it; why did you buy this book? To get more clients. Period. End of story. Are there lots of other things you'll get from reading this book? No doubt – from more confidence to more accountability, and even more friends (we'll get to that later). But, bottom line, you want more clients, and the Book Yourself Solid system delivers on that promise. In fact, every product or service you offer must have one big promise. Your job is to fulfill that promise in the delivery of your service.

A word of caution here when it comes to determining your biggest results: often, when we help explore this topic with clients who are creative service providers, they start talking about the quality of their creative work (for example, compelling copy that converts, innovative packaging design that stands out from the shelf, award-winning websites). However, the majority of clients are not interested in that. Rather, they want to understand what benefits and advantages they will see in their lives from working with you, such as a 10% increase in sales.

1.2.6 Written Exercise: Describe the biggest result you provide.

Step 4: Uncover and Demonstrate the Benefits of Your Investable Opportunities

Do potential clients within your target market see your services and products as opportunities that will give them a significant return on their investment?

They must. If your potential clients are going to purchase your services and products, they *must* see them as investable opportunities. They must feel that the return they receive is greater than the investment they made.

Our rule of thumb is that your clients should be getting a return of at least 10 times their investment in your services. It's a big number, but it's worth striving for. This return will come in different forms, depending on what you offer, but the return falls into four related categories: financial, emotional, physical, and spiritual, which we'll refer to by the acronym FEPS.

What kind of financial, emotional, physical, or spiritual return on investment will your clients get from working with you? Will it be greater than their financial, emotional, physical, or spiritual investment in your services? If so, how much higher? Two times? Twenty times?

The secret to having a successful business is to know what your clients want, and to deliver it to them.

To make it obvious that your solutions are investable opportunities for your potential clients, you need to uncover and demonstrate their benefits. What you do — copywriting, video editing, logo design, website development, interior design — are just things that you do. They are the actual services you offer. They are technically what your clients buy but not what they actually buy. They actually buy the benefits of the results you produce or help them get — financial, emotional, physical, and spiritual benefits.

For example, some of the offerings in Joana's design agency are technically these:

- Brand identity design
- Website design
- Website development
- Packaging design

However, these are still only the offerings or opportunities. The core benefits of these offerings are much deeper. Benefits are sometimes tangible results, but more often they're intangible. They are the effects your services have on your clients' quality of life. They are what make your offer an investable opportunity — the FEPS that clients can experience because of your services. They are what people buy. Don't ever forget that.

To get a stronger sense of how this works, think about this. If we asked you what you wanted to accomplish in the next 90 days, you might say you'd like to get more clients or earn more money, but what is getting more clients really going to give you? Will it give you more than money in the bank or an ever-increasing savings account?

The truth is that you don't ultimately want clients. What you really want is the financial, emotional, physical, and even spiritual benefits of having clients: financial freedom, peace of mind, time with your family, or reduced concerns about how you're going to make ends meet, and more. Are we right?

To accentuate this point, here are some more examples of the deeper benefits you'll get from reading this book:

- A paradigm shift in the way you look at marketing and sales so that you can forever create demand for your services in a way that feels authentic and comfortable to you

- Increased confidence in yourself and your capacity to handle any business challenge that you are faced with
- A feeling of pride and a sense of accomplishment as you take the actions you know you need to take and see positive results from
- Freedom from the physical and emotional stress and anxiety of not being able to cover the mortgage for the home you and your children live in
- A deep, spiritual connection to your purpose and the opportunity to be fully self-expressed
- And so much more . . .

Do you see how identifying core financial, emotional, physical, and spiritual benefits allows you to speak to and touch your target market on a much deeper and more personally and emotionally connected level? The more financial, emotional, physical, and spiritual benefits you uncover, the quicker you will start to attract new clients. People buy results and the benefits of those results. So think about the results you offer and the subsequent benefits they provide.

1.2.7 Written Exercise: What are the deep-rooted benefits your clients will experience as a result of your services?

Now do you see what clients are actually buying when they decide to work with you? Whether you're networking, writing an email, posting on social media, pitching in a Zoom meeting, or chatting on a call, always remember to articulate and re-articulate these benefits. Use words that you hear your clients use and express very specific solutions to their very prominent problems.

Even if it seems simple, it's worth repeating. If you're a branding expert and you have a client wanting to establish her personal brand and start doing something she loves, then every time you meet, remind her that her personal brand will offer her freedom so that she won't have to ever settle again when it comes to the clients she works with. This is a compelling desire for her, so remind her how inspired she is going to feel when she works only with her ideal clients. Keeping the benefits on the top of her mind, she clearly sees the fully realized vision of business and stays focused in accomplishing her goals (and sticking to the project feedback timelines).

Relax, Be Playful, and Have Fun!

If some of these business concepts are getting heavy for you, remember to look for the lightness and humor in everything you do and think of ways you can have more fun and help your clients at the same time. After all, we're just talking about getting clients, an important subject, no doubt, but not a heavy one. Start thinking about how you can incorporate more play into your life and work. Don't be afraid to:

- Be playful and quirky – be yourself.
- Be full of energy – enthusiasm is contagious.
- Help others laugh a lot – it's the best sales technique in the world.

It's been said that children laugh an average of 450 times per day, while adults laugh an average of only 15 times a day. If that's true and based on both of our experiences as parents, how did we end up 435 laughs short of a good time? Embrace a childlike sense of play and you'll be one step closer to booking yourself solid.

Clients Want You to Help Them

Begin to view your role with your clients as that of the creative director of their brand or project at hand, offering indispensable expertise and guidance. Providing anything less than insightful advice and creative guidance would be a huge disservice. Start to view yourself as a creative leader in their business.

We all want someone to believe in. Be that person and you can write your own ticket. If you view yourself as a trusted advisor, clients will never forget you. They will come back to you months or even years later. Trust is built over time, so a connection you make today may not develop until much later. Continue to share your vision, mission, and obligation to help people.

Give clients benefit after benefit and show them exactly how they can fulfill the promise of your offerings.

There is an acronym that is often used in sales — A, B, C — *always be closing*. Yuck! Sounds like cheesy sales talk to us. Instead, we say — A, B, C — *always be communicating* the benefits you offer. But first:

1. Select a target market.
2. Identify your clients' urgent needs and compelling desires.
3. Determine the number-one biggest result you help them get.
4. Uncover the deep-rooted, core benefits of that big result (financial, emotional, physical, and spiritual).

Got it? Good.

3

Develop a Personal Brand

Every time you suppress some part of yourself or allow others to play you small, you are in essence ignoring the owner's manual your creator gave you and destroying your design.
—Oprah Winfrey

Having established your target market and identified their urgent needs and compelling desires, the big result you help them get, as well as the benefits of the investable opportunities you offer, you are ready to develop a plan for deciding how you want to be known in your market – in an irresistible and unforgettable way.

You will do this by developing a *personal* brand. Brands are not just for big corporations. In fact, a personal brand will serve as an important key to your success. A personal brand will help clearly and consistently define, express, and communicate who you are, who you serve, and why you have chosen to dedicate your life and work to serving your target market so that you can attract your most ideal clients and not those who are less than ideal. Personal branding is far more than just what you do or what your website and business cards look like. It *is* you – uniquely you. It allows you to distinguish yourself from everyone else: what is unique about who you are, what you stand for, and what you do.

Branding

Your brand is certainly about making yourself known for your skills and talents, but more than that – your brand is about *what you stand for*. Successful people find their style, build a brand based on it, and boldly express themselves through that brand. Letting the world see your true, authentic worth is powerful, and it makes you memorable.

Think about some of the most successful people you know. The entertainment and creative industries offer great examples. Beyoncé's brand is centered around empowerment, artistry, and meticulous perfection, delivering powerful performances that resonate globally. Banksy is known for his provocative and socially relevant street art, creating a brand that challenges societal norms and invokes thought. Greta Gerwig, a renowned film director, has carved a niche with her distinct storytelling style, bringing nuanced, female-centric stories to life on the big screen. Each of these individuals has built a brand that resonates with different types of audiences. Some people love Beyoncé's music and performances, while others might be more drawn to Banksy's art or Greta Gerwig's films. The bolder, more authentic, and more concise your personal brand is, the more easily you'll attract those you're meant to work with.

That's how a personal brand works – it defines you, but first you must define it. Your personal brand will give you the ability to attract fun and exciting clients who understand and get you. And you get them. You can see that each of the creative professionals we described expanded their repertoire after they became well known. Well, all of them except perhaps Banksy, who continues to operate in his enigmatic, rebellious style that has always been successful for him.

Develop a personal brand that looks like you, thinks like you, and sounds and feels like you – one that is instantly recognizable as your essence. It should be:

- Clear
- Consistent
- Authentic
- Memorable
- Meaningful
- Soulful
- Personal

There are three components to your personal brand:

1. *Who and do what* statement, which is based on who you serve and what you help them do or get.
2. *Why you do it* statement, which is based on why you get up every day to do your work – what you stand for. Sure, you stand for lots of things, but you're going to choose one big one to stake your name on.
3. Your personal *tagline*. More on these three components in a minute. But first…

Should You Operate Under Your Name or an Agency Name?

This is a common question that many creative service providers ask themselves: should you operate under your own name or create an agency or business name? While it's an important question to consider (and we'll get to how to make that decision in a minute), even if you decide to go down the path of having an agency, it's crucial to develop and maintain your personal brand. Why? Because while you can scale the agency, bringing in different partners and contributors to its brand or even sell it, you will always be you. Your personal brand represents your unique vision, expertise, and values, and there will always be opportunities that are specifically for you and not your company.

When it comes to deciding whether to use your name or an agency name for your business, the answer lies in where you see yourself in the next five years. If you envision growing a team soon and scaling your business, it's important to start thinking of a brand larger than yourself. Employees often want to feel like they are part of something bigger, a team working toward a common goal, rather than just supporting an individual's personal brand. An agency name can create a sense of unity and collective purpose, which can be more attractive to potential hires and contribute to their motivation and contribution.

Personally, we recommend choosing a brand name for your agency that is not your personal name – unless you are 100% sure you want to remain a solopreneur for your entire career. This approach has several benefits, including the flexibility to scale and bring in diverse talent without the limitations of a personal brand. More important, it will be much easier to sell the agency down the road if it operates under a distinct brand name. Potential buyers are often more interested in acquiring a well-established business entity with its own identity, rather than one that is closely tied to an individual's name and identity. By creating a separate brand name for your agency, you enhance its marketability and future-proof your business for potential sale opportunities.

But your personal brand can provide flexibility. It allows you to take on opportunities that are specifically suited to you as an individual, such as speaking engagements, book deals, or consulting projects that might not align directly with your agency's focus. Maintaining a strong personal brand alongside an agency brand ensures you have the freedom to pivot or take on personal projects without confusing your agency's clients or diluting its brand.

Releasing Blocks

Before we begin to craft your personal brand, it's important to address any blocks you are inadvertently creating that may hold you back from fully expressing yourself. We know it can seem unusual to discuss personal blocks as it relates to branding, but this is *personal* branding, and this is your *life* we're talking about. You want to play the biggest game possible, don't you? The following questions can help you gain clarity about how you want to be known in the world. Consider them seriously.

> **The greatest strategy for personal and business development on the planet is bold self-expression.**

Are you fully self-expressed? We ask this because to create a gutsy, passionate, ardent, provocative, courageous, valiant, vibrant, dynamic, luminous, and respected personal brand, you must be fully self-expressed.

You can't hide behind the shingle that you've hung over your door, and you can't water yourself down in any way, shape, or form. If you do, you won't be of interest to the people you're meant to serve.

As a business owner, you probably already work *on* your business – such as setting up an automatic marketing system – and work *in* your business, serving your clients. How you brand yourself is equally critical and is a reflection of how you work *on yourself.*

Have you compromised yourself or watered yourself down in any area of your business? For example, have you been in a business situation in which you walked away feeling like you settled for less or compromised your integrity? You may be thinking, "I don't sell out. I've never compromised or sold out." If you haven't, you are unique. It's completely normal to compromise yourself from time to time.

It's also completely normal, especially when you are starting out, to wonder whether you are "ready," whether you have enough training, or whether what you have to offer is of any value. The truth is that you may never feel completely "ready," and if you get stuck perseverating about these questions, you'll never go out and find those people you are meant to serve.

While self-doubt can happen to anyone, at any time in their career, we've found that it is especially common in those who are starting out on their creative journey. Many suffer from impostor syndrome – they believe that they are undeserving of their achievements or that they are not as competent or intelligent as others might think. They worry that, sooner or later, everyone will find out. This can be incredibly damaging to their success, as it holds them back from being fully self-expressed, and as a result, they end up selling themselves short, thinking small, and being afraid to take the steps needed to move forward and build a successful career.

It will benefit you well to know exactly where you have run into trouble in the past. Working independently and starting and running your own business is challenging, and you can eliminate a lot of pain and surprise right now by acknowledging the issues you may have buried or have had a difficult time confronting in the past.

1.3.1 Written Exercise: Even though it may be a bit unpleasant to think about, list the ways in which you've sold out, settled for less, or compromised your integrity in your business, either now or in the past.

1.3.2 Written Exercise: What about the flip side? Tap into instances in your business life when you've felt alive and vibrant – fully self-expressed. Everything you did just flowed. Draw on all of your senses. What was happening at that time that made you feel so alive?

1.3.3 Written Exercise: Now compare the two areas, the ones in which you sold out and the situations in which you felt most fully self-expressed. How can you change your behavior to speak boldly and from a place of free expression so that you're working in situations that make you feel fully self-expressed? How will you communicate to make sure you stop compromising or watering yourself down in the future?

1.3.4 Written Exercise: Start with a few situations (fairly comfortable ones) in which you could practice speaking from a bolder and more self-expressed place.

1.3.5 Written Exercise: Write down a few more situations (that seem a little more difficult) that you'd like to work up to speaking more boldly about.

There are two reasons for the exercises you're doing. The first is so you can help clients understand how you can help them. The second is so you can make sure your personal and professional intentions are clear. Clear intentions allow you to gracefully and confidently move toward your goals. Conflicting intentions will undermine your success without you even knowing it. They will hold you back from your dreams. They are the mother of energy drain and confusion. From a perspective of a personal brand identity, conflicting intentions will eventually lead to a bland message and a less successful you.

1.3.6 Written Exercise: Identify one of your most important intentions as it relates to your business.
  Example: I intend to book myself solid.

1.3.7 Written Exercise: Take a good hard look within to see if you can identify any potentially conflicting intentions for the intention you identified. These are likely to be subconscious and more difficult to identify, and they are nearly always based on fear.
  Example: If I book myself solid, I won't have time for myself. Or, to book myself solid, I'll have to promote myself, and self-promotion will make me feel pathetic and vulnerable. Or maybe you want to book yourself solid but you *think* self-promotion is unappealing.

1.3.8 Booked Solid Action Step: Identifying and acknowledging your conflicting intentions is the first big step in releasing them. Awareness is key, but it is not always enough to prevent conflicting intentions from affecting and blocking our positive intentions. The next step in the process is to identify the underlying fears. Once you've identified them, you can begin to take steps to relieve them.

For this step, it's critical that you carefully choose one or two sincerely and highly supportive friends to share your new insights with. They must be truly supportive and willing to help you change. Often, as we begin to make changes in our lives, whether business or personal, some of our most dearly beloved friends and family can feel threatened by the process of change. Although they may consciously want you to be successful, they may have their own subconscious conflicting intentions and be highly invested in wanting to maintain their own comfort zone by keeping you in yours. These are not the folks you want to ask for help from to do this exercise. In fact, they're not people you want to spend much time with.

Share the intentions and their conflicting counterparts with one or two others and ask your friends to help you in recognizing whether these are genuine concerns or unfounded fears. Then brainstorm ways to address the problems.

Although you can take this step on your own, we're often too close to our own fears to see them clearly. Having a supportive friend, mentor, or professional coach who has a bit more objectivity than we do can help put them into perspective.

You Are Uniquely You

It's often those qualities that make you uniquely you – the ones that come so naturally to you that you don't even think about them – that become the best personal brands.

A student of Joana's, a young designer named Jessica, came to her feeling demotivated and unfulfilled by the work she was doing. She had been serving her clients with brand identity and web design, but the projects weren't sparking her interest or passion. It was clear she needed a change, but she wasn't sure what direction to take.

When Joana dug around to find out what Jessica could bring to the table that was unique and where her passions lay, she discovered an intriguing part of her past. Jessica used to be a model. Though she no longer wanted to model, she still loved the beauty and fashion world and the magic of photoshoots. This revelation was a breakthrough.

Through a series of back-and-forth discussions, they uncovered a path where Jessica could feel creatively self-expressed and position herself for success. They realized Jessica could leverage her deep knowledge of the fashion and beauty world to become a creative director for beauty and fashion brands. This role would allow her not only to oversee the brand identity piece but also to partner with photographers and art direct photoshoots (a prospect that made her light up).

This new direction was a perfect fit. Jessica's experience in the fashion industry, combined with her design skills, enabled her to carve out a niche where she felt passionate and uniquely qualified. She was able to transform her career by embracing her past experiences and passions, turning them into a vibrant and fulfilling new path.

You may not have a background in modeling or a specific industry, but chances are you do have something unique, maybe even quirky, that you really want to express and that others will notice and respond to.

1.3.9 Written Exercise: To know which secret quirk or natural talent is waiting in the wings to bring you wealth, happiness, and unbridled success in your business, answer the following questions:

- How are you unique?
- What are three things that make you memorable?
- What are the special talents that you are genetically coded to do? What have you been good at since you were a kid?
- What do people always compliment you on?
- What do you love or never grow tired of talking about in your personal life?
- What do you want to say that you would never grow tired of talking about when you are asked about your work?

Many times we are too close to see the qualities or quirks that stand out to others. Send a few of these questions to different people in your life to get their responses about you and your personality. Not only will you start to see some of the same truths about who you are, but you'll get back the most touching and warm emails. Give it a try.

1.3.10 Booked Solid Action Step: Send an email to five or more people (include friends, family, clients, neighbors, and acquaintances from all the different aspects of your life).

- Ask them to provide you with your top three personality traits or quirks.
- Ask for fun or unique experiences they've had with you.
- Tell them to be brave and not to be shy.

Remember that your work is likely to fail if you don't love it and share it with the world. And here's the biggie: *when you're fully self-expressed, you likely love marketing.* You won't have conflicting intentions about promoting yourself. You won't feel that the world is coming to an end when you get a rejection. You'll smile and move on to the next opportunity because your ability to express yourself is directly proportional to your level of confidence and vice versa.

With all of this new and insightful information about yourself, you should be thrilled that you've already made it through the challenge of choosing your path and being an independent business owner. That's no easy task. Keep all of these insights in mind as you begin to craft your own personal brand.

The Three Components of Your Personal Brand

As we mentioned earlier, there are three components to your personal brand:

1. Your *who and do what* statement
2. Your *why you do it* statement
3. Your tagline

Laser-beam your focus on these three aspects of your personal brand until you feel totally and utterly fully expressed when you put words to your *who and do what* statement, your *why you do it* statement, and your tagline. The process may take a day or it may take a few months. The important thing is to give yourself the time to really give thought to it all.

Your Who and Do What *Statement*

Your *who and do what* statement lets others know exactly who you help and what you can help them do. It is the first filter that people will put you through when considering your services for hire. Your potential clients will look at it to see if you help people like them in their specific situation. But is it enough to hire you? Probably not. There are other people who offer the same or similar services that help them get what they want. So, once they are convinced that you help them get what they want, they consider…

Your **Why You Do It** *Statement*

After potential clients identify with your *who and do what* statement, they will want to know if they connect with you on a personal, emotional, or philosophical level. They'll want to know if they connect with your *why you do it* statement — the reason you do what you do and what you stand for. It's the reason you get up every day to do the work that you do. It represents who you are. Those who resonate with your *why you do it* statement will feel it on a deep level and be strongly attracted to you. Your *why you do it* statement doesn't necessarily need to be wildly unique. It just needs to be deeply meaningful to you — and to the people you're *meant to serve*.

Your Tagline

Your tagline, based on your *why you do it* statement, is something you'll never get tired of hearing. And the first time you hear someone refer to you by it, you'll want to cry tears of joy. You'll formulate one simple sentence that allows people to define you in a manner of your own choosing. You'll never get tired of saying it or hearing it because it's based on what you stand for and what's important to you. And, most important, not only will it very deeply and truly mean something to you, it will resonate with the people you're meant to serve. Reading or hearing your tagline will be the defining moment people need to decide whether to purchase your services, products, or programs.

Your *tagline* lets others know what it's like to be around you. It says something about who you are at your core, and it's the essence of what you want to achieve or experience in the world. Think of it as the bigger vision that is the inspiration for what you do in your business. Your *why you do it* statement and its associated *tagline* is the way in which you want to touch others' lives in a positive and meaningful way.

Your tagline is not necessarily specific to your target market. It may resonate with many people in your target market — your ideal clients, specifically — but your tagline is not necessarily about your target market; it's about the emotional connection you make with people in general *and* with your ideal clients in your target market. Many people serve the same target market you serve, but your *tagline* is what will resonate with some people and not with others. It will resonate with those you're meant to serve.

Why have you dedicated your life to serving others? How do you want to make a difference?

> ***If you don't want to make a difference, consider making your living as something other than a service professional. The operative word is* service.**

To wrap up, let's review:

1. Who and do what statement (For example: "I help brands create visually engaging and memorable identities.")
2. Why you do it statement (For example: "I believe in the transformative power of design to connect brands with their audience.")
3. Tagline (For example: "I'm the creative alchemist who turns your brand vision into reality.")

1.3.11 Written Exercise: Start with the basics. Keep it simple and straightforward. What is your *who and do what* statement? Who do you help and what do you help them do? Refer to your target market from Chapter 2. The first time around, just come up with something accurate and clear for now — make sure a five-year-old can understand it. List as many possibilities as come to mind. Finish this statement, "I help…"

Example: I help … e-commerce business owners sell more of their products online.

1.3.12 Written Exercise: Set aside your inner critic and give yourself permission to think big — I mean *really big,* bigger than you've ever dared to think or dream before. Be your most idealistic, inspired, creative, powerful you. What is your purpose? What is your vision of what you hope to achieve through your work? Remember, your work is an expression of who you are. List whatever comes to mind.

> **1.3.13 Written Exercise:** Keeping the preceding in mind, craft a possible *why you do it* statement.

> **1.3.14 Booked Solid Action Step:** If your *why you do it* statement is not immediately and easily identifiable, get together with a group of supportive friends or associates who know you well and ask them to brainstorm it with you. It's often the things about you that are most natural and that you don't even recognize that become key elements of your *why you do it* statement. Having some outside input and a few more objective perspectives can make all the difference.

> **1.3.15 Written Exercise:** Craft a possible tagline that represents and demonstrates your *why you do it* statement.

Roma Non è Stata Construita un Giorno (Rome Wasn't Built in a Day)

Neither was Michael's personal brand. He went through many, many versions, even one a month, before he got to a *why I do it* statement and tagline that worked for him. Michael was getting caught up in trying to find the perfect brand message or positioning statement. He thought it had to be perfect because it couldn't be changed. Eventually, he realized that creating a tagline that represented what he stood for was a process and that he'd just keep changing it until he got there. If he didn't start with something, though, what would he have had? Nothing. That's what.

First, he got clear on his *who and do what* statement: "I help professional service providers get more clients."

Then he got clear on his *why I do it* statement, which was "I want to help people think bigger about who they are and what they offer the world."

What took longer was nailing down his tagline. Michael worked really hard on trying to find it. It took about six months. He thought about it every day, but the amazing thing was that it came to him by accident. He was with a bunch of people, and they were masterminding and brainstorming about their businesses and talking about what they did. He was giving the others a hard time, teasing and questioning, and asked, "Why would I hire you for that?" In the process of playing devil's advocate, one of the women gave it right back to Michael, saying "Yeah, well, why would I hire you?" Michael blurted out, "Because I'm the guy to call when you're tired of thinking small." Suddenly the whole room went silent, as if everyone was holding their breath. After a few moments, the same woman shouted out "Yes! That is *so you!*" Everyone in the room was cheering, and the air was charged with excitement.

Even so, Michael didn't really think much about it until a couple of weeks later as he was talking to a colleague about an idea he had for a social network in which people could come together to think bigger about who they are and what they offer the world. Michael was excited about it, but questioned it: "I'm not sure about this *big* stuff. I came up with this tagline that I'm 'the guy to call when you're tired of thinking small,' but I'm not sure about it. A, because it's a little cheesy and B, do you think anyone will actually care about that?"

His colleague laughed and said, "Michael, are you dense?" to which he replied, "Yes, but you're going to have to be more specific for me." She explained to Michael that she likes being around him because he helps her think so much bigger about who she is and what she offers the world.

Michael realized then that because it was so natural to him to want to help people think bigger, it didn't seem like such a big deal. Actually, it can be a bit confronting to others because he can be pretty relentless about it. So, it can push people away if they want to keep playing small. It took discussing it with others who weren't as close to it as Michael was to get the perspective he needed. The exact thing that came most naturally to him was the thing that was drawing ideal clients to him.

As Michael began using his *why I do it* statement and tagline to let others know why he does what he does, he found that the people for whom it resonated would immediately comment on how much they connected with it. Those who didn't *get* it, wouldn't. That's okay. It's all about attracting those people who are meant to work with you.

The rest will be attracted to someone with whom they will resonate, and you won't end up with less than ideal clients.

Recall the story about the old man, the boy, and the donkey (from Chapter 1). The process of booking yourself solid isn't about how to please as many people as possible. It's about how to convey your own unique message to those who are waiting to hear it. That can't be achieved with personal branding that's been watered down in an attempt to appeal to everyone. It can be achieved only through bold, no-holds-barred self-expression. It's about being uniquely you and standing for something – in a big way.

How to Talk About What You Do

A conversation is a dialogue, not a monologue. That's why there are so few good conversations: due to scarcity, two intelligent talkers seldom meet.
—Truman Capote

A primary reason that many creative service providers fail to build thriving businesses is that they struggle to articulate in a clear and compelling way exactly what solutions and benefits they offer. They don't know how to talk about what they do without sounding confusing or bland or like everyone else – and without using an elevator speech. Yes, you heard us, *without* using an elevator speech.

The elevator speech (aka the elevator pitch or 30-second commercial) reflects the idea that it should be possible to wow someone with what you do in the time it takes an elevator to go from the first to the fifth floor.

Michael has been polling audiences of thousands for years on this issue. During each speech he asks "How many of you love, love, love *giving* your elevator speech?" Maybe two out of two thousand hands go up. He follows up with "How many of you love, love, love *listening* to other people giving *their* elevator speech?"

This time, no hands go up. So what gives? If we don't like listening to or giving the speech, why is it still being taught? Because, of course, we need to be able to talk about what we do – we get the concept. However, in this case, we think that the elevator speech has been inappropriately appropriated by the service professional. Not only does it not work well, but it makes us look foolish, or, worse yet, obnoxious.

The elevator pitch was born so that the inventor could pitch a product idea to a retailer or manufacturer or the *entrepreneur* could pitch a business idea to a venture capitalist or angel investor in the hopes of receiving funding, not for the service professional to try to build a relationship of trust with a potential client over time. Venture capitalists often judge the quality of an idea on the basis of the quality of its elevator pitch. It makes perfect sense, in that situation. But this is not how a relationship develops between a client and a *service professional*. You're trying to earn the status of a trusted advisor, not trying to raise money to create some new product like metal-detecting sandals. Totally different context. Totally different dynamic.

We're on a mission to kill the elevator speech, to remove it from the business vernacular – for the creative service provider. We hope you'll join us on this mission and learn how to talk about what you do without ever resorting to an elevator speech. So, what do you do instead?

You will use this crazy concept we call a *conversation*. Weird, we know. Over the course of this chapter, we're going to teach you a Book Yourself Solid Dialogue, a creative – but not scripted – conversation that will spark interest when appropriate about you and your services. The Book Yourself Solid Dialogue will allow you to have a meaningful conversation (*conversation* being the operative word) with a potential client or referral source. The dialogue is a dynamic, lively description of the people you help, what challenges they face, how you help them, and the results and benefits they get from your services. It is also intended to replace the static, boring, and usual response to the question, "What do you do?"

The answer "I'm a graphic designer (or insert your creative profession here)" often elicits nothing more than a polite nod, comment, or awkward silence and blank stare, which always makes Joana fear they're thinking "Oh, so you spend your day doodling and playing with fonts." Once you get that response, anything more you say about yourself or your services will sound pushy. Worse yet, you could supplement the rote answer with an overblown, highfalutin, hyperbole-laden elevator speech that's supposed to make you look like a rock star in 30 seconds. Unfortunately, it's doubtful that the one-two punch of boring answer followed by excessively exuberant elevator pitch is going to compel the listener to whip out a credit card right then and there.

Instead, how about a meaningful, connected *dialogue* with a potential client or referral source? Think of it as a conversation between two people, each of whom actually cares about what the other has to say. The beautiful thing is that the interchange is based on successfully understanding why people buy what you're selling. And because of the work we did together in Chapter 2, you already know why people buy what you're selling.

You previously created your *who and do what* statement. That's a fantastic first step and an excellent tool for starting a conversation about what you do. Now you must be sure that you can captivate and actively engage the person you're talking to in a conversation that elicits questions rather than just polite acknowledgment. You must talk *with* people, not *at* them, which means listening to them, too, and really hearing what they're interested in, and what their needs are. After all, their needs may be exactly what you serve. Avoid giving a prepared script. Doing so is generally a train wreck waiting to happen. You'll see that you can have long, medium, or short conversations based on your Book Yourself Solid Dialogue that will allow you to connect with different people in different situations. You tell them about the people you work with, and then you listen to their response. You build on their response, and before you know it, you are having a conversation that is informative and inspiring – and that's the key to talking about what you do without being bland or confusing or, worse yet, obnoxious, albeit, unintended.

You are so much more than just your professional title: graphic designer, copywriter, illustrator, video editor, or other dictionary description that defines you as one of the masses.

Think about it for a moment. As a creative service provider, you meet someone who really needs your help who would also be an ideal client. The only problem is that she has a preconceived notion of what your area of creative expertise is all about, what working with a creative service provider is like, and it's not a preconceived notion that sets you up for success.

Imagine this scenario: the potential client asks you what you do. You say, "I'm an interior designer (or insert your creative profession here)." Before you know what's happened, you see the potential client's face contort, her left eyebrow lifts along with the left side of her upper lip, and her nostrils begin to flare. The potential client says, "Oh yeah . . . I worked with an interior designer once. She had a fantastic portfolio, but our collaboration was a disaster. She completely ignored my ideas and preferences, opting for what she thought was trendy. The space ended up looking stylish but felt nothing like 'home' to me. It was as if she was designing for a magazine feature, not for real people living in the space. I spent so much, only to redo most of it myself later. Now I'm hesitant to ever work with an interior designer again."

Uh-oh.

Would you like to get that kind of response when you tell someone what you do? And this can happen to any service professional, not just creative service providers. Say a stockbroker meets someone whose only introduction to stockbrokers has been the movie *Boiler Room*, a movie about stockbrokers who try to swindle innocent people out of their life's savings. Not a pretty picture.

Chances are, the prospects you'll be talking to have already worked with other creative service providers, or if they are new business owners, at least they would know someone who has. This means that their perceptions are often shaped by these direct or indirect experiences. If their only reference is a negative story, like the example given earlier, simply introducing yourself with your professional title — be it a graphic designer, photographer, or illustrator — might not make a strong impression.

How much more are you than your professional title? Your Book Yourself Solid Dialogue will allow you to set yourself apart from every other creative service providers in your field. It provides you with the opportunity to highlight the ways in which you and your services, products, and programs are unique — and do so with passion.

If your Book Yourself Solid Dialogue reads like your résumé, you'll bore people to tears, and although they may not say it, they'll be thinking, "Who cares? So what? What has any of that got to do with me?" Your potential client wants to know: "What's in it for me?"

Developing Your Book Yourself Solid Dialogue

You're going to break this down into its smallest components and gather all the information you've worked hard to compile in the previous pages. You've chosen your target market, and you've begun to develop your personal brand by crafting your *who and do what* statement, your *why I do it* statement, and your tagline. Now you're going to go back through all the exercises you've done and clean up your core message. If you've kept up on the exercises, mastering the ability to have a meaningful Book Yourself Solid Dialogue is a relatively simple process, and yet this powerful piece will make all the difference in your business and your message.

Five-Part Book Yourself Solid Dialogue Formula

Let's put it all together and create a few different versions of your dialogue: short, medium, and long. Please, please, bear in mind that we are not crafting a speech. We're just giving you some structure so that you can begin to imagine the possible content of the Book Yourself Solid Dialogue that is a *conversation*.

1.4.1 Written Exercise: Each of the following five parts has already been answered in previous exercises. All you need to do is pull the pieces into the following formula.

Part I: Introduce your target market.

Part II: Identify and summarize the three biggest and most critical problems that your target market faces.

Part III: List how you solve these problems and present clients with investable opportunities.

Part IV: Demonstrate the number-one most relevant result you help your clients achieve.

Part V: Reveal the deeper core benefits your clients experience.

You now have an outline that will help you clearly articulate what you do without sounding confusing and bland. In fact, you'll sound like a superstar because you can use this outline or framework to have a meaningful conversation with another human being. We know we're being redundant here, but it's so important that we're willing to. This is not an unchangeable script. Don't stay married to the format. Be sure to improvise. Using the structure can be helpful but you may not need to go through every element of this framework in every conversation. The person you're engaged with might end up doing all the talking and even supply your side of the dialogue accurately. Then you can just sit back and listen.

The point is, if you're prepared with these five elements, you have the required ingredients for talking about what you do so you can cook up a sweet and tasty business, booked solid with high-paying, high-value clients. (Make note of how each part of the exercises you've just done fits into the conversations that follow, and note also how each part flows as the result of a natural conversation.)

Short and Sweet

Start by trying the short version, which is essentially an expanded *who and do what* statement.

- I help [Part I]. . .[insert Part V].

Example: Checkout line at the supermarket.

MATTHEW: Nice to meet you, Joana. What do you do?
JOANA: I help e-commerce business owners sell more products.
MATTHEW: Oh, that's very interesting. My brother is in e-commerce. He sells supplements online. Do you think you could help him?
JOANA: Well, maybe! Tell me a little bit more about his business.

Now, we're connecting.

The Mid-Length Version

You can easily adapt the Book Yourself Solid Dialogue as needed. Try a mid-length version and just tighten it up a bit.

- I help [Part I].
- You know how [insert Parts I and II]?
- Well, what I do is [insert Parts III and V].

Example: Industry conference.

DELIA: Nice to meet you, Joana. What do you do for a living?

JOANA: I help e-commerce business owners sell more products online.

DELIA: That's so important . . . so many more people are shopping online these days that I would imagine it's getting tougher for e-commerce businesses to stand out from the competition.

JOANA: You're 100% right. And with paid traffic rising with it, what's happening is that e-commerce business owners are only able to do it at the cost of increasing their marketing spend. [Parts I and more of II].

DELIA: Can I confess something to you, Joana? I'm one of those people. As our customer acquisition cost is going up and up, I've been finding myself staying up all night trying to come up with better ideas for ads, tweaking our audiences, the copy, etc., but not getting the results I want.

JOANA: I hear that! But it doesn't have to be that way. In fact, before working with us, most of our clients had no choice but to increase their advertising spend every month. What we offer is a different alternative: a one-time investment that provides results month after month. Results like doubling their conversions or tripling the average revenue per visitor. [More of Part II, Part III, and Part V].

DELIA: Okay, now you have my full attention! Tell me more!

And now we're connecting.

The Long Version

Easy-peasy-lemon-squeezy. All you need to do is insert Parts I through V as appropriate:

- You know how [drop in Part I] do, are, or feel [include some of Part II]?
- Well, what I do is [articulate Part III].

- The result is [reveal Part IV].
- The benefits are [insert lots of Part V].

Example: Casual conversation at a cocktail party.

CHRIS: Hey, Joana, what is it that you do?

JOANA: Thanks for asking, Chris. Do you know how many e-commerce business owners (Part I) are facing increasingly expensive media buying, leading to higher marketing budgets just to maintain the same results? Do you know any business owners facing that?

CHRIS: Oh, yeah, I do. Actually, that's just like my sister, Jane. She runs an e-commerce skincare brand. She mentioned that her customer acquisition costs through ads have tripled.

JOANA: Oh, no kidding . . . and that's probably eating into her profit margins, or she's up all night trying to come up with ad copy or creatives that will stand out from the crowd and help lower her ad costs.

CHRIS: Exactly! I've been helping her with copywriting, but we're not seeing much change, and I'm running out of ideas.

JOANA: I hear you. It's a common challenge. It's getting increasingly difficult to lower ad costs just by tweaking creatives and tinkering with audiences. (Part II) Fortunately, I've been able to help our e-commerce clients increase their average order value, in some cases even tripling it, and boost their conversions to get more from their advertising spend. In fact, we recently helped a client add $2 million to their annual revenue without increasing their ad spend, through a one-time project with us. (Part IV) There are definitely ways around it!

CHRIS: Wow, those results are impressive! That could really ease my sister's stress, letting her focus on creating great products instead of doing constant marketing to stay afloat.

JOANA: Exactly! We don't want our clients worrying about what's outside their area of expertise. We want them focused on their area of genius, which is what got them to the success they currently have, which in turn will not only help further grow their business through the development of

> new products, but like you said, reduce their stress, and fall
> back in love with running their business. (Part V)
> Chris sighs, takes a meaningful pause, then says . . .

CHRIS: I'm so glad I asked you what you did. How can I get my sister in touch with you? She could really use your help.

JOANA: Would you like to give me your details and I'll follow up with you on Monday so you can introduce me to your sister?

CHRIS: That would be great, Joana. This way, I won't run into the risk of forgetting.

That's a pretty good way to have a real conversation with someone about what you do. Of course, we've written this scene, so it works perfectly. And, when it's in written form like this, it can feel like a script. It's not, though. In real life, it won't always be this smooth or successful. But, if you listen well, are flexible, and can adapt to the dynamic and specifics at hand, more often than not, you'll knock it out of the park.

Or Joana could start by saying "I'm the founder of Gif Design Studios, an award-winning design agency that's been running for almost a decade now. Most recently, I'm also the co-author of a book called *Book Yourself Solid for Creatives*, which comes from one of the most popular brands in the world for marketing creative service providers. Additionally, I speak regularly all over the world as an expert on design, creativity, and running a business as a creative service provider. Through my coaching business, the Ambitious Creatives, we've helped more than 15 000 creative service providers land more clients and get booked solid with their dream clients, without burnout." But then she'd sound like an arrogant, self-important jerk with a narcissistic personality disorder. These kinds of credentials and information should come out over time, when appropriate, not three seconds after someone says "What do you do?"

Once you've clearly identified your target market, understand their needs and desires, and can articulate how you help them by identifying the core benefits associated with the results of your services, you'll never be caught off guard again. We suggest you continue to refine your message over time as you learn more about what resonates with the people you're meant to serve. Then practice it over and over. We do.

Getting into a Book Yourself Solid Dialogue with Ease

Start in the comfortable confines of your home. It may take some time for your Book Yourself Solid Dialogue to feel natural. While you don't want your dialogue to sound stiff and rehearsed, you do want to practice it. The more you practice it, the more comfortable you'll get with it, the less rehearsed it will sound, and the more improvisational you will be. You get only one chance to make a first impression. Present yourself and your business in a powerful and compelling way.

Practicing in this way will help you to become comfortable with the multitude of ways in which your Book Yourself Dialogue will unfold when you're speaking with a variety of people. It is truly a dialogue, not a speech or a script, so every time you have a dialogue with someone about what you do, it will be unique. Since the people you'll be speaking with won't be reading a script, they may or may not respond in similar ways to what we outlined here, but you'll soon discover that when you know your Book Yourself Solid Dialogue well, it won't matter. You'll easily and effortlessly respond in the most appropriate way.

1.4.2 Booked Solid Action Step: Practice with a colleague or two. Call each other spontaneously to ask, "What is it that you do?" The most important principle of the Book Yourself Solid system is actually using what we teach you. Learning it is only a means to an end. Taking action will get you booked solid.

After you've practiced with your colleague, answer these questions for each other:

- Did I sound relaxed and comfortable?
- Could you sense my passion and excitement for what I do?
- What really grabbed your attention?
- What did you like best or least about my Book Yourself Solid Dialogue?

Use this exercise as the great opportunity it is to get honest, open feedback so that you can fine-tune your Book Yourself Solid Dialogue and make it the best it can be.

Be sure to speak with a lot of expression. Get excited and show the passion you have for the problems you solve and what you do in the world. If you're not very interested in what you do, no one else will be, either.

When you're passionate and excited about what you do and you let it show, it's attractive. Real passion can't be faked, and there's nothing more appealing and convincing than knowing someone is speaking from the heart.

And don't forget to:

- *Smile:* Really smile – a big, bold, friendly smile.
- *Make eye contact:* You probably won't connect with others on a deep level if you aren't making eye contact.
- *Be confident:* Use confident, open body language. Stand up straight, yet be relaxed.
- *Listen!* Stop and listen intently to the needs and desires of the person you're speaking to so that you can address whatever is most important and relevant to them. Stay in the moment and avoid anticipating where the conversation is going to go and what you plan on saying.

A well-crafted Book Yourself Solid Dialogue that is infused with your own unique brilliance and passion is incredibly powerful. Claim your passion, claim your voice, and share it with the world one person at a time.

Building Trust and Credibility

Being booked solid requires that you are considered credible within your marketplace, that you be perceived as likeable, and that you earn the trust of the people you'd like to serve. Now that you have a solid foundation, it's time to look at how to develop a strategy for creating trust and credibility so that you stand out from the crowd and begin to build relationships with your potential patients. Your strategy will be based on:

- Becoming and establishing yourself as a likeable expert in your field
- Building relationships of trust over time through your sales cycle
- Keeping in touch with clients, potential clients, and referral partners

In the first module, you spent time contemplating the people you want to serve, how best to serve them, how to express yourself uniquely through the services you offer, and how to talk to people you hope to serve about how you can help them. Now it's time to step things up a notch and look at what you have to do to earn the trust of the people you're meant to serve.

As before, we walk you step-by-step through the process, and you'll begin to see that marketing and sales doesn't have to be so hard after all. In fact, we think you'll find that it can even be exciting and fun.

Becoming a Likable Expert in Your Field

*All credibility, all good conscience, all evidence of truth
comes only from the senses.*
—Friedrich Nietzsche

Have you heard the expression "It's not what you know that's important but who you know"? There's some truth to this, but if you're a professional service provider, consider the importance of "Who knows *what* you know and do they *like* you?" If you want to establish yourself as an expert in your field, a "category authority," potential clients as well as marketing and referral partners need to know that you know what you know; and they need to like you.

Even before we discuss how to position yourself as an expert within your field, let's get down to the nitty-gritty – the standard credibility builders. The standard credibility builders are the things you need to do and have in place to appear credible and professional. Once you have all your basics covered, then and only then can we discuss how to establish your reputation as an authority in your field and look at how your likeability influences your ability to get booked solid.

The Standard Credibility Builders

The standard credibility builders may seem obvious, but without them you won't be taken seriously, so they're worth reviewing:

- *You must have a professional email address:* One that includes your domain name. joedesign@gmail.com doesn't qualify.
- Either yourfirstname@yourfullname.com or yourfirstname@your-businessname.com or similar variation is more appropriate. And, even if you don't have a website built yet, you can still purchase a domain name and use an email address associated with that domain in the meantime.
- *If you don't have a website, have one built now.* (An Upwork or fiverr profile doesn't count.) Actually, wait until you read Chapter 15 of this book, the Book Yourself Solid Web Strategy. Please don't make the mistake of assuming that your work alone is enough to get noticed. Even outstanding work needs to be seen; without visibility, it's impossible for others to recognize, trust, and reward your talents.
- *Make sure your social media profiles represent you professionally:* Think about how a potential client perceives you. What do you want them to know and what might turn them off? Learn more about how to manage your social media profiles in Chapter 15.
- *Have professionally produced photographs taken:* Display them on your website, on LinkedIn, on other social media profiles, and in promotional materials. Find any way you can to use pictures or video to demonstrate your professionalism on all promotional materials. And certainly display photographs of yourself working and showing the behind the scenes of the process or work in progress. Not having photographs readily available on your website or other marketing materials leaves your potential clients wondering what you have to hide and doesn't give them the opportunity to connect with you. Interestingly, there is some social science that suggests when people see lots of photos of you in different environments, they begin to feel that they know you when, in fact, they don't.
- *Obtain and showcase specific testimonials rather than general testimonials:* A comment from a client named H. G. that says "Pedro was

really great to work with" is not going to hold a lot of weight, and it's certainly not going to get you booked solid. However, a very specific testimonial like this from a named person carries more weight: "Ever since our new website launched, we've seen our opt-in rates go up by 20% and our average order value double! All thanks to Pedro's amazing work, which not only was incredibly beautiful, but was delivered on time and on budget." The testimonial is results-oriented. This client's satisfaction will represent the results that many of his clients want to achieve. Even better would be a testimonial from a well-known person. For example, if Pedro had done Taylor Swift's website and she offered the same testimonial, wouldn't you want to work with Pedro? You'd figure if he's good enough for Taylor, he's good enough for me. This is important because testimonials can come off as mundane and may not serve as true differentiators unless they are from people recognizable to the potential client. So, ask everybody you work with to offer specific, positive praise of you and your work and reach out to people you respect. Connect with them, and when the time is right, ask them to supply you with a testimonial of your work.

Here is an example of how you can ask your clients to provide specific, positive praise:

PEDRO: Caroline, can you believe it's been a month now since we've launched your website? How has business been since?

CAROLINE: I can hardly believe it; it almost seems too good to be true, but the last month was our best one yet. The website made me look so professional. It gave me the confidence to double my prices, and people are taking me up on it! I'm so thankful for your help!

PEDRO: I'm so happy for you. You know, Caroline, oftentimes people decide to work with me on their new website because of the testimonials they see online. Would you be willing to share your story and the results you've seen since launching it with us? It could be your story that compels someone to finally take their website to the next level.

Taking this approach when asking your clients to leave a testimonial is helpful because it tends to result in more specific, higher-quality testimonials. It also makes the client you are asking feel like they aren't just helping you but are also helping other potential clients who may be after similar results.

Bonus: Establish an advisory board: If well-known individuals will lend you their names, it will help you establish credibility within your target market. Simply being associated with other recognized experts can greatly enhance your credibility. Even if they haven't worked directly with you, their appreciation of your work and confidence in your professionalism will speak volumes.

Standards of Service

These are the basic standards of service that are essential for any decent service professional to adhere to and that your clients will expect. They help establish your credibility. The mistake that many service professionals make is thinking that these standards of service are all that are necessary to help them stand out from the crowd.

- *Quality of service:* Of course you should have a high quality of service. A potential client expects that you offer a high quality of service.
- *Methods and tools:* It's expected that you have the best methods and tools.
- *Responsiveness:* Being responsive is more than a mere courtesy — it's a cornerstone of trust and reliability. It's crucial to keep your clients informed, even when you're not ready to deliver their project. Promptly replying to their emails to set clear expectations for updates can make all the difference. The creative industries often struggle with keeping timelines and communication consistent; by setting a new standard and ensuring your clients never feel sidelined, you elevate your reputation and distinguish yourself from your peers.
- *Client importance:* Making your clients feel valued isn't just important — it's essential if you want to get booked solid. Every interaction should emphasize their importance to your business. It's more than

just making them feel important; it's about demonstrating that they are your top priority. This approach not only builds credibility but also strengthens your relationship with your clients, ensuring they understand their central role in your work.

- *Appropriate price:* Price is a signal of value, not just cost. While it's true that clients don't choose services based solely on price, setting rates that reflect the quality and value of the service you provide is crucial. Price your services too low and you'll risk raising doubts about the caliber of your service. Aim for pricing that communicates your worth and aligns with the exceptional service and outcomes clients can expect from you. More on pricing in Chapter 9.

Please do not assume that these standards of service will set you apart. They won't. They're a baseline. They're what every savvy client will expect. However, there is something very special that will make you stand out from the crowd every day of the week.

Becoming and Establishing Yourself as a Category Authority

Although being a category authority and establishing yourself as one may, at first glance, appear to be the same thing, they're not. This isn't about faking it until you make it. Before you can establish yourself as a category authority, you must *be* one. How do you do that? You truly become a category authority by absorbing everything you possibly can about the one thing you've decided to specialize in and by relentlessly honing your skills in this area.

*A **category authority** is a person who has achieved a deep and comprehensive understanding of a specific field or topic, demonstrated through consistent, high-level performance and recognition within that domain. This expertise may be acquired through formal education, extensive hands-on experience, continuous learning, or a combination of these paths.*

For many of us, the leap into learning all we can about our field can be immediately overwhelming, as the first thing we often learn is just how much we don't know. But this is a good thing. You can't seek knowledge that you don't know you need, so it is much better to first study what you didn't realize earlier that you didn't know, even if it deflates your ego. Likewise, integrating continuous practice into this learning process is crucial; it's the practice that translates knowledge into expertise.

If the thought of becoming and establishing yourself as a category authority immediately induces a sense of panic at the thought of all you'd have to learn and do, you're not alone. Or maybe you feel you already know enough to be an expert but the thought of having to put yourself so boldly – and publicly – front and center of your target market makes you want to run home for Mom's homemade chicken soup.

For some, the idea of putting yourself out in front of the people you'd like to serve in a big, bold, public way, where you'll be subject to public scrutiny, can trigger a multitude of insecurities. You'll know your dark side has taken over when thoughts start racing round and round inside your head like "Who am I to call myself an expert? What do I know? I'm such a fraud. I don't know enough yet. Maybe I'll never learn enough to be an expert. I don't even know where to begin." Or worse yet, "What if I put myself out there and fall flat on my face? What if I look silly and embarrass myself? What if everyone hates me? What if I get made fun of or criticized?" Does this sound familiar? I'll bet it does. Again, you're not alone. If you're feeling shadows of doubts beginning to loom, lock them in a soundproof closet and give control back to the bold and brilliant person you know you really are, and keep reading.

There's a big difference between being an expert in your field and being *the* expert in your field. We're not asking you to hold yourself out as better than everyone else or as the absolutely best in your field. If you do, you'll seem phony like someone who appoints themselves "the premier graphic designer in all of France" or "the number-one wedding photographer in Timbuktu," when they are actually the only wedding photographer in Timbuktu. These claims make you wonder "By whose standards? On what metrics is the statement based?" Each is over the top and likely false. We're simply asking you to be comfortable stating and showcasing your expertise.

Do I Have To?

Now that you've gotten past the shadows of doubts, if some other side of you has taken over and is whining "Do I have to?," the answer is a firm and resounding, "Yes, you do." Like it or not, becoming a category authority, an expert in your field, isn't optional if you want your business to be as successful as it can be. It's a must. Becoming and establishing yourself as a category authority will have such a powerful effect on the success of your business and will be so incredibly rewarding that it's well worth the effort and *perceived* risk (which means no real risk at all).

Becoming a category authority will:

- Create the credibility and trust necessary for potential clients to feel comfortable and confident about purchasing your services
- Gain you the visibility you'll need to reach all of your target market.
- Allow you to get your message out to the world in a big way as it raises awareness of yourself and your business *within* your target market. The idea is to be the first to come to mind when someone needs the kind of services that you offer.
- Help you gain clients and increase sales more easily and effortlessly while also allowing you to earn higher fees. It will give you the edge you need to stand out from the crowd of others who offer similar services, products, and programs. Suddenly, you'll no longer be just one of the masses.
- Make it much easier to move and expand into new markets of your choosing.
- Increase your own confidence in your ability to provide the best possible services, products, and programs to those who most need and want them.

Where to Begin

Do you remember that, in Chapter 2, we said there is a difference between your target market and your niche? Your target market is the group of people or businesses that you serve, and your area of specialty, what you become known for, is your niche.

You clarify this by first identifying what you'd like to become known for within your target market. If what you want to be known for is too broad or you try to become a category authority on too many topics, you'll overwhelm yourself and confuse your target market. A niche is focused, precise, and easy to demonstrate and articulate.

By identifying and focusing on the one thing you most want to become known for, you simplify and speed up the process, leaving no question in the minds of those in your target market about your area of expertise. This will allow you to create a synergy, not only among your services but among all the techniques you'll use to establish yourself as a category authority.

When it comes time to powerfully establish yourself as a category authority, you're going to saturate your target market using a variety of techniques that we'll discuss in Module Four, such as networking, direct outreach, referral strategies, speaking, writing, and web strategies. To do that later, it helps to focus, focus, focus, now.

2.5.1 Written Exercise: Please answer the following questions:

1. In what areas are you currently an expert?
2. In what areas do you need to develop your expertise?
3. What promises can you make and deliver to your target market that will position you as an expert?
4. What promises would you like to make and deliver to your target market but don't yet feel comfortable with?
5. What do you need to do to become comfortable at making and delivering these promises?

2.5.2 Written Exercise: Keeping the answers from the preceding written exercise in mind, if there was *one thing* you could be known for within your target market, what would it be?

2.5.3 Written Exercise: What do you need to *learn* to become a category authority in the area you'd like to be known for?

2.5.4 Written Exercise: List the ways in which you could learn the things you identified in the preceding written exercise.

Example: Books, Internet research, training programs, or apprenticing with a mentor who is already a category authority.

Even if you're already very knowledgeable about whatever it is you want to become known for, continuing to learn and staying up to date with the latest information in your field is not only a good idea but is required to remain booked solid. A good recommendation is to read at least one book a month, if not more, on your chosen subject, which will increase your knowledge, challenge you to see a different perspective, or spark new ideas and thoughts, all of which will enhance the value you provide to your clients.

2.5.5 Written Exercise: Research and list three books that meet the preceding criteria.

2.5.6 Booked Solid Action Step: Buy these three books and start reading the first one.

Making the Mental Shift

We've discussed what you need to have and do to be credible, and by now you understand the importance of becoming and establishing yourself as a category authority in a particular niche. We hope it's clear that it really helps to actually *be* an expert. You might think the logical next step would be to implement a plan to establish yourself as a category authority within your target market, but it's not. There's a critical mental shift that must take place first.

All of the Book Yourself Solid marketing strategies that you're going to learn in Module Four will put you out in front of your target market in such a big way that you will establish yourself as a category authority. First consider what you need to learn and what you need to do to establish your expertise so that when the time comes to implement the Book Yourself Solid Six Core Self-Promotion Strategies, you will *be* an expert. You will make the crucial mental shift of thinking of yourself as an expert. If *you* don't believe it, you'll have a hard time persuading anyone else to believe it.

> ***Begin to think of and refer to yourself as a category authority – an expert in your field.***

When the time comes to establish yourself as a category authority within your target market, you'll be comfortable with, and confident of, your expertise. If you already consider yourself an expert, then by all means begin including that in your current marketing materials.

Just remember – when communicating with your potential clients, be clear about what you know and clear about what you don't. People who are credible don't actually know everything, and they are just as comfortable saying that they don't know something as they are saying that they do.

There is one other very powerful mental and emotional factor that has a profound impact on your efforts to establish yourself as a category authority, one that may surprise you. We urge you not to discount or underestimate it.

The Power of Likeability

Now that you know what you need to do to become and establish yourself as a category authority, we're going to look at an even more important factor to consider: Do your potential clients like you? Do they perceive you as likeable? And I mean *really* likeable.

The fact is that if they don't, none of the rest of your efforts to establish yourself as a category authority will matter very much. That's a pretty bold statement, and it may come as a surprise to you, but bear with us as we shine some light on the subject, with the help of Tim Sanders and a few concepts from his book, *The Likeability Factor: How to Boost Your L-Factor and Achieve Your Life's Dreams.*

When you get right down to it, Sanders points out, "Life is a series of popularity contests." We don't want to admit it, we don't want to believe it, we've been told it ain't necessarily so, but ultimately, if you're well liked, if your likeability factor is high, you're more likely to be chosen and to get booked solid.

Mark McCormack, the founder of International Management Group (IMG), the most powerful sports management and marketing company, agrees: "All things being equal, people will do business with a friend. All things being unequal, people will still do business with a friend." If a potential client perceives you as the most credible and likeable, you're probably the one she'll hire. And even if all things are *not* equal, even if you aren't the candidate with the most experience or expertise, if your potential client likes you, it's your likeability that will win the day and the client.

To make choices, we go through a three-step process. First, we *listen* to something out of a field of opportunities. Then we either do or do not *believe* what we've heard. Finally, we put a *value* on what we've heard. Then, we make our choice.

With so many demands on our attention these days, we have to filter and carefully select what we give our attention to. This is why becoming and establishing yourself as a category authority is so important. Your target market and your potential clients need a reason to deem your message important enough to sit up and pay attention, to *listen* to it. If you're likeable, they're much more likely to do so and to remember what they've heard.

Once you've got their attention, they're listening, but will they *believe* what they're hearing? This is where your credibility comes into play. With so many advertising messages coming at us from every direction each day — through spam email, radio and TV commercials, and infomercials, to name a few — we've become highly skeptical of much of what we hear. If you're credible, you're much more likely to be believed.

But wait, that's not the only factor that comes into play when someone is determining whether to believe you. Again, your likeability is a critical factor in establishing trust. Think about it for a moment. You're much more likely to trust, and to *believe*, someone you like. Sanders says, "When people like the source of a message, they tend to trust the message or, at least, try to find a way to believe it."

Let's suppose you've made it through the first two steps of this process. Your potential client has listened to you and believes you. Now she must determine the value of you and your message. Consider this example:

> Imagine an indie film festival gearing up for its next big event, on the lookout for a fresh brand identity and innovative marketing materials. We have two contenders: Alex, a seasoned graphic designer known for crafting sleek, modern identities for cultural events, and Morgan, also a designer but newer to the scene with a smaller portfolio.
>
> Alex leads off with a polished presentation showcasing his previous work. His professionalism and skill are clear, but the presentation is all business, heavy on past achievements and his sophisticated style. This might leave the festival directors wandering about the room for creative collaboration.
>
> Morgan, meanwhile, starts her presentation by engaging the directors with questions about their personal connections to film and the festival's origins. She shares her own stories and enthusiasm for the project, quickly establishing a warm rapport. The atmosphere becomes collaborative and lively, setting a tone that's engaging and inclusive.
>
> Despite Alex's undeniable expertise, it's Morgan's genuine enthusiasm, her readiness for collaborative input, and her proactive approach that really resonate with the festival directors. Morgan's method highlights how likability and the ability to forge a real connection can be just as crucial as technical skill in winning new business.
>
> Your likeability factor has an enormous impact on your perceived value. Develop your credibility, establish yourself as an expert, strive to be your best and most likeable self, and you'll quickly become the best and most obvious choice for your potential clients.

6

The Book Yourself Solid Sales Cycle Process

*It is a mistake to look too far ahead. Only one link in
the chain of destiny can be handled at a time.*
—Sir Winston Churchill

Sales start with a simple conversation. It may be a conversation between you and a potential client, between one of your clients and a potential referral, between one of your colleagues and a potential referral, or between your website and a potential client. An effective sales cycle is based on turning these simple conversations into relationships of trust with your potential clients over time. We know that people buy from those they like and trust. This is never truer than for the professional service provider. We've covered likeability. Now, let's address the trust factor.

Building Relationships of Trust

If you don't have trust, then it doesn't matter how well you've planned, what you're offering, or whether you've created a wide variety of buying options to meet varying budgets. If a potential client doesn't trust you, nothing else matters. They aren't going to buy from you — period. If you think about it, this may be one of the main reasons you say you hate marketing and selling. You may be trying to sell to people with whom you have not yet built enough trust. All sales offers must be proportionate to the amount of trust you've earned.

What are your potential clients thinking?

- Do they really believe you can deliver what you say you can?
- Do they love your portfolio of sample work?
- Do they feel safe with you?
- Do they believe working with you will give them a significant return on their investment?

If you want a perpetual stream of inspiring and life-fulfilling ideal clients clamoring for your services and products, then just remember — all sales start with a simple conversation and are executed when a need is met and the appropriate amount of trust is assured.

Turn Strangers into Friends and Friends into Clients

We are continued to be surprised by how many creative service providers have been taught a marketing system that attempts to turn cold leads into paying clients with little regard for building trust and credibility along the way.

Consider the traditional cold pitch email so many of us were taught to write. Often, these emails are aimed at potential clients who, just moments ago, were completely unaware of us and our services.

If you've ever tried cold email pitches before, you know how challenging it can be to get a reply let alone persuade them to invest in your services. This approach rarely builds the kind of trust that fosters long-term client relationships.

Instead, we want to encourage you to first work on building trust and credibility with potential clients through your marketing *before* making an offer for them to become a client.

If you're doing it now, please stop interrupting people with your marketing messages and instead turn strangers into friends by adding value and friends into customers by getting permission from them to offer your products and services. In its most effective form, the Book Yourself Solid Sales Cycle not only turns strangers into friends and friends into potential clients but potential clients into current clients and past clients into current clients.

To design a sales cycle for your business, you must first understand how you're going to lead people into your sales cycle. Then you can actually build out a sales cycle process that will attract more clients than you can handle and do so with the utmost integrity.

The Book Yourself Solid Six Keys to Creating Connection: Who, What, Where, When, Why, and How

The Book Yourself Solid Sales Cycle works when you know:

1. *Who* your target clients are
2. *What* they are looking for
3. *Where* they look for you
4. *When* they look for you
5. *Why* they should choose you
6. *How* you want them to engage with you

Know your responses to these six keys and you will ensure that the offers you are making in your sales cycle process are right on target.

Key One: Who Is Your Target Client or Customer?

We've covered in depth how to choose a target market, but we're going to reiterate it here because of its importance. You need to choose whom you'd like to bring into your cycle. The more specific you are, the better. Choose one person (or organization) within your target market to focus on.

Identifying and gearing your marketing to a specific individual or organization allows you to make the important emotional connection that is the first step in developing a relationship with your potential client. When you have made the effort to speak and write directly to your ideal client in your target market, he'll feel it. He will feel as though you truly know and understand his needs and desires – because you will. That task alone will go a long way toward building the trust you desire with the clients you seek.

If you're not super clear on whom specifically you're targeting, whom you want to reach out to and attract, it's going to be hard to develop a sales cycle that works because you'll be chasing after every potential opportunity and you won't be making a strong connection with anyone.

2.6.1 Written Exercise: *Who* is your target client or customer? Describe what she is like. Get really creative with this one. List as many specific details as you can.

Example: Lorrie Morgan Ferrero, an excellent copywriter, describes her target customer like this: "Nikki Stanton, a 37-year-old divorced entrepreneur with a web conferencing business. She's Internet and business savvy. Invests most of her profit back into the business. Lives in San Diego in a gated community with her 10-year-old daughter, Madison. She's involved in her daughter's school and drives her to dance classes. Has a home office and makes approximately $117 000 a year. Jogs three times a week in the neighborhood. She loves to find bargains on designer clothes and dreams of visiting Italy with her daughter someday."

Your turn. Describe whom you'd like to attract into your sales cycle.

Key Two: What Are They Looking For?

It's important to understand what your ideal clients or customers are looking for – the kinds of products or services they think will solve their problems or help them reach their goals. It's very important to be clear on your answers because if you don't know what your potential clients are looking for, you won't know what kind of product and service offers to make in your sales cycle. We usually make offers that *we think* are relevant. It's time to put your target market first and work to truly understand what *they know* is relevant and what they actually say they *want*. Then you can decide on what you're going to offer them that will meet their needs according to the amount of trust that you've earned at various stages in your sales cycle.

> **2.6.2 Written Exercise:** *What* are your potential clients or clients looking for?
>   *Examples:* In our case, they want to give their brand an upgrade. They want new photos. They want to read a report on the latest online shopping trends. They want to attend an e-commerce conference. And so on.

Key Three: Where Do They Look for You?

Do you know where your target market looks for you? Do they search online? Do they read magazines? Do they call their friends for referrals for the kind of service you're providing? What other types of business professionals do they trust to get their referrals from? If you don't know, survey your current clients. Additionally, any time a potential client reaches out to inquire about your services, be it in person, by phone, email or text, always ask: "How did you come to find me?" If you don't have any clients of your own yet, ask a colleague who serves the same target market how her clients find her.

> **2.6.3 Written Exercise:** *Where* do your ideal clients look for you?

Key Four: When Do They Look for You?

When do the people or organizations in your target market look for the services you offer? What needs to happen in their personal life or work life for them to purchase the kind of service you have to offer? How high do the stakes need to be before they decide to purchase the service you're offering? They may be interested in what you do, and your offerings may resonate with them, but they might not need you at the moment they find you. Timing matters.

This is why the Book Yourself Solid Sales Cycle is so important. You'll want to make it easy for them to step into your environment and move closer to your core offerings over time. When their stakes rise, they'll reach out to you and ask for you. But you've got to keep the conversation going so you're right there when they need you at the right time.

> **2.6.4 Written Exercise:** Describe the situations that are likely to drive poten-
> tial clients to seek your services. *When* do they look for you?
>
> *Examples:* They've just secured a deal to have their products sold in a
> major retailer and are now seeking a new packaging design to help them
> stand out on the shelf.

Key Five: Why Should They Choose You?

That's a big question. Why are they going to choose you? Are you a credible authority in your field? What makes you the best choice for them? What is unique about you or the solutions you offer?

For this exercise, it's crucial that you set your modesty aside and express yourself clearly and with confidence – no wishy-washy answers to these questions. Think back to the last time you went in search of expert help. When you first spoke to the service provider to inquire about his services, his expertise, and whether he could help you, the *last* thing you wanted to hear was "Well, I kinda know what I'm doing. I might be able to help you. I'll give it a shot."

> *While it may feel uncomfortable at first, you've got to get comfortable saying "The best thing for you is me!"*

Granted, saying you are the best may be a bit too bold for you, but at the least you've got to be able to say "You've come to the right person. Yes, absolutely, I *can* help you. I'm an expert at what I do, and this is how I can help."

Bragging is about comparing yourself to others and proclaiming your superiority. Declaring your strengths, your skills, your expertise, and your ability to help is not bragging but expressing confidence in what your potential clients expect, want, and need to hear from you.

> **2.6.5 Written Exercise:** *Why* should your potential clients choose you? Be
> bold! Express yourself fully. This is not the time for modesty.

Key Six: How Do You Want Them to Engage with You?

Once potential clients have learned about your services, how would you like them to interact or engage with you? Do you want them to book a discovery call? Do you want them to sign up for your newsletter on your website? What is it that you want potential clients to *do?*

Naturally, you'd love for them to immediately purchase your highest-priced service, but this is rare. Most of your potential clients need to get to know you and trust you over time. They need to be eased gradually toward what they may perceive to be your high-risk offerings. It's often said that, on average, you will need to connect with a potential client or client seven times before they'll purchase from you. Not always, but if you understand this principle, you will be on the road to booking yourself solid a lot faster than if you try to engage in one-step selling. "Hi, I'm a web designer; wanna hire me today?" isn't going to be effective. That's definitely not the Book Yourself Solid way. Maybe we should call one-step selling one-*stop* selling because that's what it'll do – stop your sales process dead in its tracks.

2.6.6 Written Exercise: *How* do you want your potential clients to interact or engage with you? (Note: Establishing a line of communication is the first step in developing a relationship of trust.)

Clearly defining these six keys will help you to determine what you want to offer your potential clients in each stage of your sales cycle and will help you craft the most effective sales cycle possible. Moreover, defining these six keys will also help you tremendously when implementing the Book Yourself Solid Six Core Self-Promotion Strategies.

The Book Yourself Solid Sales Cycle Process

As a creative service provider, what you sell may have a high barrier to entry. To potential new clients, your services may be intangible and expensive – whether you think they are or not – especially to those who have not used the kind of services that you offer or who have not had good results with their previous service providers.

The Book Yourself Solid Sales Cycle is a sequence of phases that a client moves through when deciding whether to buy your services. You begin your sales cycle by making no-barrier-to-entry offers to potential clients. A no-barrier-to-entry offer is one that has no risk whatsoever for a potential client so they can *sample* your services. We're not talking just about offering free services, which is a common practice for many professional service providers. We take this concept much further with much more success.

No doubt you've heard the term "sales funnel." A sales funnel and the Book Yourself Solid Sales Cycle are different. A sales funnel drives people through a strategically designed campaign window to buy a particular product at a particular time. Sales funnels can be powerfully effective when launching products. The Book Yourself Solid Sales Cycle Process is different in that it respects the fundamental truism that clients buy services when they are ready to buy (and not necessarily when you want them to) and that clients buy in proportion to the trust and credibility that you have created with them over time.

At the time someone becomes aware of you, there is a high likelihood that they do not feel your services are necessary at that time. However, if you have done a good job cultivating trust and credibility by providing them with value over time, when something changes in their life and they become ready to buy, be it weeks, months, or even years later, they will think of you, and you will become their default choice to reach out to first.

The Stages of a Sales Cycle

In Module Four, you'll learn how to use the Book Yourself Solid Six Core Self-Promotion Strategies, including networking, direct outreach, referral, speaking, writing, and using the web to create awareness for the solutions you offer. However, rather than attempting to *sell* to a client, you will simply offer them an invitation that has no barrier to entry.

You already know that "who knows what you know" is important when working toward booking yourself solid. Do you realize how many more clients you could be serving if they just knew what you had to offer? The best way to inform them is to have at least one, if not a few, compelling offers that have no barrier to entry.

The Book Yourself Solid Sales Cycle works in a way that allows buyers to enter at any point in the process, depending on their situation. A client hires you when the circumstances in their life or work match the offers that you make. If you're a photographer, your services may not be needed right now. But perhaps, six months from now, when a potential client is planning their first event and remembers that they haven't yet booked a photographer, they'll not only want your services but need them immediately. Do you see how the stakes have changed? Chances are that if you haven't built trust with this potential client over the past six months by offering great value along the way (without expecting anything in return, mind you), it's unlikely you'll cross their mind when they look to find someone who can beautifully capture their event.

The following example will give you a framework for the process. Your sales cycle may include 3, 10, or even 15 stages, depending on your particular business model and the different services you offer. We're going to teach you the principles that govern an effective sales cycle so that you can craft one that serves your particular business and meets the individual needs and tastes of your clients and customers.

We will explain each stage and give you a real example from Joana's design agency to help you visualize exactly how each stage works. We're going to also ask you to write out your objective for each stage and how you're going to achieve your objective. This way, by the end of the chapter, you'll have completed your very own Book Yourself Solid Sales Cycle. We'll do our best to make it as easy as possible to absorb and implement the information. If you do get a bit overwhelmed, please stay with it. This is an important part of the Book Yourself Solid system, and understanding the principles behind these techniques will ensure that you're well on your way to being booked solid. In fact, we'd say it's the linchpin of the Book Yourself Solid system.

As you work through this process, remember all that you are doing is having a simple conversation with someone. You are making a connection that will build trust so that you will then be able to share your services with another person. How cool is that?

Book Yourself Solid Sales Cycle – Stage One

To book yourself solid, perform daily tasks that will keep your name in front of potential clients. In Stage One, your objective is to get a potential client to do something – go to your website, book a call, fill out an enquiry form, or perform another action that begins to affiliate them to you. To best do this, you need to create awareness for the services you offer using one or all of the Book Yourself Solid Six Core Self-Promotion Strategies. You will have your choice of six Book Yourself Solid strategies:

1. Networking Strategy
2. Direct Outreach Strategy
3. Referral Strategy
4. Speaking Strategy
5. Writing Strategy
6. Web Strategy

Your objective for Stage One of the Sales Cycle should be simple and measurable, like driving prospective clients to your website. Or maybe you want them to call you directly. It's up to you. But once you've chosen an objective, you'll choose the strategies you would like to use to achieve it.

The Sales Cycle is most effective when used in conjunction with a keep-in-touch plan. I'll show you how to do that in the next chapter.

Stage One Example: Joana's Stage One objective is to drive potential clients to her agency's website. (This is the answer to the sixth key to creating connection: "How do you want your potential clients to engage with you?")

2.6.7 Written Exercise: Book Yourself Solid Sales Cycle Stage One:

- What is your objective in Stage One of the sales cycle?

Book Yourself Solid Sales Cycle – Stage Two

In this stage you will demonstrate your knowledge, solutions, and sincere desire to provide value to your target market free of charge, with no barrier to entry and at no risk to them. The benefits include increased trust – they will feel as though they know you somewhat better.

To familiarize your prospective clients with your services, you need to offer them solutions, opportunities, and relevant information in exchange for their contact information and permission to continue communicating with them over time. What does that communication look like? You may provide a checklist, special report, or an e-book that addresses their urgent needs and compelling desires. It could be your always-have-something-to-invite-people-to offer, which I discuss in detail at the end of this chapter. No matter what you select, it should be something that speaks not only to their needs but also what you want them to know about how you can serve them.

Stage Two Example: Joana's Stage Two objective is to encourage her website visitors to download a free e-book titled *The 8 step guide to creating a website that converts* in exchange for their name and email address. Once they enter that information, they will immediately get access to the e-book.

2.6.8 Written Exercise: Book Yourself Solid Sales Cycle Stage Two:

- What is your objective in Stage Two of the cycle?
- How are you going to achieve it?

Book Yourself Solid Sales Cycle – Stage Three

Now that you've started building trust between you and your potential clients, you're going to work on developing and enhancing that trust and cultivating the relationship.

In Stage Three of the sales cycle, your objective is twofold: to continue to add value by helping your potential clients incorporate the information that you gave them in Stage Two of the cycle and to make a sale. If you gave them a free report, you should follow up with emails that help them use the content in the report to create value. Or if you invited them to your always-have-something-to-invite-people-to offer, you'll tell them more about it, make sure they know how to take advantage of it, and, of course, tell them what the benefits of participating in it will be. You should also offer them something that will surprise them. It could be a complimentary pass to a workshop you're doing or a personal note on your stationery or branded postcard with a list of books on your area of expertise that you know will speak to their urgent needs. Remember, the value you add doesn't have to be all about you. If you recommend a resource to your potential clients, they will very likely associate the value they received from that resource with you.

This is the first time in the sales cycle where you might also offer your potential clients a service or product that will cost them money: an online workshop or a consultation call. It might be one of your information products: e-book, published book, template, workbook, manual, online workshop or online course, all of which we'll get to in the book. When you send your follow-up emails, you will let your potential clients know of the opportunities you have for them that speak directly to their urgent needs and compelling desires, and you'll continue to add value without expecting anything in return.

What's important to understand is that the monetized offers you are making should not have a very high barrier to entry. You're not going to rush out of the gate and surprise potential clients with your highest-priced offer, just as you wouldn't propose marriage on a first date, no matter how smitten you are. You want to offer them something they are ready for, and if they're ready for more at that moment, they'll ask for it. Of course, you'll always let potential clients know how to view the page on your website that lists your various services, just in case they are ready to walk down the aisle.

Stage Three Example: Joana's Stage Three objective is to give those who previously opted in for her e-book a chance to purchase a website audit with Joana. During this call, she goes over the eight steps outlined in her guide and how they can be applied to the participant's own website to increase their conversions and perceived value. The session concludes with a detailed list of actionable steps that participants can implement themselves and what it would look like if they chose her services for the implementation. This moderately priced call serves as both an educational tool and a direct showcase of Joana's expertise and the value of her professional services, which often leads to the person becoming a client.

> ***All of your sales offers should be proportionate to the amount of trust that you've earned.***

As a professional service provider, you don't want to try to convince people that what you're offering is right for them. You want to provide value upon value until they decide that your services are right for them. They will get better results that way and be more satisfied with your services, a factor that is way too important to forget about.

2.6.9 Written Exercise: Book Yourself Solid Sales Cycle Stage Three:

- What is your objective in Stage Three of the cycle?
- How are you going to achieve it?

The Book Yourself Solid Always-Have-Something-to-Invite-People-to Offer

This strategy might just be the most effective marketing and trust-building strategy on the planet for the professional service provider. You'll want to consider your own always-have-something-to-invite-people-to offer as you design the first few stages of your Book Yourself Solid Sales Cycle. It might be what you choose to direct potential clients to when you use the Book Yourself Solid Six Core Self-Promotion Strategies in Stage One of the sales cycle.

People generally hate to be sold, but they love to be invited — as long as the invitations are relevant and anticipated. Meaning, they've given you permission to make an invitation.

When one of Joana's student's, Anna, who runs a paid traffic advertising agency in London catering to e-commerce business owners, learned about this strategy, she quickly implemented it and found that it quickly became one of her most effective and profitable marketing strategies.

Recognizing that many of her clients are women, Anna hosts a monthly event at her agency's headquarters specifically for women entrepreneurs who own e-commerce brands, regardless of whether they are currently running paid advertising. She invites her existing clients and encourages them to bring a friend from the e-commerce industry. Anna also extends invitations to other local e-commerce brands.

The event is structured as a mastermind gathering – a concept where small groups of like-minded individuals come together to share knowledge, support each other, and solve problems collaboratively. In the first 30 minutes, she spotlights a local e-commerce business, allowing them to share their journey, challenges, and successes. This segment not only offers valuable insights but also fosters a deeper connection among participants. Following the spotlight presentation, the gathering transitions into mastermind groups where attendees meet fellow business owners within the same industry to exchange tips. The primary goal is to foster a supportive environment where entrepreneurs help each other by sharing what works for them. At these events, Anna never pitches her services. Instead, her focus is on networking and building genuine connections. Attendees get to know Anna not just as a service provider but as a generous, knowledgeable leader eager to support their business growth. This nurturing approach strengthens community ties and organically leads to new client engagements, as attendees experience the value of her expertise and the supportive nature of her agency firsthand.

There is another added benefit of this kind of always-have-something-to-invite-people-to offer. It can serve as one of the most effective ways of establishing your personal brand. Notice how Anna's event features different success stories or challenges faced by local e-commerce entrepreneurs each month, with her agency offering a platform for these insights. A major part of her personal brand is being someone who is supportive and fosters community growth, so this helps her continue to establish and amplify her personal brand. Your always-have-something-to-invite-people-to offer is the perfect way to integrate and align your who and do what statement (whom you help and what you help them do) and your why you do it statement (the reason you do what you do).

Consider another example from early in Joana's career. Being based in Portugal with a global client base, in-person events were not a viable option for her. Instead, Joana chose to host monthly live website critiques online. Participants simply needed to drop their website links in the chat to receive personalized feedback. During these sessions, Joana didn't just critique; she gave them actionable advice on how to fix it. Attendees learned how to apply her advice to their own sites, turning each session into a learning opportunity for everyone involved.

The true value of these events was in their iterative nature. Attendees often returned after implementing changes to seek further advice, deepening both their understanding of what could make their website convert better and their relationship with Joana. For some, the scope of necessary improvements was overwhelming, prompting them to hire Joana's agency to implement the changes suggested.

These free sessions offered so much value – they were akin to individual consultations – that the word quickly spread. Attendees began to recognize common website errors and recommended Joana's critiques to peers who they saw were making similar mistakes in their websites. This organic growth not only broadened Joana's client base but also cemented her reputation as an approachable and insightful branding and marketing expert.

Are you beginning to get your own ideas on how this could work for you? The value you add in your offer meets the needs and desires of the people you serve. This no-barrier-to-entry offer is a helpful component of the Book Yourself Solid Sales Cycle. Then as you continue to build trust over time by offering additional value and creating awareness for the services you provide, you'll attract potential clients deeper into the sales cycle, moving them closer to your core offerings.

You'll notice that the two always-have-something-to-invite-people-to examples we offered are done in a group format. There are three important reasons for this:

1. You'll leverage your time so you're connecting with as many potential clients as possible in the shortest amount of time.
2. You'll leverage the power of communities. When you bring people together, they create far more energy and excitement than you can on your own. Your guests will also see other people interested in what you have to offer, and that's the best way to build credibility.
3. You'll be viewed as a really cool person. Seriously, if you're known in your marketplace as someone who brings people together, that will help you build your reputation and increase your likeability.

Please give away so much value that you think you've given too much, and then give more. A friend of Michael's in college who, when he ordered his hero sandwiches, would say: "Put so much mayonnaise on it that you think you've ruined it, and then put on more." Gross, we know (Michael believes that he has since stopped eating his sandwiches that way and his arteries have thanked him), but adding value is similar. Remember, your potential clients must know *what* you know. They must really like you and believe that you have the solutions to their very personal, specific, and urgent problems. The single best way to do that is to invite them to experience what it's like to be around you and the people you serve.

Don't be discouraged if, upon starting your own always-have-something-to-invite-people-to offer, it is not wildly successful right from the start. It can take a handful of events to get a good idea of how people in the community will respond, and consistency is key. Your always-have-something-to-invite-people-to offer should happen consistently, whether it is once a week or once a month. If it happens with a consistent frequency, it will be easier for people to know when to expect it, and as a result, you will get more people coming back again and again. Think about the world's greatest always-have-something-to-invite-people-to offer: church. It happens like clockwork, every Sunday, no matter what.

Use the Book Yourself Solid Sales Cycle to Unconditionally Serve Your Clients

You can have as many stages in your sales cycle as you need to build trust with potential clients for the kinds of offers you make. Just thinking about your sales cycle will help you clarify and expand your offerings. If you're not already established, the days of offering only one fee-based service may be coming to an end. The marketplace is too competitive and diverse. Every day another inspired professional stakes a claim and joins the ranks of free agents around the world. More and more people are rejecting corporate culture at behemoth companies and are feeling the call to stand in the service of others.

Expanding your offerings to create a Book Yourself Solid Sales Cycle may just enhance your business model – the mechanism by which you generate revenue – from only one offering with one stream of revenue to multiple offerings with multiple streams of revenue.

The Book Yourself Solid Sales Cycle is not just about getting new clients to hire you. It is designed to unconditionally serve your current clients as well. It is much harder to sell your services, products, and programs to a new client than to those who have already received value from you as a client or customer.

The most successful businesses, both large and small, know this. It's one of the reasons Amazon.com is so successful. Once you've become a customer, they know you, they know what you need, what you read, and they work to continue to serve you. The typical client-snagging mentality suggests that you make a sale and move on. The Book Yourself Solid way requires that you make a sale and ask: "How can I over-deliver and continue to serve this person or organization?" This is not a small thing.

Now it's your turn to develop your own unique sales cycle. Don't limit yourself to just the few examples I've already touched on. There are a multitude of ways to build trust with your potential clients and to ease them toward purchasing your higher price point offerings. Use your imagination and creativity to tailor your sales cycle to what works best, feels most natural, and resonates most with you.

The Book Yourself Solid Keep-in-Touch Strategy

Be well, do good work, and keep in touch.
—Garrison Keillor

You already know that, generally, you need to connect with potential clients many times before they feel comfortable hiring you. If you don't have a systematized and sometimes automated keep-in-touch strategy in place to support your Book Yourself Solid Sales Cycle Process, you may, as the saying goes, leave a lot of business on the table.

Many businesses fail for lack of a solid keep-in-touch marketing strategy. Either they bombard you with too much information and too many offers that turn you off or you never hear from them at all, which leaves you feeling unimportant and irrelevant.

Consider the experience of one of our clients, Barbara. Within a few short years she had compiled more than 5000 subscribers.

The names and emails were captured, but Barbara never really followed up with any of them until one day when she created a promotional offer to send to her list and she eagerly clicked Send. What came back were mostly emails from recipients inquiring as to who she was and how she got their email address. Barbara learned a valuable lesson that day: determine the best approach for using this strategy and build it into your keep-in-touch plans.

There is an important distinction to be made between following up with potential clients, colleagues, and others on a personal (one-to-one) level and developing an automated keep-in-touch strategy through which you broadcast electronic newsletters, send direct mail campaigns, or use other publishing platforms like social media (one-to-many).

When you've met someone and exchanged contact information, you have permission to communicate with them and to start or continue a dialogue that is valuable to both of you. However, this does not equate to having permission to add that person to your mailing list so you can send them your newsletter or other automated or broadcast messages.

All of the broadcast follow-up that you do to groups must be based on the principles of permission marketing, offering a potential client the opportunity to volunteer to be marketed to. According to Seth Godin, in his book *Permission Marketing*, "By only talking to volunteers, permission marketing guarantees that consumers pay more attention to the marketing message. It allows marketers to calmly and succinctly tell their story. It serves both consumers and marketers in a symbiotic exchange." Permission marketing is anticipated, personal, and relevant to the potential client.

- *Anticipated:* People look forward to hearing from you.
- *Personal:* The messages are directly related to the individual.
- *Relevant:* The marketing is about something the prospect is interested in.

This is essential because you want to communicate only with someone who is looking forward to hearing from you. When potential customers anticipate your marketing messages, they're more open to them. And, of course, when they have not explicitly asked you to send them things like a newsletter, and you do, it's not just possible spam, it is 100% pure spam, no matter how much you think they'll enjoy it.

With that said, once you get to know people, you should ask them if they'd like you to subscribe them to your newsletter. Tell them about it, what's valuable about it, when it's delivered, and any other relevant information. Then, if they accept your invitation to be on your mailing list, you have permission to send it to them along with special offers and other promotions.

Relevant, Interesting, Current, and Valuable Content

It's up to you to ensure that the content you share with your potential clients through your leveraged (one-to-many) keep-in-touch strategy is relevant, interesting, current, and valuable. There are six basic categories of content that meet those criteria:

1. Industry information
2. Strategies, tips, and techniques
3. Content from other sources
4. Product and service offerings
5. Cool keep-in-touch
6. Special announcements

Industry Information

Industry information that is relevant to your target market and that may or may not be widely known is excellent content to share. You'll position yourself as an expert within your industry while providing constant value to your current and potential clients. What's more, they will appreciate the information and your generosity for sharing it.

For example, if you run a web design business, you could share information about the latest technologies available to make websites more easily accessible to the visually impaired. This might not be valuable to your clients only if accessibility is something that aligns with their company values, but it also broadens their audience reach.

Including important information in your keep-in-touch strategy also makes it more likely that your potential clients will keep the information and refer to it, keeping you at the top of their mind for future support.

Strategies, Tips, and Techniques

Strategies, tips, and techniques are probably the most common type of content shared by service professionals.

Despite the appeal of this content-rich approach, many service professionals fear they will give away too much of their material. "If I provide all these great tips and strategies for free, then why would anyone ever hire me?" they wonder. Of course, there are some who will take everything you offer and never hire you or purchase a product, but they wouldn't be hiring you anyway, and you never know – they may be out in the world talking about what you do and how you help. Over the years, Joana has received countless referrals from people who are not clients just because she's helped them for *free*. Most people who eventually do hire you or buy your products will need to receive free advice and support to build the trust they need for them to believe that you can really help them. Furthermore, most people will assume that you know a lot more than what you are giving away. They'll think: "Wow! If she gives away this much great stuff, can you imagine what I'll get if I actually pay her?"

Let's say you're a personal brand photographer. You could send out tips for things that would help your potential clients prepare for their photoshoots, like "5 Poses to Elevate Your Presence and Project Confidence" and "My Top 10 Unique Locations for Personal Brand Photoshoots That You Won't Want to Miss." These resources prepare them for a successful session and also showcase your expertise and creative vision. You might conclude the email with "Ready to bring your personal brand to life with professional flair? If you need expert guidance in preparing for and shooting your new images for your brand, simply reply to this email. Let's discuss how I can help you stand out from your competition."

Content from Other Sources

We often provide current and potential clients with relevant content from other people so that we can overdeliver as much as possible. This gives us a break from continuously creating content. It also allows us to offer our subscribers more than we can offer ourselves and at the same time position other professionals as experts in their field; they appreciate the promotion.

There is a bonus as well: the experts featured often return the favor by promoting our work to the people *they* serve. Isn't that a win for everybody? It's also an easy way to create great value for the people who have given you permission to serve them when you're first starting out.

For instance, Joana often promotes content created by her agency's trusted copy partner, Delia Monk. If a client comes to Joana's agency needing a new website but doesn't yet have a marketing or sales copy, she recommends collaborating with Delia. To facilitate this, Joana includes Delia's fee in the overall project quote, ensuring that the website will have the best chance of converting not only from great design but also great copy. Recognizing the critical role of compelling copy in bringing a website to life, Joana also features Delia's resources on crafting effective copy in her newsletters.

If you're concerned that you'll lose customers or clients because you highlight other experts, please recall this Book Yourself Solid principle:

> *There are certain people you're meant to serve and others you're not. If you can help other professionals attract business through you, you're creating more abundance for everyone involved.*

Product and Service Offerings

You must make offers when keeping in touch. We generally try not to say "You must" or "You have to" because you don't have to do anything. You certainly don't have to do what we tell you to do. But, in this case, we feel comfortable saying you must make offers. Make offers that are proportional to the amount of trust you've earned, but make offers. Or don't, but if you don't, it's unlikely your business will be around for too long. With that said, making only product and service offerings to your potential clients may not be appreciated very much. Your offers must be accompanied by an over-delivery of free value. A great goal is to subscribe to the 80/20 rule when it comes to keeping in touch. That means 80% of your keep-in-touch marketing is based on giving away free content, opportunities, and resources that will help the people you serve, and 20% is made up of offers to purchase services, products, and programs that will also help the people you serve. Remember, the people who have expressed interest in your services want to know how they can work with you. Show them their options.

Cool Keep-in-Touch

We love it when you express yourself. By now you know that you will more easily and quickly attract your ideal clients when you do. This category is the cool keep-in-touch category because it can include any fun, different, unique, or exotic method of keeping in touch, some of which may expose your quirks. Please remember that quirky does not mean scary or bizarre. It means unusual, unique, and special. So get creative. Be bold. Dare to stand out from the crowd.

For example, Joana crafted a social media post that featured each team member's thoughts on what makes Gif Design Studios (her agency) stand out. The responses were diverse and reflected their individual quirks, resonating so well with their audience that Joana decided to include them in an email and even in the FAQ section of their website. This was a hit because it did more than just present the team; it offered a glimpse into their personal views and passions, transforming the perception of Gif Design Studios from a distant, business-only facade to a close-knit team passionately working through their unique perspectives.

What is your special, unique, and entertaining quirk that can be turned into a cool keep-in-touch strategy?

Special Announcements

This is a valuable method of keeping in touch if the special announcement is relevant, important, and presented as a learning tool to your target market. For example, when Joana came back from her maternity leave, she sent out an email not only introducing her newborn to her community but, more important, expressing gratitude to her clients and team for their support during her absence. She highlighted the projects that were completed and launched while she was away, demonstrating the team's ability to thrive independently, reassuring clients that the business is a robust design agency, and sparking interest in new projects. But be careful — it's often an overused category and can be irrelevant and annoying when it comes in the *all-about-me* form, like news about your company that is irrelevant to your contacts. They don't really care that you have a new logo or built a new website (unless that's the service you offer). How many times have you received announcements telling you about a new development in a company or about a change in management that you really cared about?

2.7.1 Written Exercise: What is the best kind of content to include in your keep-in-touch strategy based on your interests and the needs and desires of your target market?

Choosing Your Keep-in-Touch Tools

Once you've got great content to share with your clients and potential clients, you've got to choose how best to deliver that content to them. These are the most common methods:

- Email newsletters
- Printed newsletters (might seem old-school, but they tend to stand out for that reason)
- Podcasts
- Postcards and mailers
- Social media (Instagram, Facebook, X, LinkedIn)

Historically, email newsletters were the easiest and most cost-effective way to keep in touch with large numbers of people. However, the landscape has changed significantly in recent years. Despite the rise of free social media platforms and increasing consumer reluctance to share their email addresses – primarily due to the surge in spam – email newsletters remain unparalleled in providing direct access to our audience. While no longer the cheapest option, they ensure that messages reach recipients directly versus social media, where your posts may never be seen by your followers and you'll be subject to the whims of the algorithms, not to mention the emergence of AI.

Despite the challenges posed by new regulations and the need for great content to capture attention, the benefits of email marketing, in our opinion, continue to outweigh its costs. Paper newsletters might have some value as a marketing tool – especially for the visual creative provider – but they can be costly to print and mail. The phone is a wonderful direct outreach tool but often the most anxiety provoking of them all, so feel free to stay away from cold calling and wait to get on the phone until you've had at least one positive interaction with your direct outreach subject. We'll talk about how to use social media (Facebook, Instagram, and LinkedIn) to keep in touch with large groups of people in Chapter 15. For now, let's focus on email newsletters, which are still an effective marketing tool for:

- Building your mailing list, adding value, and marketing to your subscribers over and over again
- Selling your services while you're delivering great content and adding value
- Positioning yourself as an expert within your industry or field
- Keeping in touch with all the people who've expressed interest in your services, and reaching them all with the click of a button
- Creating a viral marketing campaign (it grows exponentially as it's passed along to others) because your subscribers will send it to their friends when they think it will help them
- Creating ongoing marketing campaigns that cost virtually nothing and reap great rewards

As you'll learn when we discuss your web strategy, your website is used most effectively as a vehicle for enticing people to opt in to your subscriber list so that you deliver value and build trust over time. Your follow-up is where you reap the financial and personal rewards of your marketing efforts.

Email Newsletter Layout

The layout of the text in your email newsletter is just as important as what you have to say. Most of your readers will not actually be reading the email. First, they'll scan it. Then, if the email seems relevant and interesting, they'll read it more carefully. Note, however, that many, if not most, of your readers are viewing your email on their mobile device. So, keep that in mind when deciding to add images or graphics.

Keep your paragraphs short. Large blocks of text are harder to scan. Finally, to make the layout support your content, consider the following criteria when writing any kind of keep-in-touch or promotional content:

- Write compelling headlines to get your readers interested.
- Use case studies and testimonials to add credibility to your claims.
- Write from your reader's point of view.
- Write about benefits, not just features.
- Read your text out loud to make sure it sounds conversational.
- Get a colleague or client to review your copy and make suggestions.
- Write as if you're speaking to one person – the person who's reading the email, not a group of people. Address readers by name to create a personal connection, using phrases like "Hey [Name], I've noticed you're interested in...," using the personalization features of your newsletter provider.
- In the spirit of diversity, equity, and inclusion (DEI), be conscious of keeping content gender neutral and bias free.
- Be specific.
- Be concise.
- Keep it simple.

Additionally, to maintain transparency and comply with email regulations, include in your email footer a line informing the recipient why they are receiving this email and provide an easy link to unsubscribe. This not only helps in preventing your emails from being flagged as spam but also ensures that your communications are welcomed, thereby protecting your deliverability.

Email Frequency

Frequency depends on a lot of factors but should be mostly based on what you're trying to accomplish and to whom you're sending the email. Some people send out weekly email newsletters, some twice a month, and others monthly or quarterly. We've even seen some daily email newsletters.

To see firsthand how we create connections with – and value for – our newsletter subscribers, go to http://BookYourselfSolid.com, http://theAmbitiousCreatives.com, or http://HeroicPublicSpeaking.com and subscribe now. Not only will you see how we do it, but we'll also be able to continue to help you book yourself solid and present yourself in the most compelling way possible.

Automating Your Keep-in-Touch Strategy

Creating a monthly email newsletter, and whatever other content and offers you plan to provide to those you are keeping in touch with, is only the beginning of implementing the strategy. It's time to:

- Build and manage your database.
- Follow up with prospects and professional opportunities.

Building and Managing Your Database

Surely you've met hundreds, if not thousands, of people over your professional life you haven't kept in touch with. Now that you're a service professional wanting to attract more clients than you can handle, you probably wish you had kept in touch with all those folks. Well, no matter. You will keep in touch with everyone you meet from this point forward – well, only the people you like and want to keep in touch with. It is encouraging, however, to reflect on all of the people you have met with whom you did not keep in touch because it shows you how easy it can be to build a database of potential clients and networking contacts if you do keep in touch.

Choosing a Database Program   To have an effective keep-in-touch strategy, you'll need a reliable and comprehensive database program. There are many database programs from which you can choose, and more than I can list here, but I'll give you a few examples and important criteria to consider as you make your choice.

There are two important differentiators that we want you to consider: sales management versus contact management. Customer relationship management (CRM) systems like Infusionsoft, Salesforce, Aweber, and MailChimp are all designed to manage not only contacts but also the sales process, to turn leads into opportunities and opportunities into clients.

Contact management systems like Microsoft Outlook and Google Contacts typically provide a way to organize your contacts. Contact management systems may provide a way to take notes on a record, but they don't provide a good way to track the sales process, which might be the most critical process in your business.

Frankly, this stuff is kind of boring on the surface, but since you're still reading and engaged, you understand the importance of it. There are some things that we need to do in business that aren't particularly fun but are wonderfully exciting when you see them working in your favor to produce sales. So, with that said, it's time to start using a real CRM system to manage your sales process, from lead generation to opportunity management to sales conversion.

Using a CRM system you'll be able to:

- *Track performance of lead sources:* It's likely that a small amount of lead generation efforts will drive the bulk of your sales.
- *Create a consistent sales process even if you have just one person working with you:* This will help you see what is driving results.
- *Increase the speed of your sales conversion:* Respond to new leads quickly, follow up frequently with emails and calls, and nurture leads that don't convert immediately.
- *Keep track of activities:* Get things done when you need to and when you say you will.
- *Report on past performance:* If you don't know what you've done, how are you going to know what you need to do?
- *Forecast future sales:* If you don't know where you're going, how will you know when you're there?

The key isn't purchasing the program to help you manage your keep-in-touch strategy, it's actually using the program to keep in touch with potential clients, current clients, and past clients. Bottom line: CRM is about managing these relationships more efficiently.

Entering Data   You certainly have to get a new lead's contact information, but that's not where most people fall short. It's that they don't actually do anything with it. You must enter and store it in the system and then continue to connect with the lead, building trust over time. The size of your database, but most important the *quality* of the relationships you have with the people in your database, is directly proportional to the financial health of your business.

Creating Automated Email Sequences with a CRM System

One of the most effective and efficient ways to automate your keep-in-touch strategy is by setting up automated email sequences in your CRM system.

For example, in Joana's agency, they have an automated email sequence of more than a dozen emails that begins when someone is entered into their CRM system as a lead. These emails are primarily positioned to provide value, build trust, and stay top of mind with potential clients.

The best part about automated email sequences like this is that once they are built, all you need to do is input the lead into your CRM system. The system will do the rest for you, sending out emails of your choosing at whatever intervals you want and ensuring that you are always keeping in touch with the leads that you've added to your list.

Getting and Following Up with Prospects and Professional Opportunities

Following up with prospects and professional opportunities is a major key to your success. It's an investment that will deliver huge returns. Your Book Yourself Solid Sales Cycle is based on the success of your keep-in-touch strategy and requires you to deliver great value. Please, we implore you to make this a top priority.

The Book Yourself Solid Keep-in-Touch Strategy is the key to ensuring that your marketing efforts are effective and successful. Keeping in touch with your potential clients is critical to developing trust and credibility, and keeping in touch will keep you foremost in the minds of your potential clients when they need you, your services, or the products and programs you offer.

2.7.2 Written Exercise: How are you going to automate your keep-in-touch strategy?

Simple Selling and Perfect Pricing

Being booked solid requires that you price your offerings at rates that are compelling to your ideal clients and that you're able to have sales conversations that are effortless and effective. It means that you must:

- Perfect your pricing strategies using the right models and incentives.
- Practice simple selling techniques so you can have sales conversations that feel as easy as a day at the beach.

Module Three consists of two chapters. These two chapters are the culmination of the Book Yourself Solid system because you'll learn how to make offers that are proportional to the amount of trust that you've earned and how to have a sales conversation that books new business. This is the ultimate goal – to get new clients so you can earn new business.

Remember how the Book Yourself Solid system works.

1. You'll create awareness for the products and services you offer using the Six Core Self-Promotion Strategies (you'll learn these in Module Four).
2. Once you create awareness for what you offer, potential new clients will check out your foundation for stability and security (you built this foundation in Module One).
3. If they like what they see, they'll give you the opportunity to earn their trust over time (you do this using the strategies you learned in Module Two).
4. When the circumstances are right, potential clients will either raise their hand and ask you to have a sales conversation or they'll accept one of your compelling offers and you'll book the business (this is the focus of Module Three).

All you have to do now is decide how to price your services and learn how to be comfortable and confident during sales conversations. Let's get right to it then!

Perfect Pricing

Price is what you pay; value is what you get.
—Warren Buffett

What is the value, for example, of having the talent and skills to help clients create a compelling web presence? Is it the length of time it takes for you to create it, the number of pages created, or how about the complexity of the design style? The answer is: D, none of the above. Unfortunately, that's how many creative service providers price their services and offerings. How should services be priced? By putting a value on what they will produce.

"But it took me a day per page to design this website," you might say. How long it takes you to design something, write something, think up an idea, or even the amount of time you spend with a client, is irrelevant. What should matter to the client is the financial, emotional, physical, and spiritual (FEPS) return on investment your service provides – remember, we introduced you to the all-important FEPS benefits in Chapter 2. Think about the value you provide:

- How much income will your services create?
- How long will what you create be a productive, useful resource for the client?
- How much pain will you relieve?
- How much pleasure will you create?

- How are you helping your client connect to their purpose or spirit?
- Will your work create substantial and long-lasting peace of mind?

No less important than the value you create is how you value yourself. This is another reason why the section on releasing blocks in Chapter 3 is critically important to your success. And this might just be the difference between simply making ends meet and earning healthy heaps of money. Remember your ideal client. Remember doing your best work. Remember standing in the service of others as you stand in the service of your destiny. You want to work with people who value what you bring to your partnership. But if you don't value it, they won't either.

3.8.1 Written Exercise: Think of a client who gave you rave reviews. Make a list of all the FEPS benefits the client received from working with you. Don't be stingy here. Think big. Now, put specific dollar values on all of those benefits. Again, think big. No, bigger than that. Because . . . hold on to your hat . . . you may just find that you have been undervaluing yourself and, as a result, underpricing your products and services. You are giving generously of your talents and skills and, it's likely, the value you provide is worth much, much more than what you've been charging.

Don't Buy into a Poverty Mindset

Maybe you think, I don't want to price my services such that people can't afford them. Or maybe it was something like, I have a new client who says they can't afford much, so I'm thinking of lowering my price for them. These thoughts don't necessarily mean you have a "poverty mindset," but they most definitely play you small. Allow your expectations to be stretched. People rarely buy professional services based solely on price. In fact, people express their values through what they buy – so let them.

Most of us express our values through the things we buy. We are what we purchase. Think about it. If you didn't know someone but came across their personal and business financial statements from the past three months, you'd know a heck of a lot about them, like what they value and how they spend their time. If their financial records show that they are at the bar every night and spend most of their money playing the slot machines in Vegas, you'd get a sense of what they value. If those records show that they spend their disposable income on collectable art pieces, purchase four books a month, and invest 25% of their income for retirement, you'd see a person with different values. We're not making a value judgment here. Rather, we're simply saying that what you spend your money on is a demonstration and representation of what you value.

Most of us want the opportunity to express ourselves through the things we purchase, especially when those things are adding value to our life or work. So please give the people you serve the opportunity to express their values by buying what you have to offer.

Only you can offer you. Whatever it is you offer, it is unique – to you. Only you can offer a particular combination of services, skills, talent, and personality. Only you can offer the exact combination of information, style of communication, and value that makes you so uniquely you. Know that. Know and accept and revel in your value. Come from a place of service. Raise your intention to be well compensated for what you offer. Expect to be paid well. Then ask for it. Not everyone will be willing or able to pay what you require, but your ideal clients will. Put out a price that makes you feel valuable and see ideal clients joyously flocking to take advantage of the great value you offer. And, practically, you can't sustain the work you're meant to do unless you are paid well to do it. Your income is a reflection of how you value yourself as well as the number of lives you impact in the world.

> **3.8.2 Booked Solid Action Step:** Right now raise your prices until it makes you slightly uncomfortable. You'll know you've reached the right number when you experience a slight feeling of nausea. That's your new price. Over time you'll grow into it – not the nausea, the price – and, over time, you'll continue to raise your prices, sans nausea.

Ask for what you are worth. But first, truly know and believe you have great value. Then others will know and appreciate all you have to offer. You have to know that what you offer is valuable, and you have to charge an amount that shows it is valuable. Only you can choose to think big about who you are and what you offer the world.

Pricing Models

Surely you've seen a number of different pricing models employed by various creative service providers. Some seem to benefit the provider and others are more favorable to the client. However, the picture of perfect pricing has each party thinking that they got the better end of the deal. If the client thinks they got more value than they paid, they'll be tickled pink, and if the service provider feels that their time, talents, and efforts are valued, they'll feel like the cat who ate the canary. The key is to figure out how to create this win-win dynamic so that both parties feel fortunate. Here are a few of the often-used pricing models used for selling professional services:

- *Time for money trade:* Clients pay by the hour or day for your creative services (for example, $100 per hour or $1000 per day). This is a straightforward pricing model, where clients pay for the amount of time they spend with you. It's a very common model and one with which clients are generally comfortable.
- *Package pricing:* Clients purchase packages that include a specified number of hours or creative deliverables, for a fixed price. This method can offer cost savings for the client compared to paying an hourly or daily rate. It also secures a set volume of work for you, ensuring more predictable revenue.
- *Flat-fee pricing:* A flat fee for a complete project with predefined deliverables. This could be designing a website with a set number of pages and functionalities or conducting a photoshoot with a start and end time, including the number of edited final photos to be delivered. Clients appreciate this model because it means that they know the full cost up front. Flat-fee pricing is ideal for projects with well-defined scopes and outcomes (to avoid the dreaded scope creep). It can also be combined with other pricing models, such as charging an hourly rate for additional hours beyond the agreed scope.
- *Royalty or licensing deals:* For creatives such as illustrators, photographers, and graphic designers who create original artwork, licensing deals provide an avenue to earn revenue from the usage rights of their creations. The client pays a fee based on usage specifics like duration of use, geographic reach, and media type. If going with this route, it is important to consider having both an agent and a lawyer

because of the complexities involved in intellectual property rights and the potential for long-term revenue streams.

- *Open-ended time for money trade:* A rate is set that trades your time for money, usually hourly, but no constraint is put on the amount of time required to complete the job. Service providers (especially contractors) like this model for the same reason that it petrifies the client — runaway time piles on additional fees. You know that 3-week kitchen remodel that's going on 30 weeks? Most people like getting unexpected gifts, but I've yet to meet someone who likes a surprise that costs them money. Imagine, instead of getting gifts on Christmas morning, you woke to find you had to pay for every box that had your name on it. Despite these concerns, this pricing model is often used in projects like software development, where the scope of work can change dynamically as the project progresses.

- *Recurring fee for an open-ended amount of time:* Commonly referred to as a *retainer,* in this model a monthly or quarterly payment is offered for a certain amount of work. Sometimes a time period is associated with the retainer, but the arrangement is typically not associated with a period of time and can be canceled at will or with some reasonable amount of notice. Retainers are beneficial for both parties as they provide a steady income for the service provider and ready access to professional services for the client. This pricing model is common among graphic designers, marketing consultants, and social media managers who provide continuous, regular services. A word of caution on this one, though; if you utilize this pricing model, we strongly recommend you put in place a service level agreement where it is very clear how the client can use this service along with any limitations or boundaries.

- *Retainer plus back-end:* This pricing model, while not applicable to all creative service providers, is sometimes used by marketing agencies and other creative providers whose work has a direct impact on revenue. Clients typically pay a fixed monthly retainer along with a pre-negotiated percentage tied to specific outcomes like increased revenue or cost savings attributed to the creative work. If the project makes money, the service provider makes money. This pricing model isn't typical but can be very lucrative. Some advertising agencies use this model. If their campaign significantly boosts the client's sales, they receive a percentage of the increased revenue. Be sure to draw up water-tight contracts with an attorney if choosing this route.

- *Flexible pricing:* This can apply to all of the pricing models. This is very common in the business-to-business market in which sales are often based on negotiated contracts. Creative service providers often offer flexible pricing, also known as *sliding scale* pricing, based on the client's ability to pay or a provider's desire to work with the client. Just be careful that you don't get into the habit of sliding down the scale too easily just to make the sale. You'll end up working a lot but for not enough money. No point in that, is there?

- *Bundle pricing:* Offering a combination of services together in a single package to increase the size of the sale can offer savings to both the buyer and the seller. The buyer gets more value for less money, and the seller gets more profit for less marketing effort. However, if you bundle your services, "Don't wrap all the Christmas presents in one box," says economist Richard Thaler. The benefits of the product or service should be enumerated rather than lumped together. So, if you buy "this," we'll also throw in "that." And, if you buy "that," we'll also throw in "this." Or, if you buy "this," you can also have "that" at a reduced price. You want to be sure the client values and appreciates each and every product, program, and service they're getting from you.

- *Penetration pricing:* Offer very low prices to get into a market. Once you've created a name for yourself, begin to raise your prices.

- *Loss-leader pricing:* This is a more common approach to selling products than it is to selling services but can be exploited by service providers, nonetheless. You can offer specific services at a very low price point to get clients in the door who will then, hopefully, buy additional products or other services at a higher price point. You may be willing to take a loss up front for a financial gain down the road. For instance, you might offer a discounted introductory design consultation, a low-cost audit of a client's website or branding, or an affordable starter package for social media management. This approach can help you build a client base by reducing the barrier to entry, particularly for clients who may be hesitant to commit to higher fees without first experiencing your work. Just beware of "bait and switch" tactics if you use this sort of pricing. We're huge advocates of letting potential clients know what your full fees are before they come in for their discounted services. This way, the client doesn't feel blindsided by pricing they were not expecting and may not be able to afford.

- *Economy pricing:* Offer the lowest prices in the market as a way of differentiating yourself. This is unlike loss-leader pricing in that all your prices are always low when you use economy pricing – it becomes part of your brand, like Walmart. In this case, you're building a model that allows more people to take advantage of your services – which, over time, can actually add value to your brand. Certainly, low prices are often perceived as low-value services, but that need not necessarily be the case. It's worth noting that it's rare for this to work well for an individual service provider.

- *Prestige pricing:* You may choose to price your services at a price point higher than is typical for your industry in order to create a sense of prestige around you and your company. You may serve fewer clients but end up making more money. This model can work well for creative service providers who have not only years of experience but have also significantly honed their craft or have received accolades for their work. In the creative industries, it is expected that the most skilled and celebrated professionals will command premium rates.

When considering which of the various preceding pricing models you are going to employ first consider your objective. You may be thinking, *Uh, are you dense? I want to make as much money as I can – that's my objective!* Well, yes, but you're reading this book to think more strategically about your business and how you grow it, so humor us for a moment. Consider the following four different pricing objectives:

1. *To maximize long-term profits:* This should be your default approach. You're building something to last a lifetime, something that will support your dreams, not to mention your family, so you always want to focus on long-term pricing. Any of the pricing models can be applied to achieve this objective.

2. *To maximize short-term profits:* This is generally chosen when you need to make a bunch of money fast. You might consider bundle pricing to sell more of what you already offer. Or, maybe, aggressive loss-leader pricing will help. Lots of options here.

3. *To gain market share:* That's just a fancy way of saying you're starting up the business or introducing a new product or service line and need to create awareness for the new service. Loss leader or economy pricing or flexible pricing models may be the way to go. They'll help you get in the game and build up a large group of ideal clients who are out in the world talking about your best work. This, of course, will bring you new, ideal clients.

4. *To survive:* Hey, look. Sometimes things get rough. You might face, say, a complete global economic recession. Sometimes survival *is* enough. This is when you employ whatever strategy you think is going to get you through to the next quarter. Do what you have to do to make it.

When to Lower Prices, Discount, and Offer Specials

The answer is not always clear, but the question remains the same: *when should I lower prices or offer discounts and specials?* Sometimes you want to offer price discounts or special packages to motivate potential clients to act. Other times, you'll feel the need (or desire) to lower prices because of factors beyond your control like economic conditions as discussed earlier, supply and demand issues, competitor's prices, or other market conditions. Or maybe, you're in complete control and have found a cheaper, more economical way to produce your services that allows you to lower your prices while increasing your profit margins. Either way, leveraging a variety of discounting tactics and other incentive devices to get clients faster and increase sales can be, to put it mildly, a godsend.

Use discounting and incentives with care. There's a fine line between over-the-top infomercial-like promotional pricing and authentic, clean, believable, appreciated-by-the-customer, and respectful use of discounting tactics and special offers. However, don't be afraid to be fully self-expressed in your sales promotions. There's nothing wrong – in fact, there's something very right about giving your ideal clients an opportunity to take advantage of your services. Remember what we said before: people buy to express their values. You're giving them an opportunity to express their values through the work you do together.

Here are some discount strategies you might like to employ:

- *Quantity discounts:* You may be able to encourage clients to buy more of your services if they can get better pricing the more they commit. For example, a studio photographer might offer photoshoot packages in tiers — basic, standard, and premium — where each tier includes more time in the studio and a higher number of edited photos. The price in studio per hour and per photo edited decreases as the client opts for more extensive packages, making the premium package the most advantageous deal. For this example, the photographer might also consider including an extra incentive for the premium package, such as a set of additional prints or a custom photo album, to further enhance the appeal and offer tangible value.
- *Pay-in-full discounts:* Reward clients who pay for your services in full with a lower rate. They will be more committed and pay less than if they pay by installments, and you will receive the full value of the contract upfront.
- *Seasonal discounts:* Encourage clients to buy at certain times of the year in anticipation of seasonal needs. Or offer off-season discounts. A landscaper can increase sales in the winter by closing the summer contracts at special off-season prices.
- *Markdowns and time-sensitive discounts:* Mark down your prices for a particular amount of time or until a certain number of sales is made. For example, "20% percent off all services booked in the next five days" or "the first three people to sign up for my gold branding package get a free upgrade to the platinum package."
- *Free services:* Give away free consultations or services as a sales tactic to get clients. Does it work? Sometimes. Should you do it? Depends on whom you ask. Some swear by it. Others have sworn off it. And yet, still others swear every time they do it because it's so frustrating. Generally, we don't recommend it. Think about it. How does it look to a potential client that you're offering free services to anybody who happens to stumble across your website — in demand, successful, and valuable or sitting around with lots of time on your hands just trying to give your stuff away for free in the hope that someone will hire you? Much more likely the latter. Credibility is built in large part on perception. And, anyway, what happened to your Red Velvet

Rope Policy? Sure, get on the phone with someone to see whether they get past your red velvet rope and give them an opportunity to fall in love with you at the same time. Learn about their needs, talk about how you can help, and book the business. In Chapter 9, you'll learn how to have effective sales conversations.

This doesn't mean there is no way to use this strategy – there is. For instance, early in Joana's freelancing career, she used this approach with great success. She cold-pitched a high-profile client, a "big fish" with high visibility, who she knew could significantly propel her career forward. In her cold pitch – which we'll cover more of in Chapter 11 – Joana expressed admiration for the client's work and offered to complete a small project at no cost, in exchange for a testimonial. The client was so impressed by Joana's work that she not only hired Joana as her graphic designer for the next five years but also became a vocal advocate for her services to her high-value network. From this single engagement, Joana generated multiple six figures in revenue from the endorsements of this one well-connected and respected client.

Clearly, when strategically implemented and carefully targeted, offering free services can indeed serve as a powerful tool to unlock significant opportunities. It's about choosing the right moment and the right client to make a calculated bet.

Additionally, here's another way Joana used free consultation sessions to produce 50% of her new business. She integrated a 30-minute free "website audit" session into her sales cycle – but only after someone had demonstrated their commitment by downloading her guide to creating a high-converting website. In the third email following their download, she invited them to a complimentary website audit. To book the session, potential clients needed to follow several steps outlined in the booking page:

- The session had to be scheduled using Joana's public calendar. She made only a few spots available on Thursday afternoons so that a waiting list developed quickly. This way she didn't look like she was sitting around twiddling her thumbs, hoping someone would show up.
- If they missed the session or didn't reschedule with 24 hours notice, they missed the opportunity and could not reschedule (again, all of this was automated).
- If they were more than five minutes late to the session, she would close the Zoom room.

- Finally, one week before the scheduled session, they had to submit a brief questionnaire about their business. This step ensured that the clients were invested in the process and that Joana had the necessary background to conduct a thorough audit. By understanding their specific challenges and objectives, she was able to highlight actionable changes that could significantly boost their website's performance.

You might think that all these rules would put potential clients off. You're trying to get clients, not force them to jump through flaming hoops. But, you know what? This approach allowed Joana to demonstrate not only her expertise but also her ability to deliver tangible improvements in only 30 minutes, making the free audit a powerful tool for converting prospects into long-term clients.

Figure out a way to use this strategy in your sales cycle and you'll get the opportunity to do something valuable, and free of charge, for your potential clients. You'll build your reputation, demonstrate credibility, and book more business. Then, once you're booked solid, you'll have so many referrals coming in that you won't need to do this anymore.

When to Raise Prices

Raise prices whenever you can, but there's no need to race to the top of the pricing ladder to be successful. Here are a few examples of why and how to do it.

- *Just for the heck of it:* Sometimes, raising prices may simply, and beautifully, lead to a much-deserved increase in profit.
- *Economic conditions:* You may need to raise prices because of inflation (rising costs unequaled by productivity gains). Inflation usually gets carried over to the consumer – which is why it's such an economic problem.
- *You're in demand and overbooked:* If demand for your services has increased – you'll be doing the Book Yourself Solid happy dance – it may be a good time to raise prices.
- *Training and skill development:* If you've recently upgraded your certifications or completed a significant training that is highly relevant to your clients' needs, it may be a great time to raise prices.

- *Upgrading your packaging:* If you upgrade your website with a complete redesign and in doing so seriously upgrade the look and feel of your brand, you can raise your prices. If you upgrade your offices, again, increasing the perceived value of your brand, you can up your prices. Credibility is, in no small part, based on perception.

Sometimes, when service providers get overbooked, they complain about it. Oh, how easily we forget what it was like when we were struggling our way up the ladder. Worse still, we've witnessed many creative service providers resist raising prices, which would have allowed each of them to work with fewer clients, for fear of losing business.

Michael used to see an acupuncturist from time to time in an attempt to reduce pain in his knee. He was likely the most experienced acupuncturist in Michael's small town and had an overbooked practice because of it. One time Michael was on the table and while he was being treated, the acupuncturist commented that he was overworked and couldn't keep up with the demand.

He indicated that he didn't want to change the model of his business, in that he still wanted to see clients himself. He didn't want to manage other acupuncturists, nor did he want to raise his prices. So, even though he had a fist full of needles at the ready, Michael said, "Why don't you just double your prices?" His answer? "But, Michael, if I double my rates, I'll lose half my clients." We'll pause here to let that sink in.

First, he wouldn't have lost half his clients, but even if he did, he'd still make the same money *and* have twice as much free time. More likely, he'd lose just a few clients but make much more money overall because of the price increase. Ironically, Michael stopped seeing him because it was too hard to get appointments that fit his schedule. So, if you're booked solid at rates that are too low, it might actually lose you clients.

If you do raise prices, it's a good idea to let clients know why. There's nothing wrong with saying that you're fortunate to be in high demand and are raising your prices so that you can give more attention to your clients. Or, that certain expenses related to serving your clients have increased and you're raising your prices accordingly. People like the truth. It's better to be open and honest with your clients, running the risk of disappointing a few of them, than be manipulative or obtuse, running the risk of damaging your reputation. Just be sure to let them know what the new rates will be and when they go into effect. Give them reasonable notice so they can adjust to the changes. And, most importantly, remind them of the continuing benefits they'll get from working with you.

On the flipside, you don't always have to carry over all costs or eke out every bit of profit on every sale. Sometimes you can earn long-term marketing juice by choosing your clients over your profit. Let's use a thriving local organic restaurant and pizza place called Jules Thin Crust Pizza as an example. At one point, the price of cheese went down. Now, the average customer is not going to know this. They might love cheese, but they don't buy it in bulk. It would have been easy, and cheesy (sorry, couldn't resist), for Jules to just pocket the extra profit from the savings. But no, instead, he put up a big sign announcing the cheap cheese and that he was lowering prices because of it. All summer, their busy season, no less, prices were reduced. Asking the owner, John, whether the cheese experiment cultured nicely or stunk up the place (sorry, again, couldn't resist), he said it was a huge success – customers loved it, as you might imagine. Now, John's not the type to boast about sales, but it's highly likely he saw more business because of his gastrointestinal-stimulus package.

Super Simple Selling

Art is making something out of nothing, and selling it.
—Frank Zappa

As a creative service provider, you may not want to think of yourself as a salesperson. You're in the business of helping others, and the sales process may feel contradictory to your core purpose. If you're uncomfortable with the sales process, it's likely that you view it as unethical, manipulative, or dishonest. Looking at it that way, who wouldn't be uncomfortable?

Many creative service providers also feel uncomfortable charging for services either that come easily to them or that they love doing. There is often a sense that if it comes easily and is enjoyable, there's something wrong with charging others for doing it.

Add the fact that creative service providers sell themselves as much as they sell services, and the whole idea becomes even more uncomfortable. It may feel like you're bragging and being shamelessly immodest.

Becoming comfortable with the sales process requires that you let go of any limiting beliefs you may have about being worthy of the money you're earning. In fact, developing the right comfort level might also require a shift in your perspective on the sales process itself.

Letting Go of Limiting Beliefs

Most people who are successful get paid to do what they do well. You don't usually become successful doing something that you find difficult. You become successful when you exploit your natural talents. Imagine Tom Hanks saying he shouldn't get paid to do movies because he's really good at it and loves it. Or J. K. Rowling saying she should write the *Harry Potter* books for free because she enjoys it.

Tom Hanks, J. K. Rowling, and anyone else you can think of who is, or was, wildly successful at what they do, work to the bone at becoming even better at what they are naturally gifted at doing. They create extraordinary experiences for the people they serve, whether it's an audience, a fan, or a client. That's why they — and you — deserve to be paid top dollar.

> *If you've been feeling like you can't, or shouldn't, be paid to do what you love, you must let that limiting belief go if you're to be booked solid.*

If you don't believe you are worth what you are charging, it is unlikely that a lot of people are going to hire you based on those fees. You need to resonate fully with the prices you are setting so that others will resonate with them as well. To do so, you may need to work on shifting your beliefs so that you feel more comfortable with charging higher fees, rather than lowering your fees to eliminate the discomfort. Understand the far-reaching financial, emotional, physical, and spiritual (FEPS) benefits that you deliver, and stand firmly in that value.

There is an old joke about a guy who gets into a cab in New York City and asks the driver how to get to Carnegie Hall, and the driver responds, "Practice, practice, practice." You're going to increase your pricing with practice. It's just like practicing a martial art or a sport or singing. Singing is a great example because your voice becomes more resonant the more you practice. At first it's uncomfortable, but over time, it becomes easier and more natural. The same thing will happen when you quote your fees. The more comfortable you feel when setting your price, the more other people will feel that comfort and the energetic resonance that comes with that comfort, and they'll happily pay you what you're worth.

Shifting Your Perspective

The Book Yourself Solid paradigm of sales is all about building relationships with your potential clients on the basis of trust. It is, quite simply, about having a sincere conversation that enables you to let your potential clients know what you can do to help them. You aren't manipulating or coercing people into buying something they have no real need or desire to buy. You're making them aware of something you offer that they already need, want, or desire.

Thinking in terms of solutions and benefits is the *aha* to the selling process. It's the key to shifting your perspective.

When you think in terms of solutions and problems solved, clients are compelled to work with you. You are a consultant, a lifelong advisor. When you have fundamental solutions and a desire to help others, it becomes your moral imperative to show and tell as many people as possible. You are changing lives.

Successful Selling Needs the Right Amount of Trust at Just the Right Time

It's no accident that we're introducing sales here in Chapter 9 – after we've taught you how to set your foundation and build trust and credibility. One of the reasons that so many sales conversations are *unsuccessful* is because they're had at the wrong time – usually too soon – before you've earned the proportionate amount of trust needed for the offer being made. Plus, your clients buy when it's right for them – when something occurs in their life that compels them to hire you. If these two factors, trust and timing, come together at just the right moment, you'll have a *successful* sales conversation and book the business. But this works only if you've built a solid foundation, demonstrating that you:

- Have a Red Velvet Rope Policy so you work only with ideal clients.
- Understand why people buy what you're selling so you know exactly to whom you are selling and what they want to invest in.
- Have developed a personal brand identity so you decide how you're known in the world.
- Are able to talk about what you do without sounding confusing or bland, or like everybody else, and without ever using an elevator speech.

If you've set this foundation, a potential client will give you the opportunity to earn his trust. But you'll only earn his trust if you:

- Use the standard credibility builders and have a high degree of likeability.
- Have designed a sales cycle that starts with no-barrier-to-entry offers including your always-have-something-to-invite-people-to offer.
- Regularly and respectfully keep in touch with the people you're meant to serve.
- Have simple lead-generating information products that enhance your credibility and speed up your sales cycle.

Then, and really only then, are you ready to have sales conversations that work.

The Secret to the Book Yourself Solid System

This simple four-step process is the secret to the Book Yourself Solid system.

1. You execute a few of the Six Core Self-Promotion strategies, which create awareness for what you have to offer.
2. When a potential client becomes aware of your services, they'll take a look at your foundation. If it looks secure, if they feel comfortable stepping onto it, they'll give you the opportunity to earn their trust — but only the opportunity.

3. That's when your plan to build trust and credibility comes into play. As a potential client moves through your sales cycle, she will come to like you, trust you, and find you credible.

4. When their circumstances dictate that they need the kind of help you provide, they'll raise their hand and ask you to have a sales conversation. You have a sales conversation the Book Yourself Solid way and book the business.

The process is simple. The process is sound. It can turn your business life around. And, most important, the process is a complete, repetitive, and self-perpetuating system. While potential clients are going through this process, you're continuing to create awareness for what you have to offer using a few of the Six Core Self-Promotion Strategies. This gets more new potential clients checking out your foundation for stability and security. They'll like what they see, stand on it, and give you the opportunity to earn their trust. You earn their trust (over time), and when the circumstances are right for *them*, either they'll raise their hand and ask you to have a sales conversation or they'll accept one of your compelling offers and you'll book the business. The process repeats itself over and over and over again. It's systematic. Once you've set up your own Book Yourself Solid marketing and sales system, it works like a charm. Just rinse and repeat.

Book Yourself Solid Four-Part Sales Formula

Now, let's talk about how to have the sales conversation. We've created the four-part sales formula for super simple selling; it practically works on its own. Why? Because, once trust is assured and a need is met, using this four-part formula during your sales conversations is a natural process for booking business. But, please, just like the Book Yourself Solid dialogue, this is meant to be an open and free-flowing conversation, not a sales script.

When a potential client expresses interest in working with you, open with a simple question . . .

Part 1: *What are you working on?* Or *what is your goal?* Or *what are you trying to achieve?* Listen. Be curious. Take your time. Once you feel certain you know what he wants to accomplish and by when, simply ask some of the following questions . . .

Part 2: *How will you know when you have achieved it? What results will you see? What feedback will you hear? What will it look like? What feelings will you have?* Again, take your time. Listen deeply. Get your potential client to connect at every level with all of the financial, emotional, physical, and spiritual benefits of the outcome he is seeking. Anchor your potential client in that place. Once you feel like the potential client has clearly articulated these benefits, make sure he is fully in the hiring frame of mind, and then ask . . .

Part 3: *Would you like someone to help you with that (achieve your goal, and so forth)?* If they say, "No," wish them the best of luck and keep in touch with him. If they say, "Yes," then offer . . .

Part 4: *Would you like that person to be me? Because, you know, you are my ideal client.* (To which they'll say, "What do you mean?" because no one has ever said that to them before.) *Well, you are someone with whom I do my best work.* (He'll ask "Why?" and you'll tell them . . .) *Because you are . . .* (Here is where you list the qualities that make them who they are and allow you to do your best work.) As you're listing these qualities, you'll see their face brighten as they sit up straight and say, "Wow. That is *so* me! Thank you for noticing." You'll say, *"So, shall we look at our calendars to plan a time to get started?"* And the answer will be . . . drumroll, please . . . "Absolutely, yes!"

Don't use the preceding phrases verbatim. Instead, just use the Book Yourself Solid Four-Part Sales Formula as a framework for a super-duper simple (successful) sales conversation.

3.9.1 Written Exercise: Practice without pressure. Try this process with a good friend or colleague and see what happens. Ask them to call you at random a few times over the course of a week and say, "Hi, I've been getting your newsletter for a while, and I think you may be able to help me. Can we talk about your services?" And, instead of doing that thing that everyone does – talk about themselves and their business for 20 minutes – ask them what they're working on or what they're trying to achieve or what problem they're trying to overcome, and you'll be into Part 1 of the Book Yourself Solid Four-Part Sales Formula. Super simple.

If They're Uncertain

What if potential clients are not ready to start working with you? No problem. Then go back into your Sales Cycle Process. You continue to keep in touch. Book Yourself Solid is not about qualifying and disqualifying leads. Book Yourself Solid takes the long view. It's about creating long-term relationships. The good news is that someday the benefits you provide will be a priority. Something in your potential client's life will change that compels them to work with you. However, if you haven't kept in touch and followed up, they'll look to someone else to help them reach their goals. But, since you're going to become a master at keeping in touch and following up, you'll be waiting in the wings, ready, willing, and able to help them accomplish their goals. (Go back to Chapter 7 and review the Keep-in-Touch Strategy if you need to.)

These are the lovely, easy steps to simple selling and booking yourself solid. Start small, end big, and remember – successful selling is really nothing more than showing your potential clients how you can help them live a happier, more successful life.

Cut the Crap Out of Selling

Traditional and trite sales tactics that include, but are not limited to, closing techniques, assuming the sale, overcoming objections, and so forth were originally developed in the late 1800s by John H. Patterson of the National Cash Register Company (who, ironically enough, was found guilty of violating antitrust laws). These contrived sales strategies, created by a convict, are still perpetuated by sales trainers. And for good reason. They give us something to do when we're lost. They provide a standard by which to measure. And the worst part is that they work – a little – sometimes. But clients detest them.

People don't buy because you want them to. If you really want to be successful when selling, listen to your potential clients. If they don't like the old, generic, overused, and clichéd tactics, why are you still holding on to them? (Maybe you're not, but you know, or work with, someone who is.)

Do what you must. Ditch the canned 1-2-3, sometimes pushy, usually insensitive, and almost always repetitive sales strategies glamorized in the past.

We've offered you the Book Yourself Solid Four-Part Sales Formula to use as a framework for your sales conversations, but there is no perfectly packaged process, magic bullet, or foolproof method to crumble every gatekeeper in your path and book every piece of business. It doesn't exist. We must be willing to learn, adapt, and listen to our potential clients.

When you do this, you'll never have to use a canned close again. But you will connect brilliantly with the values your customers want to express. Remember:

- Trash the level-setting statements and the conversation helpers and just listen while customers tell you what they really want.
- Ditch the pitch of the day and only make relevant sales offers that are proportionate to the amount of trust you've earned.
- Use the Red Velvet Rope policy and don't look at everyone as a dollar sign. Maximize your time and energy, and build credibility when you work with people you are meant to serve.

We're certain you care about what you do: the people you serve, the services you sell, and the reputation you've earned. You wouldn't be reading this book if you didn't. Do not let your guard down for one second. Think bigger about who you are and how you will serve your clients.

When you keep your focus and maintain your integrity, you'll never, ever, be put in the same category as those stereotypical, shady, smooth-talking, handlebar-mustache-twirling, sleazeball "salespeople" ready to screw over the next poor sap just to take home the commission. You're a creative service provider. Your service is important to the world. You are important to the world. Cut the crap out of selling and set yourself apart.

Pre-Qualifying Clients Using the Book Yourself Solid Super Simple Selling System

Let's end with a concrete example of how you can integrate the Book Yourself Solid Super Simple Selling process into your business. This approach will not only streamline your client intake process but also ensure every interaction adds value and builds trust with potential clients.

When Joana first encountered the Book Yourself Solid system, one of her initial actions was to dump her duds. She quickly realized the necessity of pre-qualifying potential clients to ensure only her ideal clients made it past her Red Velvet Rope. Simultaneously, she saw the need for more organic and meaningful sales conversations with those potential ideal clients.

To address both needs, she implemented a detailed pre-qualification quote inquiry form on her website. Potential clients were asked to fill out a few details about their project expectations.

If Joana and her team felt they could meet the client's expectations based on the form responses, they would confirm that the client was in the right place and set up an initial consultation on Zoom as the next step. During this call, they could address any questions or concerns about the project directly and honestly, setting the stage for a transparent and productive dialogue.

Joana found that the inquiry form allowed her team to gauge early on whether a potential client was an ideal match or a likely mismatch. This saved both her team and the potential client valuable time by avoiding unnecessary calls. If a prospective client was not a good fit – perhaps due to misaligned timelines or platform requirements – Joana's team would guide them toward more suitable alternatives.

To this day, Joana and her team believe that this pre-qualification step has spared them countless hours and avoided the discomfort of declining clients who didn't meet their Red Velvet Rope Policy. It can do the same for you.

The Book Yourself Solid Six Core Self-Promotion Strategies

You've diligently worked through Modules One, Two, and Three. You have a foundation for your creative business. You have a strategy for building trust and credibility. You know how to price and sell your services. Watch out, because you're not only on your way to liking marketing and selling, but you are now dangerously close to loving both.

By the time you complete Module Four, maybe you'll be in a full-on, mad, passionate love affair with the idea of marketing and selling. We can only hope.

Just like any new love affair, you want to give yourself time to absorb the newness of it all. Don't let the multitude of strategies, techniques, and exercises in Module Four overwhelm you. Pick the strategies that are most aligned with your strengths and run with them – you don't need to execute all of them. In fact, only three of the strategies are mandatory, whereas three of them are optional. Can you guess which are mandatory and which are optional?

The Book Yourself Solid Six Core Self-Promotion Strategies:

1. The Book Yourself Solid Networking Strategy
2. The Book Yourself Solid Direct Outreach Strategy
3. The Book Yourself Solid Referral Strategy
4. The Book Yourself Solid Speaking Strategy
5. The Book Yourself Solid Writing Strategy
6. The Book Yourself Solid Online Strategy

Give yourself an A+ if you guessed that the mandatory strategies are networking, direct outreach, and referrals. You don't survive without using those basic strategies for creating awareness for what you offer.

You might have guessed that speaking and writing strategies are optional, but are you surprised to hear that the online strategy is also optional? Yes, having a professional website that effectively starts conversations with potential clients is necessary 99.9% of the time for service professionals, but beyond that, you do not need to learn or use all of the additional online marketing strategies. If you're not web or tech savvy and have absolutely no desire to become so, then you shouldn't worry about all the various bells and whistles the Web offers. If you can outsource this, great. If you have the resources to hire people to run these efforts for you, then go for it. But, if you try to dive into the Web with no real interest or aptitude, you're sure to become overwhelmed, and fast. We know this might sound blasphemous to an expert in search engine optimization or a Facebook ad strategist, but there are many service professionals who build their business offline and send what is called direct traffic to their site rather than drive traffic from other online sources. More on this in Chapter 15, but our point is that you can get booked solid with solid networking, direct outreach, and referral strategies alone.

Start with the strategies that speak to you first. The only possible mistake you can make is to try all of these strategies at once. You run the risk of watering down your efforts, becoming frustrated with the results, or, worse, quitting before you see any results. We suggest that you use the three mandatory strategies, networking, direct outreach, and referrals, and pick one of the optional strategies, online, speaking, or writing, to start.

The mandatory strategies will ensure that you're creating awareness for the products and services you offer, and the one optional strategy will supercharge your promotional efforts. Then, over time, as you get more and more proficient with the mandatory strategies, feel free to add in more of the optional strategies. In the process, do your best to enjoy, embrace, and profit from the Book Yourself Solid Six Core Self-Promotion Strategies.

Knowing how to do something and actually doing it are two very different things. For years, we've seen many a talented service professional struggle to get clients because, even though they understood what they were supposed to do, they just didn't do it. Watching others struggle so much hurts our hearts, and solving this problem, for the people we serve, became an obsession. Thankfully, for us, and fortunately, for you, we believe we've solved the problem.

Remember, the Book Yourself Solid system is supported by both practical and spiritual principles. From a spiritual perspective, we believe that if you have something to say, if you have a message to deliver, and if there are people you want to serve, then there are people in this world whom you are meant to serve. Not kinda, sorta, because they're in your target market, but *meant to* — that's the way the universe is set up if you're in the business of helping others.

From a practical perspective, there may be two simple reasons why you don't have as many clients as you'd like:

1. Either you don't know what to do to attract and secure more clients, or
2. You know what to do but you're not actually doing it.

The Book Yourself Solid system is designed to help you solve both of these problems. Module Four will show you what to do to attract and secure more clients. But these six core self-promotion strategies must be executed every day. Yes, *every working day*. You don't need us to tell you that your future rests on your ability to execute these strategies with daily discipline. However, you might need us to help you:

- Identify exactly what you need to do each day to book more business
- Definitely get it done, daily

This module will show you exactly what to do daily. Most important, the concepts and action steps laid out in the following pages will help you create relentless demand for the services and products you offer so that you can energetically build a cadre of high-value, high-paying, inspiring clients.

The Book Yourself Solid Networking Strategy

Some cause happiness wherever they go; others, whenever they go.
—Oscar Wilde

Networking, Ugh!

It's possible that — like the thought of marketing and sales — the thought of networking may make you cringe. When most service professionals hear the word *networking*, they think of the old-school business mentality of promotional networking at meet-and-greet events where everyone is there to schmooze and manipulate one another in an attempt to gain some advantage for themselves or their business.

Who wouldn't cringe at the thought of spending an hour or two exchanging banalities and sales pitches with a phony smile plastered on your face to hide your discomfort? If it feels uncomfortable, self-serving, or deceptive, chances are all those business cards you collected will end up in a drawer of your desk never to be seen again because you'll so dread following up that you'll procrastinate until they're forgotten.

Take heart, because it doesn't have to be that way. The Book Yourself Solid Networking Strategy operates from an entirely different perspective – networking is all about connecting and sharing with others. All that's necessary is to shift your perspective from one of scarcity and fear to one of abundance and love. With the Book Yourself Solid Networking Strategy, the focus is on sincerely and freely giving and sharing and, by doing so, building and deepening mutually beneficial relationships with others. Networking is all about making lasting connections.

Making the Shift to the Book Yourself Solid Way

The first step is to change your perspective of what networking really is. Do you believe that networking has something to do with the old-school business mentality of scarcity and fear that asks:

- How can I push my agenda?
- How can I get or keep the attention on myself?
- What can I say to really impress or manipulate?
- How can I use each contact to get what I want or need?
- How can I crush the competition?
- How can I dominate the marketplace?

The Book Yourself Solid Networking Strategy (one of abundance and, dare we say it, love) asks:

- What can I give and offer to others?
- How can I help others to be successful?
- How can I start and continue friendly conversations?
- How can I put others at ease?
- How can I best express my sincerity and generosity?
- How can I listen attentively so as to recognize the needs and desires of others?
- How can I provide true value to others?
- How can I fully express myself so I can make genuine connections with others?

When we use the word *networking,* let's think of *connecting* instead. Does that help make the concept of networking more palatable? We don't get contacts, we don't find contacts, we don't have contacts; we make *connections* with real people.

> *A connection with another human being means you're in sync with, and relevant to, each other. Let that be our definition of networking.*

When people ask what the most important factor in networking success is, it's a two-word answer: other people. Your networking success is determined by other people — how they respond to you.

If you keep asking yourself the preceding value-added questions and follow the Book Yourself Solid Networking Strategy that we're about to present to you, you'll create a large and powerful network built on compassion, trust, and integrity — a network that is priceless and will reap rewards for years to come.

The Book Yourself Solid 50/50 Networking Rule

The Book Yourself Solid Networking Strategy employs the 50/50 networking rule, which requires we share our networking focus evenly between potential clients and other professionals. Most people think of networking as something you do primarily to try to reel in clients. That's not so.

While the Book Yourself Solid Networking Strategy adds value to the lives of people who could become your clients, you'll also want to spend 50% of your networking time connecting with other professionals. Networking with other professionals provides you with an opportunity to connect and share resources, knowledge, and information. Bear in mind that working solo does not mean working alone. This chapter is focused on increasing the value of your network of other professionals who can open doors of all kinds for you. You can create so much more value when other talented people are involved.

Additionally, you can strategically network with complimentary service providers. Think about who else your clients might need services from. If you're a web designer, your clients might also need a copywriter. Forming relationships with complimentary service providers can be highly beneficial. For example, when Joana started out, she joined a few networking groups of copywriters where she made friends and established referral partnerships. They referred clients to each other, creating a mutually beneficial relationship.

By diversifying your network to include both potential clients and other professionals, especially those offering complimentary services, you enhance your ability to provide comprehensive solutions to your clients while also opening up new opportunities for collaboration and growth.

Have You Got Any Soul?

The absolute best education you could ever receive on the concept of networking is from Tim Sanders in his book, *Love Is the Killer App: How to Win Business and Influence Friends* (Crown Currency, 2002).

Tim Sanders's message is that being a *love cat* is the key to business success, and it's at the heart of the Book Yourself Solid Networking Strategy. He quotes philosopher and writer Milton Mayeroff's definition of love from his book *On Caring* (William Morrow, 1990): "Love is the selfless promotion of the growth of the other." Tim then defines his idea of business love as "the act of intelligently and sensibly sharing your intangibles with your biz partners."

What are those intangibles? They are your knowledge, your network, and your compassion. They are the three essential keys to networking success.

Networking requires that you consciously integrate each of these intangibles until they become a natural part of your daily life, everywhere you go, and in everything you do. Yes, we said *daily life*. Networking isn't something you do only at networking events. It's an ongoing process that will bring terrific benefits.

Share *Who* You Know, *What* You Know, and *How* You Feel

Here's how you practically go about sharing your intangibles with your partners, potential clients, suppliers, and friends:

- *Share who you know:* This is everyone you know. It's as simple as that. Whether family, friend, or business associate, everyone in your network is potentially a good connection with someone else, and you never know whom you might meet next who will be the other half of a great connection.
- *Share what you know:* This means everything you've learned – whether through life experience, observation, conversation, or study – and everything you continue to learn.
- *Share how you feel (in ways that make other people feel better about themselves):* This is all of your compassion, the quality that makes us most human. It's our ability to empathize with others. Sharing your compassion in every aspect of your life will bring the greatest rewards, not only for your bottom line but also in knowing that you're operating from your heart and your integrity in all your interactions.

Note: Give each of these three intangibles freely and with no expectation of return. After all, that's how love is meant to operate, too. While it may seem calculated to plan a strategy around them, the fact remains that when you're smart, friendly, and helpful, people will like you, will enjoy being around you, and will remember you when they or someone they know needs your services.

Share Who You Know

To whom do you want to give your business or recommend to other members of your network? It's the people who have served you in some way; the people who are friendly, nice, smart, and helpful; the people who will go the extra mile, who give that little bit more than anyone expects, and who genuinely strive to provide the best service they can with integrity. It's the people who are upbeat, always have a ready smile, and from whom you walk away feeling supported and energized.

If you are that person in each and every interaction you have with others, whether business or personal, your network is going to grow exponentially, and those people are going to remember you and want to do business with you. They're going to link you with others in their network with whom you can make beneficial connections, and they're going to refer you to everyone they know who could possibly use your service or products.

There is one thing that is essential to consider with respect to sharing your network. You must do what you say you're going to do – always. And if you don't, apologize and make it right. If you make commitments and don't fulfill them, you'll damage your reputation and close doors that were once open to you. If you don't make commitments to connect, no one will do it for you. These habits of commitment making and fulfilling are essential to developing yourself into a masterful connector who truly and meaningfully adds value to the lives of others.

Each business day, introduce two people within your network who do not yet know each other but you think might benefit from knowing each other. This is not a referral for a specific work opportunity but rather a way to connect two people who may find some benefit in knowing each other. Maybe they both are in the same field or share some business connection. Maybe they are both into martial arts or golf. Or maybe they just live in the same town. Either way, all you're doing is creating an opportunity for connection. If they're the kind of people who value meeting others, then something special might happen. Hey, you never know. You might be introducing two people who are going to save the planet from climate calamity or fall in love and get married.

4.10.1 Written Exercise: List three people in your network who consistently support you by sending referrals, giving you advice, or doing anything else that's helpful. Then identify someone in your network for each of these five people whom you could connect them with. Whom do you know who will add value to their work or life? Is it a potential client, a potential business partner, a potential vendor?

4.10.2 Booked Solid Action Step: Try it now. Go through your address book and find two people who share something in common, something that each one of them will find relevant about the other and introduce them to each other.

The people you listed in the preceding written exercise and the people you connected in the Booked Solid Action Step are going to appreciate the opportunity to connect or the recommendation that you make, and when someone they know needs your service or product, they'll be more likely to remember you and to reciprocate.

Remember, too, that the six degrees of separation theory says that you are only six people away from the person or information you need. (In the field, your degrees of separation from anyone you need or want to connect with are even fewer.) Everyone you meet has the potential to connect you (through his network and his contacts' networks) to someone or some piece of information that you need. So step out of your comfort zone and make a sincere effort to connect with people you might not normally interact with. The more diverse your network of connections is, the more powerful and effective your network becomes. It opens doors that might otherwise remain closed.

4.10.3 Written Exercise: Think of the types of people or professions who are *not* represented in your current network. List five that would expand and benefit your network, as well as ideas for where you might find them.

Every once in a while we get some pushback from people about sharing their network that goes something like this: "But, I don't know that many people, so this won't work for me." You might be surprised to discover that you can create 45 connections from a network of only 10 people. Bump it up to 20 people and you've got 190 connections. It may seem like funny math, but it's not. It's factorial math.

Here's how it works for just 10 people.

Introduce Person 1 to Persons 2–10.

That's nine connections.

Person 2 has met Person 1, but needs to meet Persons 3–10.

That's eight connections.

Person 3 has now met Persons 1 and 2 and needs to meet Persons 4–10.

That's seven connections.

Person 4 has now met Persons 1–3 and needs to meet Persons 5–10.

That's six connections.

Person 5 has now met Persons 1–4 and needs to meet Persons 6–10.

That's five connections.
Person 6 has now met Persons 1–5 and needs to meet Persons 7–10.
That's four connections.
Person 7 has now met Persons 1–6 and needs to meet Persons 8–10.
That's three connections.
Person 8 has now met Persons 1–7 and needs to meet Persons 9 and 10.
That's two connections.
Person 9 has now met Persons 1–8 and needs to meet Person 10.
That's one connection.
That's a total of 45 connections created out of only 10 people.

If you start with 20 people, you end up with 190 connections because 19 + 18 + 17 + 16 + 15 + 14 + 13 + 12 + 11 + 10 + 9 + 8 + 7 + 6 + 5 + 4 + 3 + 2 + 1 = 190.

Your world is much bigger than you might think. And you don't really need to know much about math; you just need to know that connecting people is a good thing to do.

Share What You Know

The answers to most questions are offered in books. Even better, we get to choose what we learn and from whom. Then armed with this information, we're in a great place to share it with others, including the books themselves.

You may be thinking, "But if I'm always referring to other people's work, won't they just forget about me and get everything they need from the book or resource I referred them to?" Good question. First, if they love the book or information that you referred them to, it's highly likely they'll associate much of that value with you. They will feel connected to you because you helped them achieve a goal or change their life, or simply learn something new, the value of which is not to be underestimated. The more knowledgeable you are and are perceived to be, the more trust and credibility you'll build in your network. Reading books is, by far, the best and most efficient way to increase your knowledge. Sharing those books is an excellent way to demonstrate that knowledge and help other people at the same time.

Reading a book on a topic that is related to the services you provide offers an easy way to start a conversation with potential clients or contacts.

In fact, they may start the conversation with you instead with one simple question, "What are you reading?" Michael realized this gem of a networking technique by accident. He was born and raised in New York City, where almost every New Yorker rides the subway. You bump into friends, sit next to politicians, and sight celebrities. Plus, it's simply the best way to get around. It's also one of the best places to make new friends. Think about it; you're constantly bumped, pushed, and shoved by people you don't know. So instead of fighting all the time, most New Yorkers decide the path of least resistance is simply to strike up a conversation. If you have a book in your hand, what do you think this conversation is going to be about? You guessed it: the book. And what better way to get into your Book Yourself Solid Dialogue than to explain why you're reading the particular book you're holding in your hand.

Of course, this doesn't just apply to New York subway cars. Everywhere you go, you're running into, meeting, and connecting with other people. What if you always had a book in your hand that allowed you to share what you know about your particular area of expertise, for the betterment of the person you're talking with? We know that not every person you meet or run into is a member of your target market, or at first thought, can send you clients, but it doesn't matter. You're just finding opportunities to add value to those you meet by sharing what you know – as long as it's relevant to them.

> **4.10.4 Booked Solid Action Step:** Try it with this book. Carry it wherever you go and explain to people why you're reading it. You'll have the opportunity to talk about the Book Yourself Solid philosophy of giving so much value that you think you've gone too far and then giving more, and how it's in sync with your values and what you do as a service provider. You'll then be able to get into your Book Yourself Solid Dialogue with ease.

Ask yourself what knowledge, once acquired, would add the greatest value and make you more attractive to potential clients and business partners, and then go after learning it. Your investment in books – buying them and reading them – will pay dividends you can't even imagine.

Here are a few examples of books that will help you grow your business:

- *Profit First* by Mike Michalowicz (Portfolio, 2017)
- *The Win Without Pitching Manifesto* by Blair Enns (Gegen Press, 2018)
- *Built to Sell* by John Warrillow (Portfolio, 2010)
- *Duct Tape Marketing* by John Jantsch (Thomas Nelson, 2010)
- *Your Body of Work* by Pam Slim (Portfolio, 2013)
- *Never Split the Difference* by Chris Voss (Harper Business, 2016)
- *Lean In* by Sheryl Sandberg (Knopf, 2013)
- *Hug Your Haters* by Jay Baer (Portfolio, 2016)
- *Fascinate* by Sally Hogshead (Harper Business, 2016)

4.10.5 Written Exercise: List five books you've read that you know are must-reads for your target market. Think about and jot down the names of any specific people who come to mind for each book.

4.10.6 Written Exercise: List five books that have been recommended to you as must-reads or that you know contain information that would add value to your target market. Then go out and make the investment in at least one of them this week.

4.10.7 Written Exercise: Books aren't our only source of knowledge. As we mentioned earlier, our life experience, observations, and conversations are all sources of knowledge as well. Think about the many areas in which you're knowledgeable and list a minimum of five. Have fun with this and just let it flow. If you know a lot about skydiving, or *ikebana* (the Japanese art of flower arranging), include it! You never know what subject might help make a connection.

Let's take it up a notch. Once a week, send a book to someone with whom you'd like to develop a meaningful business relationship. Include a nice card with a note about why you're sending them the book – what it's meant to you and why you think it'll be valuable to them. Follow up three weeks later by phone to see how they're enjoying the book. This strategy is especially beneficial for those who are not particularly comfortable with small talk because now you've got something to talk about.

Now, let's take up one more notch. Sharing magazine, journal, and newspaper articles can work even better than books because the recipient of the information can consume it so quickly. Each day, send personally or professionally relevant articles to three people in your network. I know what you're thinking, *C'mon, how much time is that going to take? What do you think, I'm just sitting around with nothing to do?* No, of course not. We know how busy you are. But, if you want more clients, you need a stronger network. If you're not willing to build it, do you really deserve more clients? Just sayin'. . .

For example, if you are developing a professional relationship with Bob, a graphic designer specializing in sustainable design, and Monday morning *Fast Company* publishes an article about the latest trends in eco-friendly design, you'll be able to send the article to Bob before they even start their day. Your email will include a link to the article and a little note that says, "Good Morning, Bob, saw this article and immediately thought of you. Wonder if you've seen it? Pretty interesting when the author discusses . . . ."

You might just make Bob's day by sharing some very relevant and timely information that he might otherwise have missed. Moreover, Bob is going to feel so fortunate that you're out in the world thinking about him and his needs.

Review three publications that are relevant to your industry each day and then decide to whom you are going to send various articles.

4.10.8 Booked Solid Action Step: Try it now. Go to your favorite online publication, browse through today's articles, and when you find one that is relevant to someone in your network, send it to them with a note as suggested earlier.

Share How You Feel

In a business like yours that is based on service, people will generally not hire you unless they feel you have compassion for what they're going through.

Expressing that compassion is the first step to a successful working relationship. How do you do that? Listen attentively. Be fully present when making connections, smile as often as possible, make eye contact, and ask engaging, open-ended questions that express your curiosity and interest.

Take the time to add value to the person you're connecting with by offering information or resources that speak to their needs. If you don't have what they need, think about who in your network would meet their needs and how to go about acting as the link for them. Remember, this is done with no expectation of any immediate return.

4.10.9 Written Exercise: Note a recent situation, business or personal, when someone else expressed compassion for you. Think about how you felt following the interaction. How do you feel about that person because of the compassion they showed for you?

Can sharing your compassion be a marketing tactic? Absolutely. Do you do it manipulatively or to try to gain some favor? No, that is not the Book Yourself Solid way. You can be deliberate and developmental in the way that you share your compassion – that's not manipulative – it's thoughtful.

Send a card or an email to someone in your network at least once a week just to share your compassion. If you know they are going through a difficult time, send a note expressing sympathy. If they have just been honored with an award, shower them with praise. If they recently experienced a family triumph, like the marriage of a child, congratulate them. These simple, yet powerful, gestures make people thankful to know you. It keeps you on top of their mind. Most important, you're making other people feel better about who they are and what they do.

These Booked Solid Action Steps are your new daily and weekly networking activities, and you don't even need to leave the house to get them done.

- You'll share your network by introducing two people each day who may benefit from meeting each together. You'll come across as a real connecter, someone who thinks about the needs of others, and that's an amazingly attractive quality.

- You'll share what you know by sending one book a week, and at least two articles a day, to important networking partners. It'll make you look like a smartypants, give you something to talk to them about, and in the process build your relationship.
- You'll share your compassion with one person in your network each day, making them feel better about themselves and in the process thankful that they know you. Want to share compassion with more than one person a day? By all means, be my guest.

Let's do some more math, basic math, this time. If you adopt these habits and introduce two people each day, share articles or a book with two people each day, and share compassion with at least one person each day, that means you'll be connecting with at least five people each day (2 + 2 + 1 = 5). If you do that Monday through Friday, you'll be connecting with at least 25 people a week (5 × 5 = 25). There are generally four weeks in each month, so if you connect with 25 people each week, that means you'll connect with 100 people a month (25 × 4 = 100). Do this all year long and you'll connect with 1200 people each year. That's a numbers game worth playing. That alone can get you booked solid.

These simple, yet meaningful, networking strategies will get, and keep, you booked solid for many years to come. You just have to do it – each and every business day. I believe the Book Yourself Solid Networking Strategy is a critical key to your success.

The Book Yourself Solid Network of 90

Make a list of 90 people, a mixture of potential clients or industry professionals with whom you already have a relationship. The relationship doesn't have to be very strong, as it will become stronger over time as you work your networking muscle. If you don't know 90 people today, don't worry. Start with whoever you have. You will add to it over time.

This is your Book Yourself Solid Network of 90. This list sits on your desk. It lives on your computer and travels with you when you're on the road. Why 90, and why must you keep it with you at all times? Because your success is, in large part, determined by the quality of your relationships, keeping this list by your side will ensure that you're thinking of them, and if you make a habit of sharing your intangibles with them, your relationships will become stronger than you ever thought possible. And 90, because contacting three people from your list every day is manageable and means that you will be in touch with these people roughly once a month.

> **4.10.10 Written Exercise:** Identify a minimum of 10 and a maximum of 90 people you'd like to remain in regular contact with. This list should be made up in equal parts of peers and prospects.

Here's what you do with your list:

- Each day, reach out to the three people at the top of your list.
- Share your knowledge, your network, or your compassion with these people. You can write a quick email, send a text message, a postcard, or a handwritten note.
- After you reach out to these people, put them to the bottom of the list, and tackle another three people tomorrow. That means you'll be in contact with them every month at a minimum.
- Be flexible. If you don't see an opportunity to make a relevant introduction to the third person on your list, send them a note to say that you're thinking of them.
- Be pragmatic. You might run into somebody on your list every week at the gym. That's great. If you've had a meaningful exchange, put them to the bottom of the list. If a colleague has a birthday and they were at the top of your list last week, of course you should still wish them a happy birthday, before finding them in your list and putting them to the bottom again. It's a framework, not an exact science.
- Think big. If you have 120 or 180 people you'd like to stay in touch with on a regular basis and it's not overwhelming, go for it! Ninety is a manageable number of connections for most people, but if you're a super-connector, feel free to supercharge this strategy by adding more names.

This networking activity occurs every business day: you'll reach out to a minimum of three people, each and every day, and you'll follow up with people who reply to you, each and every day. This is critical. Dedicated, disciplined, and determined action is key to your networking success.

> **4.10.11 Booked Solid Action Step:** Reach out to the first person on your network of 90 and then add them to your follow-up system.

Networking Opportunities

The possibilities for meeting people are endless. Any time you're sharing your connections, knowledge, and compassion, you're networking. Any time you're learning more about what others do and know, you're networking. Any time you link or connect two people you know, you're networking.

Informal Networking Opportunities

These are the ones that we might not think of as networking but that we can't afford to overlook. We have dozens of these every day:

- Casual chat in line at the grocery store
- In exercise class at a gym or in a coffee shop
- Speaking with your neighbor while walking your dog

Let's take the neighbor you see while walking your dog as an example. Every day you walk the same path with your dog. Each time, you smile and chat with your neighbor as your dogs sniff each other. After a while, you begin to greet one another by name, and you know enough about him to ask after his family. He mentions he was looking forward to a special evening out with his wife the following night for their anniversary but then sighs and says, "But our babysitter canceled at the last minute. I wish [one of the phrases to always be listening for] that I knew of a good backup to call." You recall that your friend Sally seems to know every sitter in town. You pull out your phone, look up her number, and give her a call. "Sally, meet Bob. He's looking for a great sitter for tomorrow night, and you know everyone, so of course I thought you might be able to help," you say as you hand your cell phone to Bob.

Now this exchange has absolutely nothing to do with business. Or does it? On the surface, it might not seem to. However, who do you think Bob is going to call when he, or someone he knows, needs the exact service you offer? Bob is thrilled with you because you've saved his special night out. And Sally is pleased too because you've given her high praise and allowed her to show off her knowledge of who's who in the world of local babysitters. Both of them feel better following their interaction with you, and that makes you memorable. Most important, you've increased your connection factor with each of them. Your connection factor is how much trust you've built with each person in your network. The more value you add to a person's life, the more she is going to trust you.

4.10.12 Written Exercise: Think for a moment: have you recently missed any opportunities for making a deeper connection with someone? List one connection that would have been made if you had just shared your knowledge, your network, or your compassion.

Formal Networking Opportunities

These are the more formal, business meet-and-greet opportunities that can be fun and enjoyable and offer great rewards:

- Chamber of Commerce meetings
- Networking groups – CreativeMornings, American Institute of Graphic Arts (AIGA), Adobe community or Freelancers Union, for example
- Industry-specific conferences and trade shows (both related to the service you provide, and the industry your clients are in)
- Art galleries and design exhibitions

4.10.13 Written Exercise: Do some research and come up with three additional business networking opportunities like the ones I've listed that you can attend with the intention of adding value to others as well as enhancing your network.

Networking Events – What to Do

- *Arrive on time:* This is not the time to stage a grand entrance by being fashionably late or to tell any stories about why you're late. Nobody cares. If you're late and it's noticed, apologize and leave it at that.
- *Relax and be yourself:* Contrary to conventional wisdom, you don't have to fit in. It may sound trite, but be yourself, unless when you're being yourself you end the evening with your tie wrapped around your head doing a nosedive into the shrimp salad. Seriously, people want to meet the person who is out in front, who is writing the rules and taking the lead, not the one who is following the pack. So don't be afraid to be fully self-expressed. If you are, you'll be more memorable.
- *Smile and be friendly:* Both men and women may worry that smiling too big will be construed as some sort of a come-on or that they're desperate for attention. This fear of being misunderstood will hold you back. Let it go. Better to err on the side of a big, friendly smile than to be considered unfriendly or standoffish.
- *Focus on giving:* If your focus is on giving of yourself, you're going to get returns in spades. If you focus on what you can get, you will be much less successful.
- *Prepare for the event:* Learn the names of the organizers and some of the key players. Identify what and how you can share with others at the function: whom you know (without being a name dropper), what you know (without being a know-it-all), and what you can share from your heart (without making assumptions) with the people who will be at this particular event. You never know what might change someone's life.
- *Introduce yourself to the person hosting the event:* This person may be a very valuable addition to your network. Never forget to say, "Thank you."
- *Introduce yourself to the bigwig:* If there's someone you want to meet at a big seminar or event, someone famous in your industry, do you go up to them and say, "Here's what I do and here's my business card"? No. You start by offering praise. You say, "I just want to tell you your work had a great effect on me" or "Your work inspired me

to do this or that." Then the next time you are at the same event, you could say, "I would just love to hold your coffee cup." Meaning, "I would love to assist you in some way that would add value to your life or work." Or, don't wait and do it by email after you've met at the event (but read Chapter 11 before you do). They may say, "I don't think so," but what have you got to lose? Then again, they may respond by saying, "Yeah, you seem like a really genuine and considerate person. I've got some stuff you can do." Don't forget that successful and busy people always have more on their plate than they can reasonably handle. They're always looking for talented people to help make their life easier. If you can help reduce someone's stress or work level, you've made a friend for life.

- *Offer something when first meeting someone, whenever possible:* Offer praise (as in the earlier example), compassion, or a connection. When you can say, "I know someone you've got to meet" or "There's a great book I think may offer the solution to your problem," they are going to see you very differently from the person who shoved a business card in their face and said, "Let's stay in touch, dude." If you can leave the person feeling even better, uplifted, and energized after interacting with you, they're going to remember you.

- *Start conversations by asking questions:* This is a great approach, especially if you're nervous. It takes the spotlight off you and allows the other person to shine. It allows you to learn something new at the same time.

- *Identify two or three things you'd like to learn from the people at the function:* People are drawn to others who are curious and interested.

- *Make eye contact:* It expresses respect and interest in the person you're speaking with. And stay focused on the person you're speaking with. If you're speaking with Jan, but your eyes are constantly scanning the room for someone more important or relevant to you, don't you think it might make Jan feel unappreciated?

- *Wear comfortable clothing but dress well:* If you're constantly fidgeting or worrying about how you look in clothes that aren't comfortable or don't fit properly, you'll be self-conscious and others will sense it.

- *Take the initiative:* Go up to people and make friends. People love to be asked about themselves, their hobbies, or their family. This is the time to get to know a few personal tidbits that will give you the opportunity to find a common interest that makes connecting easier and more natural.

- *Offer a firm handshake:* Hold your drink in your left hand. This eliminates the need to wipe your damp hand on your clothes before shaking hands. And, guys, don't think you need to shake hands differently with a woman from the way you do with a man. A firm handshake (not a death grip) is always appropriate.

- *Be inclusive:* Ask others to join your conversations; this is very important. Don't monopolize people, especially those who are in high demand, like the speaker from the event. It makes the speaker uncomfortable. Remember, the speaker is there to meet a lot of people, too. It also annoys others who want to meet the person you're trying to keep to yourself. *Tip:* If you want to be helpful, ask the speaker if there is anybody you can introduce them to, or simply be sure to keep including people in your conversations with them. This way, you'll be seen as a very generous and open person by the others at the event, and the speaker will remember you as someone who helped them easily network and navigate the event.

- *Ask for a business card and then keep in touch:* It's your responsibility to ask for a card if you want one, and it's your responsibility to follow up. Quality, not quantity, counts when making genuine personal connections. If you race through an event passing out and collecting business cards from anyone and everyone as though there were a prize for the most cards gained at the end of the event, you'll do yourself a huge disservice. And remember, just because someone gives you his business card does *not* mean you have permission to add him to your mailing list. You do not. You can certainly send a personal email as a follow-up, and you should, but you should not and cannot start sending email blasts. You don't have permission to do that.

- *Always have a pen with you:* When you receive a business card, write a little note about any commitment to follow up, what you talked about, and any personal bits or unusual things that will help you to remember the person and to personalize future contact, and be sure to include the date and name of the function where you met.

- *A note for introverts:* Remember that networking is not speed dating. You don't need to work the whole room. Focus on creating one or two deep connections. Honor your own need for space.

Networking Events – What Not to Do

- *Don't try to be cool:* And don't overcompensate for your nervousness by bragging about your success; this is a major turnoff.
- *Don't let "What do you do?" be the first question you ask:* Let it come up naturally in conversation.
- *Don't sit with people you know for the majority of the event:* While it may be more comfortable to sit with the people you know, it becomes too easy to stay with them, and if you do, you'll defeat the purpose of being there. Step out of your comfort zone and get to know new people.
- *Don't wear cologne, perfumes, or essential oils:* Many people are sensitive to these kinds of smells, and they can be overpowering. Men seem to overdo this. If I shake your hand and your cologne transfers to my hand, you've gone way overboard. It's like marking your territory – invasively so.
- *Don't juggle multiple items:* Travel light to eliminate the necessity of juggling your coat, purse, briefcase, drink, or buffet plate. Keep that right hand free for handshakes and for jotting down quick notes on business cards.
- *Don't complain about networking or the event you're attending:* In fact, don't complain about anything. The cycle of complaining is easy to get drawn into, especially at events where almost everyone is a bit uncomfortable. While complaining is an icebreaker, it's not an attractive one. Change the subject – for example, "Have you tried the shrimp?" – or take the opportunity to recommend a great book.
- *Don't take yourself too seriously:* Remember to relax and have fun.

Online Networking Through Social Media

You're probably using social media for both personal and professional purposes, or you might be intentionally avoiding it altogether.

In an October 2009 *Wall Street Journal* article titled "Why E-Mail No Longer Rules," the writer predicted that in the next 5 or 10 years, email will become a thing of the past. He wrote:

E-mail has had a good run as king over communications, but its reign is over. In its place a new generation of services is starting to take hold. Services like X (formerly Twitter) and Facebook and countless others vying for a piece of the new world. Just as e-mail did more than a decade ago, this shift promises to profoundly rewrite the way we communicate in ways we can only begin to imagine.

He was wrong.

Yes, social media has changed the way people communicate online, but it has not replaced email communication and won't anytime soon. On the one hand, the growth of social media is good for you and your ability to exploit it for networking and marketing purposes – it's mobile, it's easy, it's quick, and it's free. You can stay top of mind by commenting on other people's posts or reacting to their stories, and that's another form of staying in touch. You can also easily send voice notes, not to mention photos and videos to keep the interaction more intimate.

On the other hand, the fact that it's easy, quick, and free is also a problem. It means more junk – more irrelevant noise clogging up the bandwidth. Additionally, depending on the person and their relationship to social media, how they use it, or how many followers they have, it might be harder to get your message seen there. So use your social media wisely and well. If you do, it will speak volumes about who you are, what you stand for, and how you do business.

Social Media – For Marketing or Networking?

Social media can be used for marketing purposes through pay-per-click ad campaigns, content marketing, promotions, and the like. However, when beginning to build a social media platform on Instagram, Facebook, LinkedIn, and others, we suggest using it primarily as a tool for connecting, relationship building, and creating value by sharing your intangibles as we discussed earlier. When we introduce you to the Book Yourself Solid Web Strategy in Chapter 15, we'll share various ways to use Facebook, X, and LinkedIn for both marketing and building relationships. It's too much to add to this chapter. Just remember the bottom line: *think relationships first, business second.*

You Are Always Networking

Your profits will come from connections with people who can send you business – whether that's by way of a satisfied client who refers others to you; another professional who has the ability to book you for speaking engagements, write about you, or partner with you; or the neighbor who appreciates your big, friendly smile and the recommendation you made for a great babysitter when he desperately needed one.

With the Book Yourself Solid Networking Strategy, the prospect of creating a phenomenal network of connections doesn't have to be overwhelming or intimidating. We all connect constantly, with everyone, every day. Now we just need to do it consciously, with greater awareness, until doing so becomes a natural and comfortable part of our daily lives.

Then follow up. Keep in touch. It is imperative that you get every one of your connections into your database and act on each relevant connection.

So You've Got Spinach in Your Teeth

We've given you a lot of techniques in this chapter about what to do, what not to do, and how to interact with others when you're networking, but there's a big difference between techniques and principles, and it's the principles that are most important to remember and begin implementing. If you can incorporate the principles, you'll naturally do well.

For example, everyone says when you meet people at a networking event you're supposed to look that person in the eye, give them a firm handshake, smile, and nod your head, but if you do that and don't take the giver's stance, it won't matter how slick you are. However, if you always take the giver's stance and share who you know, what you know, and how you feel, even if you have spinach in your teeth and your palm is sweaty, you'll be fine, because people are going to respond to who you are as a human being. In fact, they'll share their compassion with you by gently letting you know about the large piece of spinach entrenched between your two front teeth.

So what do you think? Are you ready to network your way to more clients, more profit, and deeper connections with people? Sharing your knowledge, your network, and your compassion will bring you one step closer to being booked solid.

The Book Yourself Solid Direct Outreach Strategy

You miss 100 percent of the shots you don't take.
—Wayne Gretzky

As a business owner, you'll need to proactively reach out to potential clients to make offers and to marketing partners and other decision makers to create business opportunities. In fact, the most important direct outreach you do might well be to other service professionals, businesses, and professional associations to network, cross-promote, and build referral relationships.

Let's clearly define what direct outreach is *not* before detailing exactly what it is and how to do it authentically, easily, and successfully. It is *not* spam, which has typically been considered unsolicited mail or email sent without permission to mailing lists or newsgroups. However, we think the way people now see spam has grown in scope and definition. Today, there are many more ways you can be labeled a spammer — even when you think you're standing in the service of potential clients or business associates.

As you know, spam is not the Book Yourself Solid way. It never has been and never will be. Before the advent of the Internet, direct outreach was a very common marketing strategy. I suppose it's no less common today, but unfortunately, it is often perceived as spam. You must be very careful and discerning with respect to how you use the Book Yourself Solid Direct Outreach Strategy.

You can now be labeled a spammer by sending an unsolicited email directly to a potential client that contains any kind of sales message or promotional or business offer. The same goes for cold calling. Many people just consider that another kind of spam, since it's unsolicited. Even direct outreach to an individual through Facebook, Instagram, LinkedIn, and other social media platforms can get you pegged as irrelevant or, worse, a spammer. Posting comments on a blog or other social media site, yes, even your friends' Facebook pages, can get you called out for spamming if they smack of self-promotion.

Clients now find you. That doesn't relieve you of your marketing responsibilities. You need to create awareness for what you offer so that when potential clients go looking for the kind of services you offer, they find you. If you don't like the fact that clients want to find you, rather than the other way around, then blame Google. It has changed the way customers and businesses interact. When people go searching online, they're willing to wade through junk in search of what they want because they feel in control of the process. When they find what they want, and if it's you, they'll give you permission to market to them.

Just because it's easy to broadcast our messages through email and social media platforms doesn't give us permission to force people to pay attention. We have to earn their attention – more than ever. Seth Godin, the father of *Permission Marketing*, puts it this way:

Go ahead and make what you want, as long as you stand behind it and don't bother me. If you want to sell magnetic bracelets or put risqué pictures on your website, it's your responsibility, your choice. Want to find a website featuring donkeys, naked jugglers, and various illicit acts? It's junk, sure, but it's out there. You just have to go find it. Junk turns into spam when you show up at my doorstep, when your noise intercepts my quiet.

This is why, even though it's easier than ever to make noise and get noticed, direct outreach has become trickier than ever. When you reach out, unsolicited, to a potential client or business associate about a business opportunity, their default assumption is that you're a spammer interrupting their peace and quiet. Is it fair? That doesn't matter. Until there's a cure for selfishness, one that eliminates spammers and their spam, it's the reality that we have to deal with. Don't make noise that interrupts others' quiet.

You will find yourself using the Book Yourself Solid Direct Outreach Strategy time and time again when you want to reach out to:

- An ideal client or a referral partner within your target market
- The decision maker at an organization or association to cross-promote, secure speaking engagements, submit articles for publication, and more
- The press

Or a myriad of other business development opportunities.

Direct Outreach Gone Wrong

Sometimes the easiest way to understand a concept is to see real examples of what works and what doesn't. We don't want to scare you off from doing direct outreach. Just the opposite — we want to encourage you to do more of it, but in a way that will make sure you come across as a thoughtful, considerate, empathetic, relevant, and high-integrity professional with value to add. To make sure you're always perceived this way, we're going to show you a series of direct outreach messages that went terribly wrong. We've changed the names of all of the people involved to protect the innocent, but the following are actual messages from real people. In fact, we're pretty sure they were sent by decent, hard-working professionals. Unfortunately, they haven't yet learned how to do direct outreach, and, as a result, their messages landed like a ton of bricks.

Let's start with this brick, which landed in Michael's LinkedIn inbox.

LinkedIn Recommendations

Maria Venter is requesting an endorsement for work.

Dear Michael,

I'm sending this to ask you for a brief recommendation of my work that I can include in my LinkedIn profile. If you have any questions, let me know.

Thanks in advance for helping me out.

—Maria Venter

Endorse Maria Venter. It only takes a minute. Your endorsement can help Maria Venter:

- Hire and get hired
- Win customers and partnerships
- Build a stronger professional reputation

This email was sent to you by Maria Venter (email@website.com) through LinkedIn because Maria Venter entered your email address. If you have any questions, please contact customer_service@linkedin.com.

This request from Maria is problematic for a number of reasons:

1. Let's start with the fact that Michael doesn't know her.
2. If he doesn't know Maria, why would he recommend she get hired, win customers and partnerships, and build a stronger professional reputation?
3. Michael's LinkedIn profile states that he doesn't check messages at LinkedIn. Rather, he requests that people email him at a public email address, which he lists.

What should Maria have done instead?

1. She could have started by giving Michael a recommendation first, if she thought he deserved one. It's always better to offer something before asking for something.
2. If it was important to her that they connect, she could have attempted to meet him at an event, if it was convenient for her.
3. She could have reviewed his podcast on iTunes or one of his books on Amazon. This would have been noticed and appreciated.

4. She could have sent him an email to his public email address expressing some appreciation for his work or find some other way of making
   a personal connection through any number of other activities that
   don't ask for anything in return and don't make any assumptions.

These suggestions have nothing to do with professional status. We would approach anyone this way. Of course, if the person you're reaching out to is already familiar with your work or your name, the connecting process usually speeds up. And, if you're thinking that it's just novice business owners whose direct outreach goes wrong, think again.

This next email is from a publicity and promotions manager at a marketing firm that represents supposed best-selling authors and large publishing houses. Michael doesn't know the sender or the author and has no connection to the publisher of the book. Again, we've changed the names of all parties involved.

Dear Mr. Port,

I have not heard back from you on my email below. This is a great opportunity to get your products out in front of a huge audience looking for this kind of material (our previous book campaign was seen by over 5 million people)! Not only will you be offering your subscribers an incredible package, you will also be directing more traffic to your website and building your own mailing list. Remember, there is no cost involved.

Click on the link below to view a previous campaign we put together for John Smith's New York Times bestselling book, XXXXXX: www.longurltoa salespage.com.

Please let me know right away if you would like to participate or if you have any questions.

Thank you, Andrea

Assistant Publicity and Promotions Manager

Progressive Marketing Firm, Inc.

What's so bad about a PR or marketing firm reaching out to an author to see if he'll help promote another author? Nothing. Nothing at all. In fact, one of the primary ways authors get noticed is through promotion from other authors. So, what's wrong with this one?

1. Michael doesn't know any of the parties involved, and they're sending him what is clearly a form email. It's not personalized in any way.

2. Andrea makes all sorts of assumptions about why Michael would want to promote this author. She has no idea what really makes him tick and didn't take the time to find out.

3. In the last line, Andrea tells Michael to let her know "right away" if he wants to participate. She clearly demonstrated a lack of respect or appreciation for his time, schedule, life, and so forth. It's not wrong to try to encourage someone to act quickly when promoting a product or service, but this is not such a promotion (her biggest mistake is that she thinks it is). Fundamentally, it's a request to a colleague to help out another colleague, and at this point, after all the other offenses in this email, telling him what to do and when to do it is off-putting.

4. This is actually the fourth email Andrea sent to Michael about this "opportunity." If he didn't respond the first three times, might that be saying something? And, to add insult to injury, every time Andrea sent an email Michael wrote back asking her to stop emailing him. Obviously, she ignored his requests. It just confirms his suspicion that he was added to a "list" of authors to whom they're trying to get to participate in their book promotions. That makes it real, honest-to-goodness, 100% spam.

What should Andrea have done instead? Well, since Michael didn't request any information on her promotions or the authors she represents, she could have sent him a short note to this effect:

My name is Andrea Tiffonelli. I'm the Assistant Publicity and Promotions Manager for Progressive Marketing Firm, Inc. We represent authors and help them promote their books.

I'm writing to you today to let you know that I'm a fan of your work and really loved your most recent book, Steal the Show. Before I read it, I dreaded public speaking. Now I actually look forward to it.

Again, just saying "hi" and thanks for your work. If there is anything I can do to be of service to you, please just say the word.

Sincerely, Andrea Tiffonelli

Assistant Publicity and Promotions Manager

Progressive Marketing Firm, Inc.

What works so well about this alternative version of the email?

1. She's not asking anything of Michael on her first contact.
2. She quickly tells him who she is and what she does right off the bat.
3. She offers praise and demonstrates that she is actually familiar with Michael's work.
4. She closes by offering her support with no expectation of anything in return.

This is how you start a relationship. Over time, a few more, relevant and personal interactions like this would earn her the proportionate amount of trust and credibility needed to see if Michael would be interested in getting involved in one of her author promotions. Does it take time to learn about someone and get to know one's work? Yes. But it makes your direct outreach well received, and that's the goal.

Here's another one. It's long. Very long. That is just one of its many problems. There is, however, one simple fix that could have saved this effort. Can you tell what it is?

This is Jerry Faber and I'm working with Tom Rose, The ---- Coach, looking for a few very special joint venture partners for his upcoming Quick-Start 3-Day ---- Workshop.

---- are Hot and getting Hotter! And anybody who wants to have a successful online business needs ---- as part of their funnel. So we want to offer you the opportunity to host a preview call with Tom for his highly acclaimed ---- Workshop.

Tom has been teaching this workshop for the past five years and has helped hundreds of frustrated writers become successful authors. (You can see his long list of testimonials at www.firstwebsite.com.)

I'm contacting you because Tom and I believe that you and Tom are speaking to the same target market, and that this offer will be very lucrative for you while providing great value for your list.

This opportunity pays from $200 to $1000 commission on every sale (depending on which level your subscribers register for).

For the complete details on this JV opportunity go to: www.secondwebsite.com.

Basically, here's the way this JV works.

Once you agree to do a JV call with Tom (the call is on "The Seven Biggest Mistakes People Make When ---- And How To Avoid Them" and it has converted from 11 to 22%), we'll set up the pages for the call and send you a link to all of the materials you will need to promote it, including a promo email series, blog posts, and tweets to mail to your list.

Then, over the coming weeks, we'll "drip" great content on them (unless it's the week of the Workshop. We do a final Q and A call that week).

If they buy, on or after your call with Tom through your affiliate link, you will get the following commissions.

Platinum Plus Package pays $1000. Platinum Package pays $500.

Gold Package pays $200.

You can see the sales page at: www.thirdwebsite.com.

If you're interested in doing a JV call with Tom, please let me know. You can email me directly at: jerry@gmail.com.

If you have any questions, feel free to email me at jerry@gmail.com.

Or, if you're ready to get started, email me at jerry@gmail.com and I'll send you everything you need to get started as soon as we can get the web pages set up.

Thank you for your time. We truly appreciate it – and look forward to having the opportunity to joint venture with you. And we'd like to give you a gift for taking the time to read this email:

www.fourthwebsite.com is a PDF with 28 ways to use TwitterX. We hope it helps you prosper even more!

Best Wishes,

Jerry Faber for Tom Rose

The [xxxx] Coach

P.S. If you want to know more about Tom, you can see his bio at: www .fifthwebsite.com.

You can see his videos at: www.sixthwebsite.com.

Holy cow. Where to start?

1. It's insanely long.
2. Tom and Jerry are making all sorts of assumptions about why Michael would be interested in this joint venture.

3. It's filled with hyperbole like ". . . are hot and getting hotter! And anybody who wants to have a successful online business needs . . ."

4. Jerry mentions the marketing funnel, which demonstrates that he's not particularly familiar with Michael's work because Michael writes quite a bit about how he doesn't like the philosophy behind the marketing funnel for selling services.

5. He thinks he needs to tell Michael how a joint venture (JV) like this works.

6. He gives Michael his email address three times within three sentences.

7. He wants Michael to look at six different websites.

8. He offers Michael a "gift" of an e-book on how to use X (formerly Twitter) for taking the time to read his email. Does he think Michael is unfamiliar with X and how to use it?

9. And in what might be the biggest offense of all, he tells Michael that he'll be blasting his email newsletter subscribers, tweeting to his followers, and promoting Tom's product on his blog. If Tom and Jerry think that Michael would indiscriminately promote someone he doesn't know to his subscribers, readers, and followers, for a few dollars in commissions, then it's obvious they don't know how he operates, and they don't have a lot of respect for their subscribers.

So, what should Jerry have done? Did you figure out the simple fix to this total disaster of a direct outreach attempt? If you're thinking that he should have simply sent Michael a short note asking if he even does these kinds of joint ventures, you're absolutely right. If he had, Michael would have told him that he doesn't and no love would have been lost. Instead, Tom and Jerry wasted Michael's time (and theirs) asking him to read this unrequested email about their JV opportunity. But, we do need to thank Jerry for giving us the opportunity to use the experience for the benefit of our readers. Here's what a better direct outreach attempt could have looked like:

Dear Michael,

My name is Jerry Faber, and I work with Tom Rose, who teaches courses on ----creation. I enjoy your work and really like your style. I don't want to take up much of your time so, if I may ask one quick question . . .

> I'm wondering if you ever promote products from other experts in exchange for commissions on sales. If so, would you consider learning more about Tom and a joint venture campaign we're putting together? If not, I completely understand, and I thank you for your time nonetheless. Both Tom and I appreciate your work and hope to have the opportunity to meet you at some point in the future.
>
> If there is anything we can do for you, please don't hesitate to ask.
>
> Sincerely,
>
> Best Wishes,
>
> Jerry Faber
>
> for Tom Rose
>
> www.onewebsitehere.com

Even if Tom and Jerry used this suggested letter, they're still not guaranteed a response. But they would at least have come across as professional and respectful, two of the most important components of credibility.

> Michael, please accept my friend request. Tell me about what you do. I see you have written books. What are they called? What are they about? I'm also working on a book and a project you might be interested in. I would like to discuss potential business opportunities with you.

Here's one more short one. Can you figure out what's wrong with this note? Besides the fact that Michael received it through his personal Facebook profile – which clearly states, just like my LinkedIn profile, *"Please don't contact me here. Instead, please send to* questions@heroicpublicspeaking.com."

Here, this woman asked to "friend" Michael. Of course, his Facebook profile explains what he does and lists all six of his books. So perhaps it's just ego talking, but one would hope that she would make a little effort to at least scan the page – do a little homework on him. She's asking Michael to take his time and do her work for her. Time is precious. Don't ask people to part with it. They need to offer to do so. To fast-forward the process and ask for business without building some foundation is more than just ineffective; it's a turnoff.

You Will Connect More When You've Got the Skinny

It doesn't matter if you are prospecting, screening, door knocking, outreaching, introducing, or just plain canvassing. If you do any or all of these without knowing the person or business you are contacting, you may as well be calling the president of the United States. At best, you'll find yourself winded, your time wasted, or your wares unwanted. Or, at worst . . . humiliated. No one wants to feel like a cheesy, shady, pushy, or unprepared salesperson.

So, you say at the end of the day you want to create a never-ending pool of heartwarming and bank account–filling clients? You want to capture more sales? You want to get booked solid? Make more money? Create a nest egg? Then show up front, center, and in the know with all the people you want to know. There's no minimizing your overall effectiveness and confidence when you're packin' preparation. So find out . . .

1. What motivates the person? What really gets the person's juices flowing? What makes his eyes sparkle? It might be business, family, or hobbies. Look at the photos, books, and other things sitting on or near his desk or on his website or social media pages. What is he reading, referring to others, or genuinely interested in?

2. What has the person accomplished? Do an online search. Go to her site and do a Google Image search if you don't know what her smiling face looks like yet. Who is singing her praises? Has she won awards or received acknowledgments, public recognition, or publication announcements?

3. What common interests might you have? How have your paths crossed? Express your compassion, enthusiasm, and understanding for these shared interests. Keep your focus coming back to the person. Use these common interests as a starting place to learn more about how they feel and think about the world.

4. Who are the person's peers? Do you have any mutual friends or social circles that overlap? Do you have common Facebook friends or X (formerly Twitter) followers? And are you involved in these circles? Be informed and stay connected.

5. Who is their competition? Know the opportunities and challenges they faces in their business. What challenges will you help them overcome? And what opportunities will you, ultimately, help them fulfill?

6. What unique benefits do you offer? What do others love about the way you do business? Be easy. Know your strengths. Show up as the kind of person people love being with and want to do business with.

7. What excites you about knowing or working with this person? We all want to feel appreciated, acknowledged, and respected. Share how the person's work and opinions have influenced or affected you. Stay positive, be yourself, and be complimentary.

8. What do you believe is possible for the person? No matter how confident or successful we appear, all of us have limiting beliefs. Can you see areas of business or life in which the person has been holding back? Describe in detail (but keep it to yourself, for now) the true potential you see for the person based on what they want and need. As you get to know each other, you may decide to share what you see.

9. What is your current status or role in the person's life? Don't over-rate or exaggerate who you are or why the person should work or connect with you. Be realistic about what you bring to the table and how you see the relationship unfolding. The best relationships grow slowly and with a foundation of trust.

10. How can you become an indispensable asset to the person? Do you truly know how and why the person should know or work with you? Do you believe that her life will be happier, easier, fuller, richer, or just plain better with the benefit of you and your services?

Sales offers aren't always sensible. Connecting isn't always cool. Even if your proposition seems picture perfect . . . life, decisions, and relationships are always wrapped up in underlying influences. Some of these foundational influences we can see quickly at first glance, while others take a bit more time.

But, when you show up knowledgeable and prepared, you address the human needs of the people you want to serve, and you are closer to meeting both the other person's needs and your own. You might have a shot at getting what you ask for. Plus, aren't conversations just easier and more fun when you know and share these commonalities? Doors stop slamming. People start playing, and they start paying, too.

Direct Outreach Done Right

Joana is no stranger to receiving direct outreach from copywriters eager to collaborate with her design agency, Gif Design Studios, which doesn't have any in-house copywriters. Yet, one particular email stood out to her, ultimately leading to more than $100 000 worth of business referrals within the first year of their connection:

Subject: That extra copywriter you (don't know) you need . . .

Body:

Hi Joana,

I love all the training and tips you've been giving on Insta recently (packed with value!) – and I have been fangirling all over your Ambitious Creatives Booked Solid sales page. I am currently in another mastermind until December but look out for my name if you run it again next year!

But I'm emailing you today to see if I can help you . . .

I love what you've created at GIF Design Studios. I was recently writing a website for a web designer and I analyzed your website and feedback as part of my research process. Let's just say it was love at first click!

I love the designs you've produced but more than that I adore the tone of voice and attitude of your brand. So many cogs go into creating such a successful agency and it looks like you have a wicked team to cover all bases.

But I was curious as to whether you collaborate with copywriters – or if you might need some extra (writing hands) on deck at times?

I am a qualified conversion copywriter (writing personality copy with detailed attention to tone of voice is my bag). I would love to offer you and your clients the same attentive process that I deliver to my private clients.

I am poised and professional enough to work directly with your clients but also a team player who's happy to hang behind the scenes, making you look brilliant. (You can get an insight into my process by reading my three-step plan here if you are curious.)

I have worked with many web developers and designers who have said some very lovely things about me (spoiler alert: they love my wireframes).

For example, Kayleigh Hall, Design Consultant and CEO of Hall Creative, said: "Delia makes my job so much easier! Her wireframes have completely spoilt me from a design perspective. And my clients have been over the moon with the tone of voice work she's produced. Seriously good stuff."

"She is also a real expert in conversion copy – she speaks with conviction, has sound rationale with every decision, and is a real strategist."

So, what do you think Joana? Need a hand on any projects you've got coming up?

Cheers,

Delia

PS Fancy a 20-minute virtual coffee – with zero pressure – to have a chat about how I might be able to help you? You can book a slot on my calendar here. I would love the opportunity to "meet" you!

PPS Want to vet me first? Wise. You can get an insight into my writing style and process by reading my secret three-step plan to writing websites here.

What did Delia do right in this email that led to her getting more than six figures in referral work from Joana?

She opens the email with a personal touch, acknowledging Joana's recent work, demonstrating that she has taken the time to understand Joana's work and interests

Delia expresses genuine admiration for Joana's work and the tone of Gif Design Studio's brand, which helps to establish a positive connection and rapport.

Rather than making a generic offer, Delia specifically asks if Joana collaborates with copywriters or needs any additional writing support. She shows consideration for Joana's potential needs without making assumptions or being pushy.

Delia succinctly outlines her qualifications as a conversion copywriter and explains how her skills can complement Joana's team, highlighting her experience and the value she can bring to Gif Design Studios.

By including a testimonial from a client, Delia provides social proof for her capabilities and reliability, making her more credible and trustworthy.

Providing links to her process and writing samples, she further makes it easy for Joana to vet her work, building trust.

Finally Delia's suggestion of a 20-minute virtual coffee chat is a low-pressure way to initiate further conversation, making it easy for Joana to agree to a casual meeting.

To be clear, it wasn't just Delia's email that led to all the referrals Joana sent her way. Her website and work examples played a significant role in convincing Joana that Delia might be the right fit when extra copywriting support was needed. But it was Delia's email that stood out in Joana's crowded inbox and prompted her to book a call. That initial meeting secured Delia her first project with Joana. From there, Delia's exceptional service and results led Joana to send even more work her way.

Remember, the goal of these emails isn't to make a sale but to get a reply. Sometimes, asking for a meeting right away can be too much too soon. Take it one step at a time. Focus on what will move the conversation forward, rather than trying to land the client with just one email.

Using the Book Yourself Solid Direct Outreach Strategy is all about making personal connections. Whichever of the following direct outreach tools you employ, you should be reaching out to others from the heart, in a way that is genuine and authentic for you.

Only One Link in the Chain of Destiny Can Be Handled at a Time

There are lots of different tools that you can use to reach out to other people. You can write emails, letters, or postcards. You can reach out to people through social media sites, including, but not limited to, Facebook, X (formerly Twitter), and LinkedIn. You can use the phone. And you can do what we call the whatever–it–takes direct outreach, as long as it doesn't get you arrested, like parachuting into the backyard of the CEO of Google because you think you have a great service to offer his company. It will get you noticed but also get you arrested.

These tools can be instruments with which you can make beautiful music or they can be weapons of mass destruction. It just depends on how you use them. Our mantra is Winston Churchill's quote: "It is a mistake to look too far ahead. Only one link of the chain of destiny can be handled at a time." Keep that on the top of your mind as you progress through the direct outreach process and you'll be able to avoid desperate direct outreach measures. You'll build trust over time instead and end up swimming in success.

When reaching out to others, you'll go through multiple stages of relationship development. At each stage of the process you'll, ideally, build more trust and earn more credibility with your new friend, much like the Book Yourself Solid Sales Cycle Process that you learned in Chapter 6. And, just like the sales cycle, no relationship will develop in the same way. There isn't a secret formula that will guarantee everyone will love you and do exactly as you want, but there is a way to know whom to contact when, how to make contact, and whether to do it again – and the method requires a well-developed social intelligence.

Socially Successful Conduct

When asked "What other marketing books should I read?" in addition to some of the books listed in the previous chapter, we also recommend *Social Intelligence: The New Science of Human Relationships,* by Daniel Goleman, a popular science writer. Why a book that draws on social neuroscience research to help learn how to market and sell professional services? Because, social intelligence can be defined as a person's competence to comprehend their environment and react appropriately for socially successful conduct. And socially successful conduct is what ensures successful direct outreach.

Understanding the concepts people use to make sense of their social relations can help you understand things like, *What situation am I in and how do I talk to this kind of person?* You can also learn rules that help you draw references like, *What did he mean by that?* as well as plan your actions so you can decide, *What am I going to do about that?*

You may or may not like this concept, depending on your interpretation of self, but your ability to succeed in many entrepreneurial endeavors is, in large part, based on your self-awareness and social savvy. Being able to understand yourself and what's going on with others and then skillfully responding to them is a question of social intelligence, not how many different clever pitches you've memorized or methods you've got on hand to impress someone with.

According to Goleman, humans are wired to connect, neurologically speaking. Holy rapidfire synapses, Batman. That means you are wired to market and sell. But really, all brain function aside, you've already got the mental crampons to do the steep climbing and naturally scale to the top of your class.

Marvel at this. The news gets even better. Goleman doesn't believe that these competencies (the ability to connect) are necessarily innate, but rather can be learned capabilities, if worked on and developed to achieve outstanding performance. There's nothing phantom about your direct outreach success. To perform at your highest level and enhance how you connect to real people in the real world, increase your social intelligence. With diligence, reflection, and the commitment to improve, set aside time to study your:

- *Self-awareness:* The ability to read your own emotions and recognize their impact on others while using gut feelings to guide decisions.
- *Self-management:* Involves controlling your emotions, impulses, and the ability to adapt to changing circumstances.
- *Social awareness:* Your ability to sense, understand, and react to others' emotions while comprehending social networks.
- *Relationship management:* The ability to inspire, influence, and develop others while managing conflict.

While you are at it:

- Toss the trite sales pitch and never formulate another "smart" thought. Develop the keen ability to listen and hear what others truly want and need.
- Tear up the How-to-Get-Anything-You-Want-in-Three-Easy-Steps manual and increase your empathy by entering into the realm of others' feelings.
- Step away from the PowerPoint presentation and study your self-presentation so you can foster credibility, trust, and connection confidence.

Social intelligence is defined as a person's competence to comprehend his environment and react appropriately for socially successful conduct. This brand of intelligence is therefore *the* most important component of your direct outreach strategies.

Understanding the concepts people use to make sense of their social relations can help you improve your social awareness, presence, authenticity, clarity, and empathy. Bottom line: you'll be more attuned to the needs and desires of others, which will make you more relevant and influential.

The Book Yourself Solid List of 20

Make a list of 20 people with whom you'd like to develop professional relationships. These are people whom you do not yet know – influencers within your target market who can help you get booked solid. This is your Book Yourself Solid List of 20. Much like your Network of 90, this list never leaves your side.

It sits on your desk. It lives on your computer and travels with you when you're on the road. Why 20, and why must you keep it with you at all times? Since your success is, in large part, determined by the people within your industry who are willing to refer others to you or to put you in front of your ideal patients or endorse you, you need to keep these people at the top of your mind. Keeping this list by your side will ensure that you're thinking of them and, if you do, you'll begin to notice opportunities to connect with them and get to know them. And 20, because it's a large enough number to keep your focus expansive but narrow enough that you won't feel overwhelmed.

4.11.1 Written Exercise: Identify a minimum of 3 and a maximum of 20 people you'd like to reach out to directly and personally. (For now, this list should focus on people who you want to add to your network, not potential clients. You can start another list of 20 just for potential clients if you'd like.) At this moment, you might not think you can fill out your list of 20, but now that you know what you need to do, you'll start to take notice of the people you should add to this list. You'll see in a minute how your list can grow far beyond just 20 people.

Here's what you do with your list:

- Each day, reach out to the person at the top of the list.
- After you've reached out to this person, if you connect with them, take them off your List of 20 and start sharing your network, your knowledge, and your compassion. Generally doing so once a month is acceptable. Then add a new person to the bottom of the list so you always keep the list at 20.

- If they don't respond to you, move this person to the bottom of the list and they will take the twentieth position. The person who was in the twentieth position will move up to the nineteenth spot, and each person on the list will move up one more position. If the person who moved to the bottom of the list because you didn't hear back from them the first time doesn't respond a month later when they move back into the first position and you reach out to them again, then take them off the list. Continuing to contact someone when you're getting no response isn't good form, as we've already discussed.

This direct outreach activity occurs every working day: You'll reach out to one new person, each and every day, and you'll follow up with people you've already reached out to, each and every day. This is critical. Dedicated, disciplined, and determined action is key to your direct outreach success. Remember, the Book Yourself Solid List of 20 is your wish list. They are your list of 20 people who could have a significant impact on your business through their referrals, introductions, and advice. Do this daily and you'll be booked solid in no time flat.

4.11.2 Booked Solid Action Step: Reach out to the first person on your list of 20 and then add them to your follow-up system. Then add a new person to your list of 20.

Making Your Case

When you get to the point in a relationship at which it's time to make your case for something you want, usually after the initial courtship, the next step is to expand upon your reason for contacting them and make your case. To do this, there are three things that others take into account, whether consciously or unconsciously, when they consider a proposal you make:

1. Is it going to be successful?
2. Is it worth doing?

3. Is this person able to do what she says she can?

If you get a resounding "Yes!" for each question, you're in. If your reader raises an eyebrow at even one of the questions, you've probably gone as far as you're going to go with this person. For your direct outreach to be effective, all the questions must be answered in the affirmative. Also, to make sure all your bases are covered before you make any calls or send out any letters or email, ask yourself the following questions:

- Do I connect with the reader about one of their accomplishments?
- Do I indicate that I will follow up?
- Do I know how I'm going to follow up?
- Am I being direct without pushing?
- Am I being real in the message?
- Am I clear about the next steps?

Whatever-It-Takes Direct Outreach

You can do a lot to grab attention, but attention is valuable only if it shows you off in a light that's flattering. If you're a creative soul with a strong and developed sense of play, you'll have a lot of fun conceiving of and executing no-rules attention-grabbing direct outreach campaigns. Because, yeah, there may be a time when someone you really want to connect with is just not paying attention.

Twenty years ago, when Michael was a vice president at an entertainment company, he had a boss who swore, literally, every which way till Sunday that he had to get a particular executive at a big cosmetics firm to agree to sponsor one of their events. The only problem was that the executive wouldn't take Michael's calls. Michael tried to explain to his boss that he didn't think they were the right fit for their company, but his boss disagreed and directed him to make it happen.

After a few more weeks of trying to get a meeting with the executive, Michael was about to give up when his assistant, the toughest gatekeeper he'd ever encountered, let slip that the executive was out to lunch. Just making pleasant conversation, Michael asked, "Oh, yeah? What'd he go for today?" "Chinese. It's his favorite . . .," she replied, without thinking much about it. "Okay, thanks. Have a nice day!" he said, and hung up.

The next day Michael had a $250 order of Chinese food delivered to him at that exact same time. Inside the order was the proposal for the project. Twenty minutes after the food arrived, he called the executive. This time he was put right through. Michael asked, "Will you take a look at my proposal now?" "No," the executive answered. "Why not?" Michael asked. "Because I don't like any of the dishes you sent over." "What do you like?" he asked. "Moo Shoo Chicken with Mandarin Pancakes." Michael said, "If I send these over tomorrow, will you read my proposal and take a meeting with me?" He said, "No, but I will read your proposal. If I like it, then I'll take a meeting with you." Michael said, "Great. When would you like me to follow up?" The executive told him, and they said goodbye. As it turned out, the executive did like the proposal and subsequently took a meeting with Michael, but they never actually made a deal. It turned out that their two companies really weren't a good fit. But they became friendly, and the executive introduced Michael to one of his first clients after he left the corporate world and started his own business. You just never know.

Here's another example of whatever-it-takes direct outreach. A client was trying to connect with a meeting planner at a large multinational corporation and couldn't get the planner to give him the time of day. After all his other direct outreach attempts failed, he sent her a coconut with a note that said "You're a tough nut to crack. How about it?" She was still laughing when she called him to schedule an appointment.

Think creatively about what kind of fun, outrageous, no-rules attention-grabbing direct outreach strategies would work for you. Really let loose and let the ideas flow freely.

4.11.3 Written Exercise: Jot down one wild, wacky, and unique way to make a personal connection, especially with anyone you've been unsuccessful connecting with in the more traditional ways.

Direct Outreach Plan

There are many ways to connect with potential clients, but none of the concepts we laid out is effective without a plan. After you identify a person or organization you'd like to reach out to, what do you do? Do you create a plan and then execute the plan? No? Well, that's okay because now you will and you'll be delighted with the success your new plan will bring. Each day, when working with your Book Yourself Solid List of 20, here's how to keep it simple:

1. Identify the individual you're going to reach out to.
2. Choose the steps you'll take to connect with her.
3. Create a schedule for your initiatives.
4. Execute the plan.
5. Evaluate the plan.

Patience and Persistence Pay Off

Remember that there is no *trick* to direct outreach. The magic formula to direct outreach, if there is one, is a consistent and open course of action throughout the life of your business. Direct outreach, like networking and keeping in touch, is something that must become a part of your regular routine. It takes time, but if you're patient and persistent, you *will* book yourself solid.

The Book Yourself Solid Referral Strategy

For it is in giving that we receive.
—Saint Francis of Assisi

Imagine enjoying deeper relationships with every client you work with while attracting three or four times as many wonderful new clients as you have right now. The key lies in generating client referrals. By starting an organized referral program, you can immediately connect with an increasing number of potential new clients.

Think for a minute about how you seek out high-level services or products. Perhaps you need a new lawyer or accountant; or maybe you want to put a new addition on your home. It's not likely that you make your choice of service provider based solely on a Facebook ad or a Google search. The likelihood is that you will look for a referral from someone you know, someone who has had an experience with the particular service you seek. This is why having an organized referral program is so important for your success.

Because your clients enjoy and respect working with you, they will be eager to recommend your services to their friends and family. In fact, the vast majority of your new clients already come to you as a result of word-of-mouth referrals, either directly or indirectly.

You can increase your referral quotient exponentially. How many referrals do you get without a referral system right now? Now triple or quadruple that number. That is the potential increase in clients you could be working with as early as next month. Referral-generated clients are often more loyal, consistent, and better suited to you than any other category of potential clients you could find.

Quick Referral Analysis

Let's look at how you've already received referrals. By identifying a situation in the past when a client or colleague, or someone else altogether, referred a client to you, you will recognize patterns that will help you consistently produce the results you desire.

4.12.1 Written Exercise: Start by remembering the last time a quality referral came to you:

1. From whom did the referral come?
2. What was the referral for, specifically?
3. Did the referral need your services immediately?
4. How were you contacted – by the person making the referral or the potential patient?
5. Had you educated the referrer about your services before he made the referral?
6. How did you accept the referral and follow up?
7. Is that new referral a continuing patient today?

You may have already noticed some of your strengths in generating referrals, or perhaps parts of the process need a little of your attention. Either way, we're creating an easy and profitable process.

Finding Referral Opportunities

Referral opportunities are all around you, and most are slipping through your fingers right now because either you aren't noticing them or you aren't acting on them. Pay close attention and mentally seek out every possible situation in which you could see yourself asking for referrals.

> **4.12.2 Written Exercise:** Create a referral-tracking log based on the seven questions in the preceding written exercise and begin to track daily referral opportunities. Your referral-tracking log should focus on the details of your referral interactions. Doing so will help you see what works and what doesn't work in the referral process. If you study these interactions, you can learn from them and adjust your behavior accordingly while significantly increasing your referral quotient. You're going to be pleasantly surprised at the plethora of untapped referral opportunities that are appearing before you every day.

Beginning the Referral Process

Are you ready to begin working with eager new clients who have heard about your expertise and seek the benefits you offer? Never forget how profitable and prosperous your business can be. How committed are you? Are you convinced that this is something you absolutely must do?

Step 1: Identify Your Clients' Benefits

Keep their benefits in mind when you speak to your clients about referrals. These are the reasons they work with you and why they would want others to do the same. Refer to the work you did in Chapter 2.

> **4.12.3 Written Exercise:** Create a list of the benefits your clients will experience by working with you. Keep going until you've exhausted all the possible benefits.

Step 2: Identify Why Others Would Refer Clients to You

What are the emotional, social, and professional benefits that go along with being someone who refers people in need to those who can help?

Examples: They feel great helping their friends improve their business in a specific way. They feel special having made a positive influence in their friends' lives. They feel important and knowledgeable about something. They feel connected and accepted when they introduce friends and business associates to a high-quality professional. They feel confident that they are a valuable resource in their friends' lives and that they sent them to someone who is qualified, committed, and well liked.

4.12.4 Written Exercise: Bring to mind your two best clients and list the reasons they would want to refer their friends and family to you. Again, think in terms of benefits. How did they feel after having referred their friends and family?

Step 3: Identify the Types of Referrals You Seek

Examples: Family members, friends, neighbors, acquaintances, work associates, business owners, executives, and so on.

Don't forget your Red Velvet Rope Policy of working only with ideal clients with whom you do your best work.

4.12.5 Written Exercise: Write down the types of people you want your clients, associates, friends, and family to refer to you. Your friends and family may have no idea whom to refer to you.

Step 4: Identify the Places Where Your Referrers Meet Ideal Referrals

Your goal here is to help your clients and other acquaintances understand who in their lives will benefit most from your services and where they cross paths with these people. You are helping them get a clear picture of the people in their lives who must meet you and work with you. With these two things in mind – whom your referrals should be referring and where they will meet them – you have all you need to start on the referral path.

Examples: At the office, taking the kids to school, neighborhood events, sporting events, lunch appointments, after-work socializing, charity functions, the gym, political events.

4.12.6 Written Exercise: Write down the places where your referrers would meet or connect with good referrals for you.

Step 5: Clarify and Communicate How Your Referrers Make a Referral

Let's focus on how to help your referrers have a simple conversation with a potential referral that will effectively connect them to you and your offerings. You can't leave this to chance. Being able to articulate what you do in a way that makes you stand out from the crowd and truly connects you to the people you're meant to serve is not only necessary, it's essential for booking yourself solid.

What do you want them to say? How do you want them to talk about what you do? What specific words and phrases do you want them to use? Do you want them to say that you are "the best"? Do you want them to mention that you recently received an award for a recent project? Get very specific. Think of yourself as a one-person public relations (PR) firm. You decide how you want people to talk about you.

If you do not have a formal referral process in place, it is likely that your current clients don't actually know how to refer people to you. No matter how badly they might want to send referrals your way, if they are confused about how to do so, it's much less likely that they will refer people to you. For this reason, creating a process that is simple, consistent, and able to be clearly communicated to your potential referrers is very important.

4.12.7 Written Exercise: Write down how you'd like your referrers to refer their contacts to you.

Step 6: Ask for Referrals

If you want to increase your referral quotient by 50%, the best strategy is to ask for referrals. This is the simplest part of the Book Yourself Solid Referral Strategy, as well as the most important. The preceding and following exercises will help you ask effectively. Please make sure to complete these exercises thoughtfully before you run off and just ask for referrals willy-nilly. What you can start with today is seeking out opportunities for referral conversations. Here are a few excellent situations that naturally lead to a referral conversation:

- Your ideal client thanks you for work well done.
- Your ideal client asks you for more services.
- Your ideal client asks for clarification on a process or concept.
- Your ideal client describes a past problem that you helped fix or goal you helped them achieve.

And here are some obvious situations:

- Your ideal client mentions a friend or business associate who's been facing the same challenges your client faced.
- Your ideal client mentions they are going to an industry conference for a few days (and you serve businesses or individuals within that industry).

Or you can create the opportunity for a referral conversation by:

- Thanking clients for their energy and enthusiasm during your project
- Clarifying their goals or making a suggestion to work on their own
- Asking clients how they are feeling about the work you're doing together or about past challenges
- Complimenting clients on their business achievements – always

Once you get clients talking, ask them about the value they get from your work together. Use this as an open door to have them talk about how your services could benefit other people or organizations they have relationships with.

Imagine this: You've been on a creative journey with a client who was once struggling to establish a compelling brand identity. Through your work and expertise, they now have a powerful, cohesive brand that resonates deeply with their target audience. That's a powerful transformation.

Now let's take this a step further. What if you could frame the referral conversation in a way that positions your client as the hero of their own story? They've walked this path, they've overcome this challenge, and they know there are others out there who are still struggling.

By encouraging them to refer someone who is in the same boat they were when they first came to you, they're not just passing along a name. They're offering hope. They're saying, "I've been there; I now have a brand that has positioned my business for success, and so can you."

This approach doesn't just make them more likely to refer to you. It empowers them to make a difference in someone else's life. And that's a story worth sharing.

Step 7: Facilitate the Referral Connection

Offer to meet, consult with, or advise anyone who is important to your clients. Let them know that you want to help educate their friends about the benefits of your services.

Ask them to make the introduction today. There are times when you can take the burden of calling or sending the email off of your referrer. Not because your referrer doesn't want to make the referral happen but because life sometimes gets in the way. People are busy, and they can get distracted by other tasks on their to-do list. If *you* actually make the connection and do the follow-up, it's sure to happen.

The same is true any time you personally meet potential clients. They say they're going to call you, and even if they have the best of intentions, things come up that get in the way, and you don't get a call. So I suggest that when you meet someone you really connect with and who has expressed interest in your services, you contact them; don't wait for them to contact you.

Step 8: Follow Up with Referrals and Referrers

Contact new referrals and introduce them to what you have to offer – in a meaningful, connected, and helpful way. This is where your always-have-something-to-invite-people-to offer comes into play. It gives you a really easy way to start a conversation with the potential client and extend a no-risk, no-barrier invitation that is compelling and attractive. All you have to do is make a generous invitation and you've started the Book Yourself Solid Sales Cycle.

When beginning a relationship with potential clients, consider the following:

- Schedule private consultations to eliminate any uncertainty or hesitation they may have about trying your services.
- Learn about any past experience with creative services that they may have had and, most important, what they hope to achieve.
- Tell them what to expect, how you work, and the benefits they will experience.
- Include administrative details too; what to have available, if anything. Help clients feel as comfortable and prepared as possible.
- Share case studies that demonstrate how your work has helped grow your clients' businesses.
- Invite clients to work with you, and remember the Book Yourself Solid Super Simple Selling System. Offer a specific date and time that suits their schedule.

Practice Your Referral Presentation

Speak with lots of expression, get excited, and show the passion you have for the benefits your services can offer.

- Smile.
- Be confident.
- Open your heart.
- When your potential clients starts speaking, hush up and listen.

4.12.8 Booked Solid Action Step: Make the commitment to ask for referrals every day for five days straight.

Are you as excited as we are about the dozens of potential clients you're going to meet? Just think about all those potential clients who've been searching for and waiting to be introduced to an expert like you. We hope and expect that you will serve your potential clients and community by immediately starting to ask for client referrals. Once you start speaking with your potential clients on a deep and personal level, they will see you as far more than just your title. They will see you with more value, dimension, and a higher level of respect.

This meaningful connection is the key to achieving a greater level of prosperity and personal satisfaction. It's the Book Yourself Solid way.

Who Wants What You Want?

While some of your clients, friends, family, and colleagues may refer others to you without your having to ask, many won't. As we mentioned earlier, it isn't that they don't want to; they're just busy with their own lives and it hasn't occurred to them. While it may feel awkward at first to ask for referrals, give it a try. You'll be surprised at how willing they are to do so once you've brought it to mind. Certainly, if they've worked with you, they'll want their friends, family, and business associates to experience the same great benefits they have. And they'll enjoy being able to help you as well. When someone has a positive effect on one's life, even in small ways, it feels good to give something back, and referrals are a great way to do it.

Other Professionals – The Other Source of Referrals

Other professionals who offer services and products that are complementary to your own, and work with your target market, are ideal sources of referrals. That's why we spent so much time on the 50% of your networking strategy that focuses on other professionals. When you operate from a perspective of abundance and cooperation, rather than from scarcity and competition, it becomes easy to reach out to others to develop relationships that can be mutually beneficial.

> **The more you refer to others, the more they'll be inspired to refer to you.**

Many service professionals have a formal referral group with five or six other professionals who serve the same target market but offer complementary services and products. Each member of the group works to send referrals to each other member of the group. If you join a high-integrity referral group, you'll greatly extend your referral reach. You'll also build your reputation by having others talk about you and your services.

Affiliate Fees and Rewards Programs

Reward those who refer others to you. A reward could be anything from a formal affiliate program, through which you pay cash for referrals, to coupons for discounts on your services, products, or programs or highly personalized gifts.

Cash-based referral programs can be highly effective and are commonly used among service providers. These programs are particularly beneficial when partnering with professionals who have complementary skills, creating a synergy where clients might need both services for their business. For instance, a copywriter collaborating with a web designer, or a web designer working alongside a web developer, can offer a comprehensive solution that meets the client's needs.

However, it's not always the preferred approach when your clients or past clients send referrals your way. Finding a way to show your appreciation and reward for the referrer is essential nonetheless.

We recommend doing it through gifts. Not gift baskets or gift cards. They're too trite. Instead, focus on personalizing gifts based on the recipient's hobbies, interests, and passions. For example, Joana secured a meeting with a very large company in Portugal through an old family friend. They were competing against other large national agencies and probably wouldn't have even been invited to pitch for the job without this connection. After landing the big job, Joana knew her contact was a big fan of wine. She had a couple of bottles branded with both Gif Design Studios' logo and the client's, with the title "Cheers to new beginnings," and sent them to the office for everyone to share. Joana's contact was thrilled because he appreciates good wine, and it also made him look good in front of his peers for recommending Gif Design Studios. This thoughtful gesture set the tone for the level of client care Joana's agency provides, reinforcing that they made the right choice in hiring them.

Say you charge $1000 per month for your services and you currently have 10 regular clients. You're currently earning $10 000 a month. Now let's say that you receive 10 referrals at $1000 per month. That's another 10 clients for another $10 000 a month. If you give a referral fee of 10%, you'll be paying each referrer $100 per referral for a total of $1000 in referral fees. Would you spend $1000 to make $10 000 for a profit of $9000 and a new monthly income of $19 000, almost double what you were making? Of course, you would.

However, are people really going to make a concerted effort to send you referrals because you're offering them $100 per month? We haven't found that to be the case. It's rare that someone will make a referral simply because you're offering a small referral commission or reward. They'll do it because they believe in you and what you stand for. The fee or reward is just a nice bonus that makes them feel appreciated. Additionally, if you do a good service and make their contact's life easier, you just make them look good, and who doesn't like that?

Strike While the Iron Is Hot

Nurture the relationships you develop with those who refer others to you, and *always* follow up right away on any referrals you get. You'll then create not merely satisfied clients but raving fans by delivering your best work. Before you know it, you'll be booked solid.

The Book Yourself Solid Speaking Strategy

It usually takes me more than three weeks to prepare a good impromptu speech.
—Mark Twain

The Book Yourself Solid Speaking Strategy is an extremely effective way to get in front of potential ideal clients to demonstrate your knowledge, talents, and strengths. But it's not for everyone. It's not mandatory. There is no reason you should use this strategy unless you'd like to speak to groups of people, large or small. You're not a more impressive person because you want to speak in front of others. In fact, many do it just for the approval of the audience or to sell something to them instead of being in service of them and reaping the rewards of that service. There is nothing deficient about you if you don't want to use this strategy for marketing yourself.

The wonderful thing about sharing your knowledge is that it's rewarding for both you and your audience. They will leave your presentation or event with a kick in their step, feel a little smarter, and think a heck of a lot bigger about who they are and what they have to offer to the world. You've also given them an action plan that will help them implement what they learned from you. You will benefit because you'll know you've helped others, which is the reason you do what you do. And you'll increase awareness of your services at the same time.

To get in front of your target market, you can promote yourself or have others promote you. When you promote yourself, you're inviting your target market to something that is going to help them solve their problems and move them toward their compelling desires. When you are promoted by others, your surrogates put you in front of your target market. You may want to travel both routes.

We won't address the details of being a professional speaker, someone who makes a living speaking to organizations, but rather how you can use public speaking to create awareness for what you have to offer and get booked solid. If you're interested in becoming a professional speaker, pick up a copy of *The Referable Speaker: Your Guide to Building a Sustainable Speaking Career: No Fame Required* (Page Two Press, 2021). And, if you'd like to uplevel your public speaking skills, dig into Michael's *Wall Street Journal* best-selling book, *Steal the Show: From Speeches to Job Interviews to Deal-Closing Pitches, How to Guarantee a Standing Ovation for All the Performances in Your Life* (Houghton Mifflin Harcourt, 2015). Moreover, if you'd like more help with your public speaking, visit Heroic PublicSpeaking.com for resources and information on our training programs and events.

Self-Promotion

Of course, all of the Book Yourself Solid Six Core Self-Promotion Strategies require that you promote yourself in one way or another. Even using the Book Yourself Solid Speaking Strategy to get other people to put you in front of your target market requires that you promote yourself to the person who is going to give you that platform.

First, let's look at pure self-promotion, such as inviting your target market to events that you produce, not necessarily big workshops or conferences, but simple, community-building, meaningful, enlightening events at which you can shine, show off your services, and build your reputation and credibility in your marketplace. These types of speaking and demonstrating events might fall into the category of an always-have-something-to-invite-people-to offer, or they may be one-off events.

Webinars and Online Meetings

Start a monthly or weekly call for potential clients to learn the benefits of working with you. Prepare a new, timely, and relevant topic every time. Pick up a magazine in your industry and use one of the articles to inspire your topic, invite guests to discuss their area of expertise, and ask your clients to tell you what they'd most like to hear about. The rest of the call will naturally flow into a Q&A session. Here are a few ideas to get you started and to spark your inspiration and creativity for your own unique ideas:

- Offer a monthly or weekly Q&A on your field of expertise. No planning is necessary; just show up and shine.
- Offer an online workshop sharing tips and best practices for getting started with your service. For example, if you're a personal brand photographer, guide participants through planning a shoot, from selecting the location to setting up lighting and perfecting poses.
- Host monthly or quarterly online sessions offering real-time audits specific to your services. For example, if you're a copywriter, provide live copy critiques; if you're a web designer, conduct web design audits. Operate on a first-come, first-served basis, with participants submitting their links in the chat for immediate feedback. This not only demonstrates your expertise but also builds trust and engages potential clients.

If you're doing a webinar or online meeting, it won't cost you a dime after you've paid for your meeting software. Record each session and put it up online, on social media, or on your website. Highlight small sections and share them as snippets online. Those who couldn't make the actual session will still have the opportunity to listen to it and benefit from it. Archiving and sharing the calls is also a wonderful way of immediately establishing trust and credibility with new web visitors and attracting new prospects to check you out.

Demonstrations and Educational Events

These opportunities are similar to conference calls except that they're conducted in person. For creative service providers, demonstrations and educational events are an excellent way to reach potential ideal clients since your work often has a tangible or visual component. This approach is also a great alternative if you feel that virtual events don't speak to your strengths. This format is another opportunity to get creative and express yourself. Here's how to make the most of these events:

- Host an open house or live demo at your studio, or any other venue. Invite potential clients along with your current clients, friends, and colleagues who know the value of your services and can share their experiences.
- Offer a weekly creative challenge where clients and potential clients can participate. Encourage them to bring a friend each week. Plan a new activity, such as shooting reels for their business, writing their next newsletter, or designing their next social media posts, followed by a social event to foster networking.
- Host a no-cost or low-cost morning retreat. Be playful and adventurous. It doesn't have to be expensive, just creative. Allow clients to get to know you and meet other people with similar interests and goals. Make it as simple as serving tea, whole fresh fruit, and scones and share your wealth of knowledge.
- Start a niche club. Consider cool stuff clients would enjoy. Think about activities that you love. Start a creative brainstorming club, weekly play group, or fun family outing. Michael met a dentist who organizes bike rides – of the Harley Davidson variety. He gives out bandanas for everyone to wear. And, yes, they are black with a big white tooth on them. It's not a coincidence that most of the folks who participate in these regular rides are also his clients.

Introduce these offerings at the end of your Book Yourself Solid Dialogue. Add "I'd like to invite you to __________" or "Why don't you join me and my clients for a fun, playful __________." Try out different venues and topics until you discover the one that works for you. Remember, the difference between the typical client-snagging mentality and the Book Yourself Solid way is that the typical client-snagging mentality plays it safe so as not to look foolish. The Book Yourself Solid way asks "How can I be unconventional and risky so as to create interest and excitement for my services?"

You will never be at a loss for different things to try or experiences to create for your clients and potential clients. You want to invite as many people as possible to these events for three important reasons:

1. You want to leverage your time so you're connecting with as many potential clients as possible in the shortest amount of time.
2. You want to leverage the power of communities. When you bring people together, they create far more energy and excitement than you can on your own. Your guests will also see other people interested in what you have to offer, and that's the best way to build credibility.
3. You'll be viewed as a generous connector. If you're known in your marketplace as someone who brings people together, it will help you build your reputation and increase your likeability.

Podcasting

Starting a podcast can offer a great way to amplify your voice and establish yourself as a trusted authority, while also building meaningful connections with your audience.

Right about now, you might be wondering, "Why should I invest my precious time and effort into creating a podcast when there are already countless podcasts out there?" It's a fair question, especially if you're thinking you need to create a podcast with a national reach. However, as a creative service provider, your aim isn't necessarily to have a podcast with a massive reach. Instead, you can focus on creating a podcast on whatever topics are of interest to your ideal client in your local area. Often, when we are coaching people through launching a podcast, one of the first challenges they bring up is not knowing how, or where, to find guests. Since you are implementing Book Yourself Solid principles, finding guests will become much easier; you're going to be meeting more people and making more friends. Having a podcast that features guests can be a great way to open up doors with people you would like to get to know better.

For example, your Network of 90 (as discussed in Chapter 10) would make for excellent guests, and since they serve the same group of ideal clients, having them on your podcast will be an exciting opportunity.

Additionally, you can leverage your podcast as you look to develop relationships with people on your List of 20 (go back and read Chapter 11 if you need a refresher).

As you reach out to people on your list, beginning the conversation by offering to have them as a guest on your podcast can serve as a great way to bridge the gap between them not knowing who you are, to them seeing you as a generous, likable person who is offering them something valuable.

Another benefit of podcasting is that it will give you a ton of content that you can repurpose for use on social media (more on that in Chapter 15). If you are going to start a podcast, it's important you have a consistent schedule and stick to it.

4.13.1 Written Exercise: Create three ways that you can instantly add value to your potential and current clients by way of an invitation.

Getting Promoted by Others

Now let's address the second approach: getting promoted by others to speak or demonstrate. If you're speaking for exposure, which I believe is very effective for many people, you probably won't be paid up front for most of the speaking you do, except possibly an honorarium and travel costs. You're doing it for the opportunity to address potential clients and to interest them in your offerings. There's an assumed trade involved. You receive marketing opportunities, and the association or organization that brings you in to speak or demonstrate gets great content that serves their constituents. The key is to balance the two. If you are invited to speak and you spend 90% of your time talking about what you have to offer, you won't be well received, and you certainly won't be invited back. However, if you don't make any offers at all, you'll be sure to miss great opportunities for booking yourself solid. When Joana first adopted this strategy, she started by guest speaking at her clients' events. This approach turned out to be incredibly effective. Remarkably, the year after she began speaking, 50% of her annual business came from just one speaking engagement she had done the previous year.

Booking Your Way Up

If you would like to be promoted by others, you need to develop trusting relationships with decision makers at associations and organizations that serve your target market. In the business world, these people are often called meeting planners. At your local associations, these people may be called communication or education directors or something altogether different. Bottom line: they are the people who can get you in front of your target audience.

There are thousands of associations and organizations that serve your target market. For example, colleges and universities all across the country sponsor executive extension courses, community learning programs, and all kinds of management and small-business seminars and workshops. And to create comprehensive programs, the colleges and universities will often invite guest experts, like you, to make a presentation on their area of expertise. Trade associations and networking groups all need speakers to address their memberships, and this phenomenon continues to expand in the public sector as well as becoming a big part of the local communities they serve. The most potentially rewarding venues will offer you audiences that include potential buyers for your products and services. Some of the venues or organizations may even have name recognition that is prestigious like a university club or well-known business networking group.

There is a general hierarchy of associations and organizations that can sponsor you and your services. I start the list with the lower-level organizations and associations and work up to the highest-level organizations and associations. The lower-level organizations are usually smaller and less prestigious, but don't let the hierarchy fool you. You can get booked solid by speaking in front of members of the lowest-level associations and organizations, but you don't necessarily have to start with the lowest and work your way up. It may help to have previous speaking experience with some of the lower-level associations and organizations for you to get booked with the higher-level associations and organizations.

Level One

Your entry point to speaking and demonstrating is with local community groups or organizations, co-working spaces, libraries, and different industry meetups. Some of these groups serve a particular target market, but most are made up of individuals who share similar interests. They're good places to find potential clients and great places to work on your material and practice speaking and demonstrating in front of other people.

> **4.13.2 Written Exercise:** Identify several Level One groups or organizations that you can contact.

Level Two

Seek out local for-profit business groups, learning programs, and schools, including schools of continuing education and networking groups like Business Network International, Vistage, universities, and others.

These organizations are higher up the value scale for you because they serve more targeted groups of people who are really there to learn what you have to offer. Furthermore, they tend to be slightly more prestigious than the local not-for-profit community groups.

> **4.13.3 Written Exercise:** Identify several Level Two groups or organizations that you can contact.

Level Three

At Level Three, you'll be speaking at local and regional trade associations. There are more local and regional trade associations than you can count or ever speak to in a lifetime. Do a quick search on Google to find associations for everything from home-based businesses, electricians, and computer programmers, to lawyers, and family winemakers. Local and regional trade associations and organizations are excellent opportunities for you to connect with your target market because you know the exact makeup of your audience.

> **4.13.4 Written Exercise:** Identify several Level Three local or regional trade associations or businesses that you can contact.

Level Four

From here you're just going to keep moving up the trade association ladder, from local and regional trade associations to national trade associations and then to international trade associations. There's even a Federation of International Trade Associations (FITA).

4.13.5 Written Exercise: Identify several Level Four national or international trade associations that you can contact.

How to Find Your Audiences

Most of the information you'll need about associations and organizations that serve your target market is available online. An obvious statement, we know. They're easy to find but it can sometimes be difficult to identify from a website whom to contact, but it's the best and cheapest way to start. If you're serious about using the Book Yourself Solid Speaking Strategy as your go-to marketing strategy, you can also pick up a copy of the *NTPA: National Trade and Professional Associations of the United States*. It contains the name of every trade association, its president, budget, convention sites, conference themes, membership, and other pertinent information. You might also consider referencing the *Directory of Association Meeting Planners and Conference/Convention Directors* and the *Encyclopedia of Associations* at your local library. If local libraries still exist by the time you read this, that is.

4.13.6 Written Exercise: Identify the decision makers for the organizations you chose in the previous written exercises. Put them on your List of 20 and then go through your network to see who you know who might be able to connect you with these decision makers or someone else who might know these decision makers.

> **4.13.7 Booked Solid Action Step:** After reading this chapter, contact these decision makers using your newfound direct outreach strategies and begin getting booked to speak.

Get Booked to Speak

Meeting planners and their respective counterparts get lots of offers from people like you to speak to their constituents. That's why it's critical that you follow the Book Yourself Solid system. If you have a strong foundation and a trust and credibility strategy in place for your business, you'll understand why people buy what you're selling. You'll also know how to talk about what you do and have a clear idea of how you want to be known in your market. With these elements in place, you'll be able to have effective sales conversations and establish yourself as a likeable expert within your field. Additionally, by creating brand-building, self-expression products, you'll not only attract all the clients you want, but you'll also earn the respect of decision makers at the associations and organizations where you'd like to speak.

Do your homework. If you're going to contact a meeting planner or education director, make sure you know as much as you possibly can about their organization. You'd be surprised at how many people overlook this step and cold-call these meeting planners without having done their homework. The meeting planner knows it within minutes of the conversation.

Talk to organization members first, if possible. Learn about their urgent needs and compelling desires. They know best what they need, so learn it from them and then reach out to the decision makers. You'll get booked a lot faster that way. Even better, have a member or board member refer you, if possible. How much do we love it when other people talk about us so we don't have to? So much.

Send an email first and follow up with a call. And as always, be friendly, be relevant (meaning that you offer your services only if you can really serve the group), have empathy (step into the shoes of the meeting planner), and be real (no big sales pitch).

What You Need to Present to Get Booked

Each meeting planner, depending on the organization and type of event they're planning, will ask you to submit different materials in order to be considered. If you're trying to get booked at the local community center, a simple phone conversation may do the trick. If you're trying to get booked to speak at the largest conference in your industry, more is expected. In this case, you'll be asked for a video, session description, learning objectives, speaking experience, letters of recommendation, general biography, introduction biography (which is what is used to introduce you right before you present), and more. Even if five organizations ask for the same materials, it's likely each one will ask for them in their own special way. Here's a word to the wise: make sure you follow instructions. People, especially meeting planners, like that.

Your Invitation to Speak

When invited to speak or present a program, a preliminary meeting or phone call usually sets the stage for further interaction with the person responsible for the program. During the initial contact, you and the meeting planner can usually nail down the topic to be covered and the length of time expected for the presentation. From the time you receive your invitation to the time you write thank-you notes, knowing the key players and how to connect with them is vital.

Know Your Audience

Start by considering your audience. Do as much research as you can on the people who will be attending your presentation so that your learning objectives can be directed right at their needs and desires. Work to understand the culture of the group you're speaking to so you can understand how to best communicate with them. Your audience will influence your choice of vocabulary (technical jargon) and may even influence how you dress. Knowing your audience well will also help you decide how much background material you need to deliver for you to effectively communicate your message.

Ask if you may have an opportunity to interview some of the leadership personnel (and even more exciting, some of those who will be attending the seminar or conference) to determine who they are along with their personal goals and agendas. Will they allow you to involve them in the presentation?

Setting up for success in advance will remove much of the stress of preparation, and it'll give you more confidence when delivering the actual presentation. Once again, a reminder that a strong foundation leads to super performance.

Know Your Audience – Questionnaire

Experience has proven that at this point it is appropriate to present a questionnaire that gives you background information specifically tailored to this particular audience. Developing various forms to help you present effectively and evaluate your performance gives you the professional edge when talking with the person in charge of the program.

The kind of forms you can create might include:

- Pre-questionnaire – to know your audience in advance
- Audience evaluation forms
- Follow-up forms

Be Prepared

Of course, you will find out where your presentation is to be held and what audiovisual equipment will be available to you, if any. While slides can be valuable, especially for visual creatives, they must be used thoughtfully to enhance your message rather than detract from it. Avoid overloading slides with bullet points, which can distract and disengage your audience.

Clarify how long you'll be speaking and what your audience will be doing before and after your presentation so you can incorporate that information into your planning. It's even a good idea to end a few minutes early. You'll find that, even when you bring down the house, your audience will appreciate a little extra free time.

Don't forget to remind the facilitator of your requirements closer to the presentation date. Remember, he is juggling a lot of information. Your presentation may be a small part of a larger conference.

Know Your Speaking Venue

Ask to visit the speaking site. As a guest speaker, an appointment with the conference chair, facilitator, or meeting planner is important, as you probably will have only one chance to determine several factors:

- Room setup, speaking area, time of access to facility and meeting room.
- Location of restrooms.
- Setup and breakdown time allowed for your presentation – staff help?
- Your technical and physical needs – who provides what?
- Back-of-room sales – permitted or not?

Remember Your End Goal

If your goal is to get hired, focus on what really matters to your audience. If it's busy business owners who need effective solutions to grow their business, don't waste time teaching them "how" to do what you do. They don't have the time or the desire to master your craft, which you've spent years perfecting.

Instead, explain why your service is essential and how it can transform their business. Use compelling stories and case studies to illustrate the potential impact. Paint a vivid picture of the benefits they'll gain by understanding the power of your service.

For instance, Joana's first talk was for an audience of e-commerce business owners. Her session, titled "Bad Design Can Kill Your Business," highlighted common design mistakes she knew many in the audience were making. She showed how these errors were turning customers away and hurting conversions, making a strong case for the value of professional design services. Through her presentation, Joana helped change their perception of design from a tool to "just make things pretty" to a serious tool that can boost sales.

By focusing on the "why" instead of "how" and demonstrating the real-world impact of your expertise, you make a compelling case for why they should hire you.

Steal the Show

Now that you're going to be booked to speak, you need to put together a presentation that steals the show. Keep your presentation as simple as possible. To be an effective speaker, you need to either teach your audience something that they don't know or haven't yet fully realized – but will really value learning – or give them an experience that changes the way they see the world. Ideally, you want to do both.

When putting your program together, start by considering your venue, the primary learning objectives, and the amount of time you have with your audience. We know how much you have to offer, and we know you want to give so much value that you knock people right out of their chairs. Believe it or not, you'll do that by delivering a reasonable amount of content rather than an overwhelming amount of content. It's likely that your audience is going to be rushing from somewhere else and then rushing to somewhere else after you've finished. So simplicity and clarity is a winning approach. Again, it's important to never run overtime. Even if you get a standing ovation and they scream, "Encore! Encore!" you must still end on time. Only amateurs run over their allotted time.

Develop Your Introduction

Your introductory bio needs to do one of two things, or both. Demonstrate that you've done what they want to do or know what they want to know. If it does, the audience is much more likely to listen to you right from the get-go. The fact that you live in New Jersey, have a spouse, 2.2 kids, and a dog, isn't important to them. If you have 11 children and have climbed Mt. Kilimanjaro, well, that's interesting and should be included. Remember that your written bio and spoken introduction bio are different. The spoken introduction bio should read naturally and be brief and to the point.

Who will introduce you? Send your introduction in advance, but take at least two copies with you, as it will probably have been lost amid all the conference preparation papers. Go over the introduction with the facilitator in advance and explain that you do not want ad libs. Be sure the person introducing you knows how to pronounce your name correctly and that any other information is clearly understood. If your name isn't easy to pronounce, writing your name phonetically in your introduction and asking the presenter to say it out loud a couple of times is a sensible precaution to take. Take this seriously even if you think you have a name that is easy to pronounce. Michael has been introduced more than once as Michael Porter, the esteemed author and Harvard Business School professor. The person introducing you may be a sponsor or some other VIP, and until you become better known, may not know you from Adam and, frankly, may not care. Michael's last name is *Port* (just one syllable).

Know Your Material

The best way to give the impression that you know what you're talking about is to really know what you're talking about. You must understand your subject very well and be able to answer related questions. On the other hand, it is impossible for anyone to know everything. If you're asked a question for which you don't know the answer, there is no shame in answering, "I don't know, but I'll find out and get back to you." Or you might ask if someone in the room knows the answer. Very often, you'll find that someone does.

In preparing your presentation, take the time to survey friends, clients, and others in your network who represent the kind of people to whom you'll be speaking. Learn as much as you can about what others are saying about your topic and make sure that your presentation passes the "so what" test. Deliver it to a test audience and make sure they don't say, "So what?" at the end of the presentation.

Wrap Up and Follow Up

Be sure those participants have your contact information and that you have contact information for participants where possible. Your follow-up strategy will also include thank-you notes and personalized gifts to those who helped make your presentation a success: the person or organization that invited you to speak, the facilitator who introduced you, anyone else who helped with room preparation, and so on.

You may want to remind the organization of the availability of follow-up materials as part of your keeping-in-touch plan. Make notes of what you learned so that you can apply it to future presentations and particularly to the current organization, should you be asked back again.

Fifty Public Speaking Performance Tips You Can't Afford to Ignore

Use these tips when you're preparing for a presentation. However, if you haven't yet read Michael's book, *Steal the Show,* but you're about to read these tips, please know that *these are just tips,* snapshots of a more comprehensive process for developing speeches and performing with professionalism and passion.

Our suggestion is to, no matter what kind of presentation you're preparing for, take a few moments to review the following items as a checklist to ensure that you're ready to steal the show.

1. *You don't have to tell them what you're going to tell them.*

    You've probably heard this one before: "Tell them what you're going to tell them. Tell them. Tell them what you've told them." That's not bad advice. But it's not always the case. If you're going to make your audience sit up and pay attention, wouldn't it be worth doing something that every other speaker *isn't* doing? Try a *pattern-interrupt* instead. Open with a surprise, a shock, or an interaction. Open with something that makes a connection or something that entertains or something that leaves you exposed. Be different. Be memorable. It's often the journey that's exciting. If you already know where you're going, you might not pay as much attention along the way.

2. *Cut, cut, cut.*

    We often see (and you often see) extraneous detail added into stories and speeches that disrupt the flow. Cut to the meat. Cut to the chase. Include specifics at critical parts of the story. You don't need to pad out your speech to make an impact. Instead, you need to focus — with intention — on what's important. Your audience needs a lot less information to get to the "aha" moment than you might think.

3. *An entire story is designed to serve the end.*

   Whatever precedes the punch line must serve the pay-off. See Tip 2. Does the audience need to know what color socks you're wearing or how long it took you to get to the venue? The only things that matter are things that serve the story.

4. *Establish right away that you know what the world looks like for them — and what it could look like.*

   Vividly paint the picture. Meaningful speeches are transformational experiences for your audience. Start out by showing "This is what you've got today, and this is how it could be." This builds immediate rapport and hooks the audience's interest. You know them. You understand them. You've got their back and you've got a better way.

5. *Reward them for contributing in some way.*

   Don't encourage interaction just to ignore it. Your audience isn't made up of chimpanzees: they don't need treats (although, they'll appreciate them). They're intelligent beings, who do, however, need some acknowledgment.

   Imagine being asked to participate in something — whether it's holding a door open for a friend or running a project — and not even getting a nod of thanks in return. You start to feel bad right away.

6. *Use open hands with your palms up instead of your finger for pointing.*

   Sometimes the finger looks like a gun. It also feels accusatory even if you don't mean it to be. Instead, extend your hands with your palms up as if offering up alms. It's more gracious, more inclusive, and more giving.

7. *People say "yes" when we've affected them intellectually, emotionally, or physically.*

   Can you include those three elements in your presentation? Can you give your audience intellectual gristle to chew on? Can you make them gasp or cry or laugh with an emotional connection? Can you get them physically engaged (you can tell by the way they're sitting) with your ideas and message? If not, learn how and start today.

8. *Make sure to unpack your ideas.*

   If you say you're going to share something, you need to follow through. Enough said.

9. *Use props.*

   What can you show or demonstrate or depict with objects rather than words? Can you stimulate your audience visually as well as aurally? Props aid recall: If you want to be remembered, you can be visually arresting (without dying your hair) by using props to drive your points home. Most speakers don't do this. That's just one of the reasons why you should.

10. *Use contrast and extremes to create excitement and keep attention.*

    Contrast can be emotional, physical, and structural. This basic technique is integral to every great play and film and every great piece of music. Consider your performance like a roller coaster ride. Can you take me to the edge of a cliff before artfully lowering me, with love and care, to a safe place? Can you make the highs higher and the lows lower?

11. *Keep moving forward.*

    Never let your energy drop. You're on stage to take your audience to their final destination. Keep your foot on the gas pedal. You'll have uphill moments when your speed slows but the power and intensity increase. You can be both calm and energetic simultaneously. The great actor does this brilliantly. You, as a speaker, need to do this as well. The best way to be effortlessly spontaneous is to rehearse to the point of mastery. How often do you have to stop to think about "spontaneously" adjusting your shoelaces? Never. When you know your material, you can deliver it like it's the first time every time you perform it.

12. *Stand and land.*

    Let your punch lines, point lines, and purpose lines land. That means you don't move while you're delivering them. You remain physically rooted to the spot so that your body reinforces the gravity of your words.

13. *You can move and talk at the same time.*

    People do it all the time in real life. The idea that you can't walk and talk at the same time is ridiculous. But don't sway, and don't move when you're landing your most important points (read 12 again, *Stand and Land*).

14. *Don't say "I'm glad to be here."*

     Show them that you're glad to be there instead. Your audience should see it in your actions and hear it in your words. Besides, what's the alternative? That you're pissed off that you're there?

15. *Don't tell them you're going to tell a story. Just tell the story.*

     If you do, it's likely that they'll prepare themselves to judge the story. When people find themselves *in a story*, they are usually more engaged. People are driven by their curiosity for answers. Stories stimulate that curiosity. If you can create a sense of wonder for the listener, you can take them on a journey of exploration and insight.

16. *Be conscientious about connecting the dots or you'll lose your audience.*

     If you're presenting a series of interconnected concepts or stories or characters, make it as simple as possible to understand. Remember: Even though you know your material inside out, your audience is hearing it for the first time.

17. *Give them time.*

     If you like to encourage note-taking during your performance, make sure you give people enough time to write down what you want them to write down. Spell things out if necessary. You'll lose your audience very quickly if they've got their heads stuck in their notebooks or laptops and you're already on to your next point.

18. *Never apologize for the amount of time you don't have.*

     The minute you apologize for what they're not getting, your audience will start to feel that they're missing out on something. They should feel that the amount of time you have is the perfect amount of time. You can blow their minds in just a few minutes. Look at all those great Technology, Entertainment, Design (TED) talks for inspiration.

19. *Let them go early.*

     Audiences always like to be let out a few minutes early – even if they love your performance. There are no prizes for endurance in performance. Let them leave a few minutes ahead of schedule; they'll thank you for it.

20. *Enlist the self-proclaimed experts in the room.*

     There's often somebody in the audience who knows more than you – or thinks they do. Get them on your side. Talk them up. Kill them with lavish praise. It'll help knock the chips off their shoulders and get them to support you and your message.

21. *Embellishment is positively okay.*

    You'll paint a more vivid picture with brighter colors. Be honest, but embellish to help the audience gain better insight or to make a story more entertaining. You can combine multiple stories into one story if it produces a better result. Go for what is most dramatic and effective to get your message across. This is different from lying. Lying is something you do to make yourself look better.

22. *Remember that they don't know what you know.*

    It's the first time they've heard your info. Don't assume prior knowledge if you're not sure. It can only help your message if you're comprehensive and to the point.

23. *Don't use acronyms.*

    Or, if you do, explain them the first time around. Take the time to make them clear.

24. *Show them what the world will look like if they don't change.*

    Make it clear that if they don't follow your advice, or come with you on your journey, their world will probably remain the same as — if not get considerably worse than — it is today. Just do this respectfully and without hyperbole.

25. *Study stand-up comedy.*

    Watch stand-up comedians for their approach. Watch their setup, delivery, and pay-off. See how they own the stage. Stand-up comedians can even turn a water bottle into a tool for creating magic moments.

26. *Be careful using idioms.*

    Across cultures — even cultures that share a language — there are big idiomatic differences that can turn your message opaque for an audience that doesn't "get it." If you're an American talking to a British audience about bangs, bleachers, boondoggles, or fanny-packs, you've likely lost them already.

27. *Don't make jokes about difficult topics.*

    Stay away from jokes that are awkward, insensitive, or otherwise confrontational. If you want to make yourself the butt of your jokes, that kind of self-deprecating humor can work very well. This doesn't mean you can't lighten up the mood when talking about difficult subjects, but that's different from poking fun or making jokes at other people's expense.

28. *If you tell them you care about something, you also need to tell them why.*

    It's not good enough to say "I'm a strong proponent of women's rights." It may seem obvious, but you've got to hook them in with *your* reasons. Your why is what makes your beliefs more powerful and your case stronger.

29. *Boom, boom, BANG.*

    The rule of three is one of the most important performance techniques you can use to grab attention and make people laugh. It's powerful, it's potent, and it packs a punch. (See what I did there?)

30. *Understand stage blocking.*

    You need to remain physically open so everyone in the room can see you at all times. That means you don't hide or turn to face anybody other than your audience, unless it's for some theatrical effect.

31. *Deliver big moments center stage (usually).*

    Centering yourself physically on the stage is the same as bolding and centering a headline in a newspaper. It says: "This is important—pay attention." When you designate center stage as the pivotal place for your performance, you can more effectively use the rest of the stage to support your main message. There are always exceptions to this concept, so be sure your staging works before the big day.

32. *That said, don't head straight for center stage.*

    When getting onstage for the first time, avoid making a beeline from one side of the stage to the other before turning to the audience to start your speech. Doing so looks stiff and clunky.

33. *Learn how to rehearse.*

    Rehearsal is the key to a successful performance. It's also the most effective method for reducing anxiety and calming pre-performance anxiety. If you know what you're going to do because you're well-rehearsed, you'll feel more prepared and, thus, less anxious. It's not just repetition, but training. If you have to stop a rehearsal, start back up at the exact same emotional, physical, and energetic state. Otherwise, you'll lose the through-line and arc of the speech.

34. *When you land a joke, bask in the glory.*

    If public speaking is notoriously difficult, making people laugh when you're performing is devilishly tough. So, when you nail a joke, be sure to bask in the moment.

35. *Voice and speech training are not something you master in an hour.*

    It takes some time. Michael studied voice and speech daily for three years at New York University's Graduate Acting Program, and he's still learning. Voice and speech training can make you sound more substantial so people will pay attention to you. It can also help you manage your nerves.

36. *Don't push.*

    Pushing is a theater term for overacting. When you push, you can't show emotion. When you push, the work feels false and self-absorbed. It's insincere. Insincerity is the enemy of truth. Truth is integral to performance.

37. *Just because you're feeling it doesn't mean they are.*

    Major emotion for you as the speaker doesn't always translate to major emotion for your audience. It's only in rehearsal and practice that you find out what works and what doesn't. You might be moved to tears while your audience is bored to tears. Big difference. Your job is getting the audience to think differently, feel differently, and/or act differently. How you feel doesn't matter. Achieving your objectives for the people in the audience does.

38. *Get everything in before the audience claps.*

    Then, take a bow and get off the stage. Don't let them see you doing housekeeping or making routine announcements. It breaks the theatrical experience. Avoid the dreaded line that you often hear after the clapping starts, "Oh, I forgot, there's more thing I need to tell you."

39. *You can also stay onstage at the end if you invite them to join you there.*

    That way, you're hosting the party. You don't want them grabbing you in the restroom: Nothing dissipates magic like a damp handshake in the gent's restroom.

40. *Anyone can make a sexy sizzle reel.*

    Meeting planners want to know you can hold the stage for an extended period of time. Make sure you can show them a video of 5–15 minutes of continuous performance in which you deliver a strong message and truly engage the audience. Any good editor can piece together a bunch of good lines from different speeches but it doesn't tell the audience that you can hold and own the stage.

41. *Get right to it.*

   Most speakers waste time on too much exposition and preparation and the audience starts thinking, "Let's go already." Instead, hit the accelerator hard and launch straight on. Let them know what they're in for by what they experience from you in the first 30 seconds.

42. *Stop using the storyteller voice.*

   It's false. Tell a story to 10 000 people the same way you'd tell the story to your best friend. Don't use some dramatic made-up voice. Study your favorite speakers. They make you feel like it's just you and them in the room.

43. *Simplify.*

   You have no time for self-indulgence. You must be clinical and surgical with your material and your message. Don't use overly obfuscating verbiage when you can say things simply. See what we did there? We get attached to bits that really don't further the story or resonate with the audience, perhaps because they're funny or easy for us or have a special meaning to us. But it's not about us. It's never about us. It's always about them.

44. *You don't need to slow down.*

   Most speech teachers tell you to slow down. Sometimes that makes sense. But if you're worried about speaking too quickly, you're focused on the wrong thing. Instead of slowing down, focus on pausing. Speakers who speak too slowly have a soporific effect. Great orators can speak quickly, but they pause at the right place. That creates rhythm. Audiences can easily absorb the important points if you offer them the power of the pause.

45. *If you have to explain a joke, it's just not funny.*

   No joke gets funnier with explanation. Choose a better joke or let go of it altogether.

46. *Never turn your back to the audience.*

   Unless it's intentional to make a point or convey an emotion, of course. When you need to move upstage (that's toward the back of the stage, away from the audience), walk backward if possible. Try not to turn your back on them.

47. *Never yell at your audience.*

   This shouldn't need saying, but we sometimes get so fired up about what we believe in that we start shouting at the audience.

Be aware of how you're coming across. Also, if you need to get everybody's attention after a coffee break, for example, simply raise your hand and stand silently. People will get it and follow. If you yell at an audience to come back to their seats, you'll lower your status and potentially create some animosity with the audience members.

48. *If you think you're going to rise to the occasion, don't bet on it.*

Under pressure, you don't rise to the occasion; you fall back on your training. If you think you're going to somehow be inspired to come up with the right material during the speech without significant preparation, don't bet on it.

49. *Have fun.*

Some speakers will often book a speech and then worry that they didn't prepare for it and wind up frustrated at how poorly they're giving it. That's not a particularly powerful place to be when performing. No audience has more fun than the speaker. If you enjoy giving the speech, they will be much more relaxed receiving it from you. You can make mistakes, lose your place, and even trip all over yourself, and still steal the show.

50. *Read* Steal the Show.

Read *Steal the Show: From Speeches to Job Interviews to Deal-Closing Pitches, How to Guarantee a Standing Ovation for All the Performances in Your Life.* It's a *Wall Street Journal, USA Today*, and *Publisher's Weekly* best-seller. And, the president of Starbucks, Howard Behar, said, "*Steal the Show* is the most unique and practical book on public speaking ever written." So, there's that.

Many Rules Are Made to Be Broken

But to break the rules of performance, you need to know what the rules are. You need to know why they exist and exactly why you're breaking them. When you break the rules with a real purpose, you can achieve a better and more effective result.

Be prepared if you want to make life-saving, world-changing speeches. That's what *Steal the Show* can do for you: make you a much, much better public speaker and performer in all aspects of life.

A performance can be about wowing an audience, but it can also be about simply connecting with one person. Most important, you don't have to be an entertainer to be a performer. And you don't have to think of yourself as a performer today to use what we teach here and in *Steal the Show* tomorrow.

To Speak or Not to Speak, That Is the Question

It's important to be aware of what your talents are and to not use the speaking strategy if public speaking isn't one of your strengths, which isn't to say you can't get better at public speaking and performing – you can. You integrate what you learn by melding your first presentation into your second, and so on. However, I wouldn't suggest using the Speaking Strategy as one of your primary self-promotion strategies if you really aren't comfortable speaking in public or just don't want to.

Having said that, we'd like to make a key distinction: even if you're feeling stage fright at the thought of public speaking, that doesn't mean you don't have the ability to be a good public speaker. Michael, one of the most accomplished professional speakers in the world, is nervous before almost every single speech he gives. He'd be worried if he weren't, because it's natural to feel nervous in such a situation. If you're drawn to speaking and would like to give it a try, then by all means, go for it.

> *If you feel called to share a message, it's because there are people in the world who are waiting to hear it.*

Your job is to work hard to find the people who are waiting to hear your message and not let the naysayers – the people who don't like what you're doing – deter your from finding those you're meant to serve. This principle can drive you and keeps you going when the going gets tough. It prompts us to say again to you, if you feel called to speak, to share your message, there are people out there waiting to hear it.

The Book Yourself Solid Speaking Strategy is a great way to establish yourself as a category authority, get your message out to the world in a bigger way, and allow you to reach more of those you're meant to serve.

The Book Yourself Solid Writing Strategy

Words are, of course, the most powerful drug used by mankind.
—Rudyard Kipling

Article writing is an effective way to create awareness for your services and build your reputation. Using the Five-Part Book Yourself Solid Writing Strategy you'll learn how to write effective articles and post them online, one of the most effective ways to generate traffic to your website.

You'll also learn how to analyze some of the different offline writing markets and the steps to get editors to publish your articles. Writing articles and publishing them online and offline will help you establish your reputation as an expert while generating interest in your products, programs, and services. By publishing online and offline, you will imprint your position as a category authority as widely as possible.

If you consider yourself a writer, you're going to say, "Yes, this Book Yourself Solid Self-Promotion Strategy is for me, and I'm going to jump on this right now." If you don't picture yourself as a writer, you might be inclined to skip this chapter, but please don't. Even nonwriters can learn to write effective articles.

Michael's fourth-grade teacher said he had the worst spelling she had ever seen in her 25-year career in teaching. Many years later, when he told one of his childhood friends that he had sold a book to a big-time publisher, his friend questioned how he could do that without his help. He still had an impression of Michael as the kid who didn't even like to write five paragraphs for a high school essay. But he wound up writing a lot more than five paragraphs – and a few good ones, too.

The point is that we don't want you to miss out on this important self-promotion strategy simply because you think you can't write. If you can speak, you should be able to write well enough to use the Book Yourself Solid Writing Strategy. You're not writing the Great American Novel here. You're writing to educate the people you serve and promote the services you sell. Even if writing isn't one of your natural talents, it's a skill that can be learned well enough for you to master the Book Yourself Solid Writing Strategy and can be improved upon through practice.

How to Get Out of Writing

Does the thought of having to write an article still make you cringe? Okay, we get that. There are two other ways to gain the benefits that article writing provides without going anywhere near a keyboard:

1. Hire a ghostwriter.
2. Collaborate with another subject-matter expert who likes writing.

Ghostwriters are professional writers who will custom write an article for you on the subject of your choice for a fee. Your name and business information appear in the byline. Sure, it costs a little, but it's still a comparatively inexpensive marketing tool. And once you've got it, you can use it in many different ways:

- Send it to related websites and newsletters that accept submissions
- Publish it in your own newsletter
- Upload it to your own blog and announce it to your mailing list
- Submit it to print publications that cater to your area of expertise

You can get a lot of mileage out of one article, especially if it's of professional quality.

Collaborating with another subject-matter expert who likes writing is another way to get the word out about your services. If you know someone who can write well, consider pitching a joint venture to this person. You provide the expertise, and they provide the writing skills to prepare an article based on your supplied information. Then both of your names and website addresses appear together in the author's box at the end.

This sort of collaboration is a great way to solve the I-dislike-writing problem while effectively promoting two businesses at once.

The Five-Part Book Yourself Solid Writing Strategy

The publishing part of the article writing strategy really isn't that scary. What most people find daunting is the actual writing of the article. So, let's start with how to do that.

Part 1: Deciding on the Subject
Part 2: Choosing an Ideal Topic
Part 3: Creating an Attention-Grabbing Title
Part 4: Writing Your Article
Part 5: Getting Your Article Published

Part 1: Deciding on the Subject

What is your subject? A subject is a broad category of knowledge – design, marketing, fashion, business, society, and recreation are all subjects. It's possible you already know a great deal about the subject of your article, or maybe you're curious about a new subject and want to expand your knowledge of it. To help identify a direction for your writing, ask yourself these questions:

- What am I passionate about?
- What interests me on a personal level?
- What is the scope of my expertise?
- What life lessons have I learned?
- What is my target audience interested in learning?

Answering these questions will help you find good subjects. Of course, you should always remember the golden rule of writing: write about what you know. If you feel stuck, it might be because you've strayed from a subject that relates to your products, programs, and services, since this is probably what you have the most knowledge about. Or, it might be because you're trying to demonstrate that you're smart by attempting to write like an academic.

Don't forget to explore your personal interests as well. Consider subjects based on hobbies, family, community involvement, or charity work. Your life experiences can provide you with endless ideas for article writing.

4.14.1 Written Exercise: List three subjects you would feel comfortable writing about on the basis of your passions, your personal interests, your areas of expertise, the life lessons you've learned, and what your target market is interested in learning. Once you've chosen one subject area to write about, you're ready to narrow it down to an ideal topic.

Part 2: Choosing an Ideal Topic

A topic is a specific, narrow focus within your subject area. Subjects such as design, marketing, and business are too broad to write about, especially since article pieces are usually between 500 and 3000 words. Have you ever noticed that most articles and books (other than reference materials) are focused on a narrow topic? The reason is simple – it makes the writing (and reading) more manageable.

Let's say you're writing about marketing. You might choose a topic like how digital marketing evolved from traditional marketing methods, the role of social media in modern marketing strategies, effective content marketing frameworks, or the growing importance of the growing impact of video in engaging audiences.

The following examples demonstrate how to narrow a broad subject area to reach a focused topic.

From Broad Subjects to Focused Topics
Marketing → Video Marketing → Creating Compelling Video Content to Boost Engagement

Marketing → Social Media Marketing → Effective Strategies for Instagram Marketing

Design → Sustainable Design → Eco-friendly Materials for Modern Interiors

Design → UX Design → Enhancing User Experience Through Intuitive Interfaces

Design → Typography → Choosing the Perfect Font for Your Brand

---

4.14.2 Written Exercise: List three focused topics you would feel comfortable writing about based on the subjects you chose in Written Exercise 4.15.1.

Determine your objective for writing: Now that you've chosen a focused topic for your article, you need to establish a clear purpose or objective. Are you writing to inform, persuade, explore new territory, or express your personal opinion? Knowing your objective will help you zero in on the content of your article. Ask yourself these questions:

- What do I want to teach the reader?
- What life experience do I want to share?
- Do I want to venture into new territory?
- How do I want to be known?

Let's examine these questions in more detail. One of the most popular types of article is the how-to article, in which you teach your readers something. This is a great place to start, especially for new writers, because you can simply tap in to an area of expertise you already have, cutting out the need for hours of research. Likewise, sharing an experience that taught you a life lesson is another straightforward way of telling a story that can really affect people.

Or you can do the research on a brand-new topic, educating yourself and your readers at the same time. This keeps the writing process fresh and interesting for you.

Articles that provide links within the content to good resources (perhaps pages of your own website) are a great way to help your readers while establishing yourself as a reliable source of information.

Deciding now what sort of expert you want to be known as will help you determine the objective of your articles. Let's say you are a copywriter focused on working with online course creators. Writing a series of articles on how to write compelling long-form sales pages to sell online courses is a great way to tap into your existing knowledge base while establishing a reputation for yourself as a copywriter who understands the intricacies of the online education market. That kind of credibility can drive new business to your door without spending a cent on advertising.

Understand your target audience: So far you have narrowed your subject to a focused topic and established your purpose for writing the article. Now it is time to consider your reader.

As we discussed in Chapter 2, your target market is a group of clients or prospects with a common interest or need that you can meet. The same is true for the target audience of your article – a group of people united in their common need for the information you have to share.

To zero in on who they are, ask yourself these questions:

- What do I know about my audience – income, age, gender?
- How educated is my audience – specialized, literate, minimal education?
- How much do they already know about my topic?
- What do they need to know that I can teach?
- Are there any misconceptions about my topic that I can clear up for them?
- What is my relationship with my target audience?
- How else can I help my readers?

Digging deep to ponder and answer these questions about your readers will help you develop a mental picture of their lives and their needs. Let's say you decided to run in a marathon, but you've never run in one before. You know there must be thousands of other people out there just like you who would like to run, get fit in the process, and just feel the satisfaction of knowing they can do it. Your target audience in this case would be people who are highly motivated, health conscious, open to challenges, curious, and willing to try something new. Defining them was easy because they are just like you. Of course, writing about this would only be worthwhile as a self-promotion activity if these were the people you wanted to serve.

If you know that people in your target market need simple information on the topic you want to write about, and you can describe them as we just did, that knowledge will help you to define:

- *What* you will tell them
- *How* you will tell them: your tone, vocabulary, and style of writing

Hot buttons: Another way to understand more about your readers is to study the emotional hot buttons that make all of us tick. Knowing what these buttons are can help you choose topics and write articles to tap in to your audience's basic interests in life. Now that you have a topic for your article, it's time to start writing.

Part 3: Creating an Attention-Grabbing Title

Creating attention-grabbing articles can make a big difference in whether it gets read or not. In fact, some writers say it's the most important part because without an arresting title, no one will bother to read the rest of your article. Here are some additional tips to help spark your creativity when writing attention-grabbing titles:

1. Select a few choice words that sum up the main point of the article. Example: *How to Renovate Your Kitchen without Spending a Fortune*
2. Tell the reader what they will learn. Use specifics: "95 percent of all" or "two out of three." Example: *New Study Reveals 75% of Users Judge a Website's Credibility Based on Design*
3. Hint at the solution your article provides. Example: *Capture Stunning Portraits Without Expensive Gear*
4. Use questions in the title to involve the reader. Example: *Is Your Brand Design Not Attracting Your Target Audience? Find Out Why*
5. Curiosity is a powerful tool, so consider a teaser title. Example: *What Do Blockbuster Movies and Viral YouTube Videos Have in Common?*
6. Promise results. Explain how your article will solve a problem for the reader. Example: *How To Write Headlines That Sell in Five Minutes*
7. Promise to teach them something using phrases like "How To" or "Five Steps to Improve." Example: *How to Pick Your Website Platform in 5 Easy Steps*

Optimize your title: If you're writing an article on how to launch a website, then you want people who are looking for this type of information on a search engine to be able to find your article. So you would do keyword research first to determine the most likely phrases your readers would use – for example, *how to launch a website, website building tips, how to design a website* – and then include one or two of those terms in your article title. If you determined that the keyword term *website design tips* is searched on more frequently than *how to launch a website,* you might write a title like this: "Website Design Tips for Beginners." Or you might even incorporate two popular search terms into one heading: "Website Design Tips: How to Launch Your Website Successfully."

Search engines place a lot of emphasis on words they find in headings, so including your keywords here is vitally important to getting your article found on the Web.

4.14.3 Written Exercise: Create three titles based on your topic choices. Remember, titles need to summarize in a few words what your article is about and be intriguing enough to make people who are interested in that topic – and even those who aren't – want to read more. If you can fit it into your top keyword phrase, so much the better.

Part 4: Writing Your Article

The introduction: The introduction contains the nugget of your story, a short capsule that summarizes what's coming in the body of the article. It builds on the topic already presented in the title and explains why that information matters to the reader, which is why it's so important to know who your target audience is.

Some writers tend to back into their story by dropping their lead nugget down to the third or fourth paragraph, but this is a dangerous tactic. In nearly all cases, the first paragraph of your article should reflect the title, elaborate on it, and hint at all the juicy information to come.

Your introduction is also the place where you set the tone for the entire article, so be sure to speak directly to your readers using the words they use frequently. A casual style will endear you to your readers much more than an academic or technical style of writing. Above all, a strong introduction presents ideas that entice the reader to keep reading.

A compelling introductory paragraph answers everyone's most pertinent question: what's in it for me? Know how your information will benefit your readers and express that in your opening statement to them. If you can't imagine what benefit they will gain from your article, it may be wise to go back and refine your topic.

> **4.14.4 Written Exercise:** Write your lead-in paragraph by presenting the most important information first. Remember to address the topic presented in your title and explain to your readers what they will gain from your article. Here's where you get to appeal personally to the readers by telling them how you can help them learn something new, solve a problem, or simply entertain them for a short while.

The body: The body of your article is where you fulfill the promise made in your title and lead-in paragraph by expanding on your theme. Here are a few tips to make the writing of this, the longest part of your article, easier:

- *Try to stick to one idea in each sentence and two or three sentences in each paragraph:* Concise bits of information are much easier for your readers to handle and are much less intimidating than long blocks of writing.
- *Use subheadings:* These are like mini-titles that explain what's coming next and help break up the writing into manageable sections. Subheadings also help you organize the presentation of your information, somewhat like an outline. Put them in bold text or all capitals to make them stand out.
- *Use lists:* Giving your readers information formatted with bulleted lists, numbered lists, or any other visual device also makes the writing easier to read. The bottom line is that even the people who are very interested in your topic are in a hurry and want to get the goods fast.
- *Be consistent with your layout:* If the first item on your list of bullet points starts with a verb, make sure the first word of every item starts the same way. For example, in this list of five points, each opening

sentence – the one in italics – starts with the imperative form of a verb: try, use, be, optimize.

- *Optimize your body copy:* The keyword phrases you selected for your title must also appear throughout the body of your article if you want searchers to have a better chance of finding it. Repeating these phrases just often enough to be effective without going overboard is an art form, so aim for a level of keyword frequency that reads naturally.

Going to the trouble of optimizing your article's body is worth the effort for two reasons:

1. It helps your article get listed higher in the search engine results than other content, especially if other writers don't include relevant keyword phrases in their articles.
2. It will satisfy people doing the search because you've helped them find information that speaks directly to their needs. And people (you) who help other people (your readers) get what they need are often thought of very highly and remembered.

So you can see that adding relevant keyword phrases to the title and body of your article helps both you and your readers.

4.14.5 Written Exercise: It is time to write the body of your article. You need to elaborate on and fulfill the promise made in your introduction by backing up your statements with facts. Refer to the points listed earlier if you get stuck. And remember that you don't have to get all the words perfect in the first draft. Much of writing is about rewriting and editing. At this point, concentrate on the broad strokes and allow yourself to enjoy the process.

The conclusion: Have you said everything you wanted to say? Then it's time to wrap it all up. The conclusion is easy because it's simply a summing up of everything you just wrote. The point is to leave your readers with an easy-to-remember summary of your main theme so that it is reinforced in their minds.

If you were simply to finish your article on point nine of a list of tips, your readers would feel they were left hanging. It's human nature to crave a satisfying ending to a story. You can leave them on an even sweeter note if you share with them how they can best use the information to their advantage, and you can offer a few words of encouragement.

Write a conclusion using these guidelines:

- Restate your main points, wrapping them up in a neat summary.
- Encourage readers to try your advice.
- End on a positive note.

4.14.6 Written Exercise: End your article with a strong closing. Write a conclusion by summarizing your key points from the body of the article and tell the readers how they can best use the information you just gave them.

The author's resource box: This is where you get to take a bow, share something pertinent about yourself or your business, and invite your readers to take an action. It's also an important opportunity to offer your services.

At the end of every article is a separate paragraph of about five or six lines (this depends on the guidelines of each publication, so check with them before submitting). This resource box or author's bio can be used in several ways. Most authors put the following information in their resource boxes:

- A brief explanation of who they are and their expertise.
- A line or two about their business or the special offer they want to promote.
- A call to action that prompts readers to either phone, click a link, or make contact in some other way.
- *Optional:* The offer of a gift or other incentive to motivate action.

The key to writing your resource box: To make sure your resource box is effective, clearly invite action and explain why this action would benefit your readers. This applies to whether it's signing up for a free report, a complimentary consultation, a newsletter subscription, or simply a visit to your website to learn more about your products, services, and programs or to read more of your scintillating articles!

> **4.14.7 Written Exercise:** Create your author resource box. Remember to include your area of expertise, your business or offer, a specific call to action, and pertinent contact information and links.

Let it simmer and proofread: Now take that article you have so carefully and lovingly created – and ignore it. Set it aside for *at least* a day. Return to it later and take the time to read it out loud. This is when any dropped words or weird phrasing will become apparent. Check your grammar and spelling. Polish your work to perfection. Ten rereads are not excessive; each time you'll see something that could be said better, tighter, or more accurate. Always read your writing out loud. Many people – like me – will hear errors that their eyes don't see on the page.

A word about spelling checkers: your word processing program has a spelling and grammar checking function. Use it, but don't depend on it. You could use a spelling checker and still make spelling errors. For example, you might have typed *here* when you meant to type *hear*. The English language is a mess, and although they're getting better, most spell checking programs can't comprehend which word you meant to use or should have spelled differently based on how you used it. Also, share your articles with others and accept their help to spot any spelling or grammar problems that you may have overlooked.

> **4.14.8 Booked Solid Action Step:** Compile all the accumulated elements of your research and writing to complete one article of 500–750 words on the topic of your choice, including the resource box. When it's polished to your satisfaction, share it with friends, colleagues, or a writing group to gain valuable insight on your writing progress.

Part 5: Getting Your Article Published

This is when the fruits of your writing labor pay off. After you have completed writing your article, you'll want to search for websites and the publications that will help share your writing with the world.

Getting published online: The Internet offers a number of unique environments to display your written work, thereby generating traffic to your website, building your credibility, and increasing visibility for your products, programs, and services. Here are some examples:

- Niche websites and blogs
- Facebook, LinkedIn, Medium, and other social media sites
- Numerous online magazines
- Email newsletters

Let's take a closer look:

- *Niche websites and blogs:* The owner of a niche website or blog requires quality content written on specific topics relevant to their audience. The web owners' agenda is to keep their website fresh with articles that cater to their targeted readers; they look to writers like you to supply them with this free content.
- *Facebook, LinkedIn, and other similar social media platforms:* LinkedIn provides you with the ability to publish your content. When you click "Write an article" on your homepage, you are redirected to a blog-like platform in which you can create your content and upload a header image. You can create a hotlink that will enable you to lead capture. Public Facebook pages and other social media platforms allow you to do the same.
- *Numerous online magazines:* There are hundreds of online magazines that serve your target audience, and they're constantly trying to find content providers like you to fill their "pages."
- *Email newsletters:* Electronic newsletters come in all shapes and sizes on varied topics. You write the content, share it with these publishers, and immediately gain access to their readers who are also your target audience. The publisher gains credible content without needing to write the articles, and you reach a larger group of prospective customers.

Where should you start? Consider your target audience and where they're most likely to spend their time online. These are the hot spots you'll leverage to display your writing on a consistent basis. However, before you start the submission process, there are a few more details you need to consider:

- *Researching relevant environments:* Locate the specific environments that cater to your target audience, familiarizing yourself with the article submission guidelines.
- *Creating an article summary:* Write a short synopsis of your article.
- *Choosing keywords and keyword phrases:* Make a list of your keywords and keyword phrases. (These should be the same keywords and key-word phrases you used to prepare your title and article copy for the search engines.)
- *Listing the word count:* Some content sites will require a word count of your article. The total word count usually includes all words plus the title and resource box that make up your entire piece.
- *Checking your spelling and grammar:* Check your article before sub-mission. I agree with Mark Twain, who said: "I don't give a damn for a man that can spell a word only one way." Unfortunately, not everyone agrees. One misspelled word can really turn people off.
- *Preparing an email:* Write a letter to the publishers detailing what your article is about and why it would benefit the content provider's readership. Insert a copy of your article into the body of the email correspondence.

4.14.9 Written Exercise: List five online magazines that serve your target market.

4.14.10 Booked Solid Action Step: Submit your article once you've followed the preceding Book Yourself Solid Writing Process.

4.14.11 Written Exercise: List five email newsletter publications that serve your target market.

4.14.12 Booked Solid Action Step: Submit your article once you've followed the preceding Book Yourself Solid Writing Process.

Consistency is the key to writing and publishing articles as a marketing tool. The idea is to saturate your target market so when a potential client is searching for valuable information, your name and articles come up again and again within the search engines' results.

Getting published in print: Once you're comfortable with sharing your written work online, you might consider branching out and offering articles to print publications. Writing for the print market can be a more competitive process, but it's also very rewarding.

Plan your print publishing strategy:

1. Think big but start small.
2. Request the writing guidelines.
3. Analyze the contents.
4. Write a query letter.
5. Send the letter.
6. Follow up with the editor.

Let's examine each step in more detail.

Think big but start small: Rather than going for the large mainstream magazines, shoot for the small, focused publications such as local newspapers and magazines, trade journals, or neighborhood community newsletters. These publications are more likely to accept your work and even help edit your articles for suitability.

Once you've been accepted to write in one of the smaller publications, you can build your portfolio of printed pieces and approach the larger markets. This is important because many large-publication editors won't consider your writing ability unless they can see you have been previously published. It's similar to when you're trying to break into the speaking circuit: you start at the local level, step up to the regional level, then move up to the national level, and finally go to the international level. It's the same concept when you're trying to get your writing in print publications.

Request the writing guidelines: Never submit articles without understanding what the publication is looking for and accepts. You need to be aware of word count, spacing format, style, and the type of information each publication is looking to include. For more detailed information on writing guidelines for thousands of print publications, pick up a copy of *Writer's Market 100th Edition,* by Robert Lee Brewer (Writer's Digest Books, 2021).

Analyze the contents: Your chances of getting an article accepted for print will greatly improve if you take the time to become familiar with the publication. Either purchase a subscription or several back issues; then analyze the contents by looking at items such as article length, the tone of the writing pieces, the topics covered, the balance of short articles versus long, and how many illustrations or photos were used.

Write a query letter: Now that you know which topics you want to write about and have identified the publications you want to write in, it's time to write a letter to send by email. A query letter is basically a proposal that pitches your article idea. You can send a query letter about an article that has already been written or an article that hasn't yet been created, as a way to feel out the publication's enthusiasm for your idea.

Your query letter should follow the rules of a good business letter. It must immediately grab attention and convincingly sell your article idea. Use bullets to list key points for easier reading.

Follow up with the editor: After sending your query letter by email and waiting the appropriate time for a response, follow up by telephone. Your objective is to inquire whether the editor is interested in your article and if they require additional information. If the editor's response is no, don't be pushy and try to change their mind. Instead, ask if there is a different slant to the article that might be of interest or whether they know someone else who might be interested in your piece.

4.14.13 Written Exercise: List three print publications that serve your target market.

4.14.14 Booked Solid Action Step: Submit your query letter to the print publications you identified in Written Exercise 4.14.13.

Help Editors Help You

Every publication has an insatiable hunger for good content. They're looking for articles that will inform and entertain their readers – pieces that will help them improve their lives, whether it's how to save money, lose weight, build self-esteem, or build a shelving unit.

Most editors need good writers who also happen to be experts in their field – like you. They usually have to pay top dollar to staff writers or freelancers to provide it. So if you can give them good articles at no charge, the publication saves time and money, and you get great exposure.

A solid relationship with an editor can help you gain insight to:

- What type of information is being considered for future publication
- What kind of story may be needed in the future
- How to strengthen your chances of being interviewed to write a particular story

Consideration goes a long way in the print publishing business. You'll discover that the most vital component for building relationships with editors is listening and providing the best information to meet their needs. If you stay in contact with them and consistently work to supply them with good stories, you'll successfully build relationships that will provide publicity for you and your business over time.

4.14.15 Written Exercise: Decide on an ongoing schedule for submitting your articles. This can be weekly, every other week, or monthly.

4.14.16 Booked Solid Action Step: Schedule the time you'll need to write and submit new articles and then do it.

It's important to learn the art of delayed gratification. While it's natural to want instant results, this is a process, not a magic formula for overnight fame and fortune. One of the greatest mistakes we see creatives make is giving up too quickly when their initial efforts don't produce immediate results. It's the cumulative effect that will pay off, so be consistent and be tenacious. Don't give up.

15

The Book Yourself Solid Web Strategy

The Internet is becoming the town square for the global village of tomorrow.
—Bill Gates

Having a strong online presence is indispensable for today's creative service providers. Why? Well, you know this, but we'll say it anyway – the Web is a powerful tool for starting and continuing conversations with potential clients. So, yes, you need a brand-building website that starts conversations with potential clients to turn them into current clients. That said, using online marketing as a primary strategy for promoting your services is not essential, nor is it necessarily effective for marketing your creative services. The Web can be *very* effective, but hardcore Internet marketing is not for everyone and every business. If the highly specialized Internet marketing gig is not right for you, then it won't be effective.

If you don't want to become an Internet marketing maniac, don't. Mastering tactics like search engine optimization, pay-per-click advertising, and the many other tools are for those who want to spend their time online. If that's not where your passion lies, you'll quickly become overwhelmed, and the last thing you, or we, want is for you to feel overwhelmed.

If you are simply not driven to spend your energy learning a new technology but you still want to leverage the power of the Internet, hire or partner with others who have the skills, talents, and desires that you do not. But, there is something for everyone in this chapter – novice and expert alike – so we've divided this chapter into three parts:

Part 1: Designing Your Website
Part 2: Getting Visitors to Your Website
Part 3: Building Your Social Media Platform

The Web is an extraordinary vehicle for self-expression. It offers huge opportunities for sharing who you are and what you offer, as well as the privilege of connecting with others. There is a learning curve, but all great opportunities require that we learn something new. Two of the most important rules for doing big things in the world are learning in action and working with others.

Learn in real time and in action. Don't wait until everything is perfect to go out and do what you want to do. If you wait for perfection to go out in the world and do big things, it's unlikely you're going to get there – or get anything done, for that matter. Many people hold themselves back because they think they have to know everything about how to do something before they actually do it. This is not true. You can learn while doing.

You cannot learn how to run or become a better runner without actually running. You can certainly read an article about how moving your arms in a particular way can help your stride, but until you put the tip into action, you won't really know or experience its truth. The same is true for marketing or any other new skill you're interested in learning. As you embrace each of these self-promotion strategies by learning in action and working with others who have more experience than you, you will be pleasantly surprised at what you're able to accomplish in a very short time.

PART 1

Designing Your Website

Design is not just what it looks like and feels like.
Design is how it works.

—Steve Jobs

In this first part, we walk you through the purpose and benefits of having a website, how to structure the content on your website, the most critical components your site needs to have, what to look for when hiring help, and the biggest mistake most people make online. We'll try to make it as easy to understand as a day at the beach – or at least a day at the beach with your laptop.

Purpose and Benefits of Having a Website

There are numerous purposes and benefits to having a website and developing a strong online presence, many of which we're sure you've considered. Your own website:

- *Positions you as an expert:* Having your own website increases your visibility, credibility, and trustworthiness.
- *Builds your brand identity:* Your website represents you and your business in the marketplace.

- *Reaches a global marketplace:* If you have a service available on your website, you'll expand your geographic marketplace from your local neighborhood to the entire world should you want to.

- *Creates a 24/7 passive-revenue profit machine:* The Web never sleeps, which means you can turn your computer and website into a cash register around the clock, and many, if not all, of the processes can be automated.

- *Builds your database:* A website can instantly increase the effectiveness of your sales cycle by building a targeted list of potential patients who have given you permission to follow up with them. A website with an opt-in feature allows you to provide value while building your database (by offering something of value in exchange for email addresses). Remember, your visitors must see your offers and your services as opportunities worthy of their investment, even if that investment is as small as an email address.

- *Allows for filtering out unsuitable clients:* All of your marketing materials can guide potential clients to your website, where you save precious time by allowing them to familiarize themselves with you, your services, and your process before they contact you for more information. They can then determine whether they feel they'd be well suited to work with you.

- *Provides an opportunity for bold self-expression:* Your website is a fantastic vehicle through which to express yourself. It is an extension and a representation of you and what you offer.

The Biggest Mistake Most Creative Service Providers Make Online

Before diving into the technical aspects of what makes a great website, let's address the biggest and most common mistake creative service providers make: believing their work will speak for itself. This often leads to the creation of what we call a *portfolio website*. Does this sound familiar? Your logo at the top left, with a heading like "Hi, I'm Jen. I'm a web designer based in London." Then there's a feed of photos showcasing your work.

At the bottom, you might have a vague call to action like "Have a project you want to bring to life? Let's chat!" next to your email address or a simple contact form.

While it might seem that showcasing your work should be enough to attract clients, this approach can actually hold your business back. Here's why: a portfolio website often fails to address the fundamental questions potential clients have. They may admire your work, but without context, they're left wondering, "Can this person solve my problem?" or "What specific services do they offer?" or "Are they even available for hire?" If it's too hard for them to answer these questions, they'll move on without making an inquiry, opting for a competitor who clearly addresses their concerns.

To effectively attract and convert clients, your website needs to do more than just display your work. It must clearly articulate what you do and for whom, tell a compelling story that resonates with your ideal clients, and guide them toward taking action, such as inquiring for a quote.

So, what should you include on your website to effectively attract and convert clients? Let's dive into the essential components that will make your website not just an engaging showcase of your work but a powerful tool for growing your creative business and getting you booked solid.

Essential Elements for an Effective Website

To transform your website from a static portfolio website into a dynamic, client-attracting powerhouse, you need to include a few key elements. These components will help you clearly communicate your value, attract your ideal clients, and encourage them to take action.

Clearly Communicate What You Do and for Whom

Imagine a potential client lands on your website. Within seconds, they should know exactly what you offer and whether it aligns with their needs. Too often, creative professionals focus solely on showcasing their craft without clearly communicating how they can solve specific problems. Your headline and introductory text must immediately convey your services. For instance, instead of saying "I'm Jen, a web designer," try "Grow Your Food Blog with High-Converting WordPress Sites." Follow with a subheadline like "Engage

4.15.3 Written Exercise: Create a detailed case study that showcases your expertise and attracts your ideal clients:

- Choose a past project where you achieved significant results.
- Identify the specific challenges the client faced.
- Outline the strategic steps you took to overcome these challenges.
- Detail the results you delivered, including visuals, relevant data, and client quotes.
- Present the case study in a compelling narrative format.

4.15.4 Written Exercise: Reflect on what you want your calls to action to be and what questions you want to use in the form as a filter:

- Determine the primary action you want visitors to take on each key page of your website (e.g. "Schedule a Free Consultation" or "Get a Custom Quote").
- Identify the questions you need in your form to filter potential clients. Consider what information is essential to determine if they are a good fit for your services (e.g. project details, budget, timeline).

Maximizing Your Website's Potential

Your website can make you look like a superstar, offering valuable content, experiences, and opportunities for your target market. With a professional, up-to-date modern design and loads of great content that serves your target market, you will position yourself as an expert and the go-to person in your field.

As challenging as the journey to website success may seem right now, you might be pleasantly surprised that the work you've already done in the book has set you up for success. Your website is your opportunity to decide and control how you're known — your tagline boldly expresses why you do what you do. Your site should speak to the values of your ideal clients and demonstrate how dedicated you are to your target market, their needs and desires, and the number-one biggest result that you help them get, along with the financial, emotional, physical, and spiritual benefits they will receive from investing their time with you.

Your website also demonstrates your platform and helps you build trust and credibility. Also, each of the Six Core Self-Promotion Strategies can be integrated into the way you promote and use your site. Your website can help you start a conversation with a potential client by offering free information products or experiences for new potential clients, and it's an effective way to introduce them to your sales cycle so you can build trust over time. Your site is an avenue through which you can offer various pricing incentives for your products and services, leading to super simple sales conversations with ideal clients.

Here are some specific ideas of how you can integrate the Book Yourself Solid Six Core Self-Promotion Strategies right into your site:

- *Networking Strategy:* You can invite people to join you on various social network platforms like Facebook, X (formerly Twitter), LinkedIn, YouTube, and so forth. You can also use it to connect with new people every day through your subscriber list, blog posts, and "Contact Me" forms.

- *Direct Outreach Strategy:* You can use direct outreach to get to know others in your field by commenting on their posts and also asking them if you can reprint some of their blog posts. You can even offer to write posts for them to publish on their blogs. Not only is your website a great tool for starting conversations with potential clients, it's a great way to start conversations with influencers in your industry. It's often the first thing a potential business associate will review when they are evaluating you and your relevance to them.

- *Referral Strategy:* You can implement the referral strategy by writing blog posts or articles that refer to another colleague who can help your clients with a particular problem they may be having for which you are not the expert. Or, you can create a resource page in which you profile various referral partners. Your newsletter is another opportunity to offer referrals.

- *Speaking Strategy:* You can advertise your teleseminars, classes, and events on your site. You can also feature your podcast through your website.

- *Writing Strategy:* A blog can be integrated into your site, and you can have a page with articles that help position you as an expert in your field. You can submit articles to article banks or directories that will help drive traffic to your site and enhance your status as an expert.

By integrating the core self-promotion strategies into your site, you will attract potential clients with whom you will build trust and who will ultimately become ideal, life-fulfilling, and career-making clients.

Choosing Your Platform

Now that you've come this far in the book, you're probably eager to put everything you've learned into action and get to work on your online presence. If you're not updating an existing website and are starting from scratch, you might be feeling overwhelmed by an important decision: with so many options available, where should you build it?

Choosing the right platform is a critical decision that will shape your business's presence and growth. Your website needs to do more than just look good – it must function seamlessly, integrate with your existing tools, and scale as your business evolves. While we won't name specific platforms – since the landscape evolves quickly – the principles for choosing the right one remain the same.

Start by assessing your needs. Do you need advanced features like e-commerce, blogging, or client booking systems? How well does the platform integrate with other software you use daily?

Next, consider the balance between ease of use and customization. If you prefer a hassle-free setup with minimal technical demands, look for platforms with intuitive, drag-and-drop interfaces. These are great for getting online quickly but might limit your customization options and scalability. On the other hand, more customizable platforms offer greater flexibility but may require a steeper learning curve and more hands-on management.

Budget is another key consideration. Website platforms range from free to premium services with varying costs. Be aware of potential hidden expenses, such as hosting, premium themes, plugins, and transaction fees, if you plan to accept payments via your website. Additionally, consider whether the platform includes hosting or if you'll need to purchase it separately. Align your choice with your business needs and financial resources without compromising essential features.

Support and community are crucial. Reliable customer support can save you time and frustration, especially when you encounter technical challenges. Trust us, there's nothing worse than investing time and resources into building your website on a shiny new platform only to discover a year later that you're stuck with bugs and no support. Look for platforms with a vibrant community of users and developers who can offer a wealth of resources, from tutorials to plugins, that enhance your website's capabilities.

By carefully considering these factors, you'll be equipped to choose a platform that not only meets your current needs but also scales with your business as it grows. Remember, the goal is to create a website that showcases your work as well as drives your business forward, setting the stage for sustained growth and success.

Hiring Help

Building a website, even in today's world, can be quite the task, and getting the right help can make all the difference. Whether you're a web designer in need of a developer's expertise, a developer seeking a designer's creative touch, or a copywriter who needs both, working with experts can elevate your website to new heights (and save you a lot of time too).

Let's talk about bartering for a moment. While generally we don't recommend bartering – since getting booked solid with noncash projects isn't the goal here – there are strategic exceptions. Swapping services can be a savvy solution for building your website and testing potential referral partnerships. Imagine telling a client "Tom developed my website after I designed it, and it's working great. You should work with him too!" This kind of endorsement builds trust and shows your commitment to their ongoing success.

However, if time is not something you have in abundance, you might prefer to go for a straightforward transaction. In that case, hiring professionals can be a smart investment. Hiring help allows you to focus on your strengths while experts handle the rest. Professionals bring specialized skills that can transform your website into a powerful business tool. They stay current with the latest trends, ensuring your site is visually appealing, functional, and user-friendly. This not only saves you time but also accelerates your website launch so you can focus on what you do best.

If, after reading this, you're still unsure about hiring help and prefer to take a stab at building your website yourself, you might want to check out Joana's Website in a Day Kit, which includes all the templates you need to help you write, design, and launch your website in just one day, without any copywriting, design, or coding skills required. For more details, visit https://theAmbitiousCreatives.com/website-in-a-day-kit.

Now you know how you want to *design* your website. Next up is learning how to get people to land (and stay) on your website. You're in the right place. Turn the page and you'll be on your way to traffic school – where you'll learn how to direct traffic, quickly (and safely) to your site.

PART 2

GETTING VISITORS TO YOUR WEBSITE

I think the Internet is uniquely suited to this free market idea . . . we all need each other.
—Pete Ashdown

Here is where we look at how to create a steady flow of traffic to your site and how to convert that traffic into business. We'll cover the nine most important and easy-to-understand tried-and-true techniques and strategies for generating more traffic to your site, along with the two essential principles of *visitor conversion*, so that when someone does visit your site, they give you permission to keep in touch (market to them).

A word of caution: just because we're sharing nine techniques doesn't mean you have to implement all of them. In fact, some of Joana's students are consistently booked solid using just one of these strategies. Whether you choose to master one or explore several, it's important not to feel pressured to do everything at once. Find what works best for you and your business, and remember that even small efforts can lead to significant results.

Optimize Your Site

Search engine optimization (SEO) is all about how to get the search engines to notice your site and, ideally, to give you a good ranking. Then, when someone searches for what you're offering, your listing will be displayed in a high position in the search results. SEO is a big topic. Entire books are written about it, so we'll touch on only the basics, and if you choose to make SEO a primary traffic generation strategy, we trust that you'll continue your learning elsewhere.

Make sure your site is optimized with the best keywords, that is, words or phrases that your target market types into the search engine to find what you provide, along with the proper metadata, including descriptive keyword-rich page names. Because every search engine has different criteria for ranking websites, and none of them actually wants you to know what these criteria are, the most effective strategy for SEO is to build content-rich pages that your visitors want to see, pages that are legitimately filled with the same keywords and phrases they use to search for what you are offering.

How do you determine what keywords and phrases will help you drive the most traffic? You focus on the urgent needs and compelling desires of your target market. What would a potential client type into a search engine to find what they're looking for? The best keywords and phrases are the emotional, benefit-filled terms that:

- Have the most number of searches
- Have the least amount of competition
- Draw targeted traffic that is ready, willing, and able to invest in your services

In fact, there are a number of tools that tell you exactly how many people are searching on your chosen keywords and phrases. Google offers a free keyword search tool. To find it, just search on Google for "Google Keyword Planner." When you find the right keywords and phrases for your site, optimize your site using these same words and phrases. Understanding your best keywords is essential for the success of all your online marketing.

4.15.5 Written Exercise: Identify the top five keywords and phrases for your site.

Leverage Your Email Signature

One of the most often overlooked methods of promoting your services is through your email signature file. This is the information that you put at the close of your email. It's a simple and effective way to tell people about what you have to offer and to encourage them to sign up for your newsletter or any other no-barrier-to-entry offer that you make.

You could consider asking a question in your signature file and include a link to your site where the answer to the question will be waiting.

4.15.6 Booked Solid Action Step: Create a compelling email signature and begin using it immediately.

Participate in Online Communities

There are hundreds of thousands, if not millions, of groups online discussing the issues of the day: discussion boards, forums, social networks, and others. Getting involved in the communities in which your target market hangs out offers you an opportunity to become a leader of the community by offering advice, support, and any other value. Many of these communities give you the opportunity to create a profile that displays your bio, email address, website address, and more. When you make a (good) name for yourself in a community made up of your target market, members of that community will be compelled to visit your website to learn more about you and how you are able to serve them. You find these groups by searching Google. Input the various keywords and key phrases that your target market would use to find communities built around their industry, situation, needs, and so on.

Participating in online communities offers immense value beyond just knowledge and support. These platforms can position you as an expert in your field and attract potential clients to your business. Whether you join free forums or paid membership groups, these communities provide opportunities to connect, share, and grow your business.

> **4.15.7 Booked Solid Action Step:** Find the most active online communities that serve your target market and are focused on topics you know a lot about. As a member of the group, you can make intelligent, thoughtful posts that add value to the discussion topic. You might answer other members' questions or you might suggest helpful resources or simply provide your opinions on issues that relate to your industry. And you never know – you may learn a lot by reading what others have to say.

Cross-Promote Through Marketing Partners

This is one of our favorite online marketing strategies because it allows you to partner with, and promote, other people you think are fabulous while they do the same for you. We've talked about how important it is to get other people to talk about you so you can quickly build trust with new potential clients. Well, cross-promoting through marketing partners is the best way to do so.

If your colleague sends out an email to their newsletter subscribers endorsing your services, their subscribers are more likely to trust you. When you promote them, the same will be true. It makes it much easier to build relationships with potential clients that way. It's just like meeting a great friend of a great friend of yours. You love your friend, and if your friend loves that person, you assume that person is great. The same goes for cross-promoting online (and offline).

You can cross-promote on multiple levels: with another service professional who serves the same target market or with larger associations and organizations. For example, if you're a copywriter specializing in online coaches and consultants and you develop a relationship with a design agency that already serves 300 clients within your target audience, they can promote your services to their clients. Imagine the influx of project inquiries and the potential new clients who could turn into actual clients. The possibilities are limitless.

When Delia Monk, a talented copywriter, cold-contacted Joana, Joana immediately saw her potential and began referring her to her agency's clients. Later, Delia mentioned her online course designed to attract clients.

Recognizing the opportunity, Joana promoted Delia's course to her newsletter subscribers and Instagram followers, with an agreement to split the revenue. This collaboration not only increased Delia's course sales but also brought her more clients from Joana's audience through the free workshop promotion. It was a mutually beneficial partnership that showcased the power of cross-promotion.

Here are some other strategies to consider:

- Co-produce special promotions you could not afford on your own.
- Have a contest with the prizes contributed by your partners. For the next contest, roles change, and you contribute your product or service as a prize for a partner's contest.
- Give customers a free product or service from a participating partner when they buy something that month from all of the partners listed on a promotional piece.

Online cross-promotion has the potential for a big marketing pay-off because partners can successfully expand through one another's client or client base. Both you and your marketing partners can gain an inexpensive and credible introduction to more potential clients more effectively than with the traditional lone-wolf methods of networking, advertising, or public relations.

4.15.8 Written Exercise: Come up with several of your own unique ideas for cross-promotions and identify who might be a good marketing partner.

4.15.9 Booked Solid Action Step: Reach out, connect with, and share your ideas with the people you identified in the preceding exercise.

Use Tell-a-Friend Forms

A significant percentage of your clients will come from referrals. If your current raving fans are telling others about you offline, don't you think they would like to tell others about you online as well? Well, they can with a tell-a-friend form. Imagine that a visitor to your site likes what they see and believes they have a friend who could benefit from your services, too. People use social sharing buttons regularly – Facebook, LinkedIn, and so on – but with a click on your tell-a-friend link, they can refer your site directly to that friend. You can even customize it so that it automatically sends a personalized email promoting your site and its web address.

It's an amazingly simple and effective strategy. Again, you're getting others to talk about you and help build trust between you and a potential client.

4.15.10 Booked Solid Action Step: Create, or hire someone to create, a tell-a-friend form and begin using it.

Leverage the Power of Online Reviews

If you poll people on how they choose a creative service provider, you'll find that a referral from someone they trust tops their list. However, in the absence of direct referral, positive online reviews are usually the next best thing.

Think about it for a moment, if you are in need of a new dentist and you don't have a direct referral from someone you trust, what's your first step? If you're like the vast majority of people, it would include a web search that leads you to click the first search result with the highest number of positive online reviews.

Currently, Google and Yelp are by far the most popular and most used platforms for people to find businesses based on online reviews. If you focus on just one, go with Google. As you know, it's the most popular search engine in the world.

Having more positive online reviews than any other creative service provider in your area can give you a big advantage over your competition and can generate a substantial amount of traffic to your website. If you are serious about getting online reviews on sites like Google or Yelp, don't leave it up to chance.

Unfortunately, most people are more likely to leave a review after having a negative experience than they are after a positive one. However, this can be easily overcome simply by asking clients to leave feedback. Every time one of your clients expresses appreciation for the transformation they have experienced, ask them to share their story on Google or Yelp. To make it easy, you can send them a link that points directly to the page where they can enter their review.

Take Advantage of Online Press Releases

The Internet has unleashed so many new opportunities to connect with your target market and get free publicity online. Online press releases are one marketing tactic often underused, yet effective for increasing web traffic. Online publicity opportunities can improve your site's search engine ranking while, at the same time, enhance your credibility and increase exposure to media outlets.

Consider using online press releases to increase traffic to your website. You may:

- Increase traffic to your website quickly (usually within 24–48 hours).
- Boost your credibility – it increases the know, like, and trust factors.
- Make you stand out from the crowd because it's a marketing tactic that few small business owners use.
- Deliver traffic for months and years to come because online press releases are permanently indexed by search engines.

So, what's the difference between an online press release and an offline press release? When a small business has news, online press releases are the fastest and easiest way for the media to find them. Sites like PRWeb.com and PRNewswire.com take your press release and place your news directly on leading sites like Yahoo! News, Google News, Ask.com, and other sites, which reach hundreds of thousands of news subscribers and media publications, including bloggers, journalists, and consumers. Online press releases can increase traffic to your website and increase your search engine rankings. For small business owners, PRWeb.com is by far the most feature-rich and affordable service. (Please note: We have no financial or personal connection to this service.)

Your press release must be well written and targeted. To optimize your press release for online distribution, use keywords for your business throughout the body of the press release so that when someone does a search on your business or topic, your press release shows up prominently in search engines. Keywords should be used in the headline, subtitle, and body of the release.

If you're not a writer, you can easily outsource press release writing to a freelance writer or PR agency. Many sites have press release distribution services (some may require a waiting time of 24–48 hours), most have a fee, but some offer various free options as well.

Another useful tool is an online press kit. You can add a page to your website titled "Press Kit" or "Media Resources." The page should include a personal bio, company bio, any press releases written, article placements, and a professional photo of key business personnel. In addition to adding a page to your website, you can also host your press kit with online press page services. Journalists and bloggers frequently visit these sites for story ideas and interviews.

4.15.11 Booked Solid Action Step: Write a press release about the most impressive result one of your clients achieved and submit it to PRWeb.com. You can get tips at the site on how to craft a solid press release.

Profit from Pay-per-Click Advertising

Using pay-per-click ads on search engines can be an effective marketing tool. Pay-per-click means that you pay a fee for each person who clicks the ad. You may be surprised to realize that this is the first time we've mentioned spending money on advertising. Until now our other online strategies haven't cost much besides time. You should not be spending much, if any, money online to generate traffic. If you show up in the top five regular search results for your keywords, you certainly don't need to pay for clicks. But if you're not in that top five, this is a great way to get targeted exposure for a small investment with the potential for a big return.

Pay-per-click ads on Google allow you to connect with prospective clients as they're searching for services or products like yours. You create an ad and choose keywords that, when entered into the search engine, will bring up your pay-per-click ad along with the regular search results. You pay only when someone clicks through to your site from the pay-per-click ad.

The position of your ad (highest to lowest) is determined by your bid price, the amount you're willing to pay for a click (the exception is with Google, where your position is determined by a combination of your bid price and your click-through rate). You really need to be on the first search page for your pay-per-click ads to generate significant traffic. Of course you can affect your position by modifying your bid. But don't worry – you can cap the amount of your daily spending so you don't exceed your mortgage payment in pay-per-click ads. The other great thing about being in the top three positions on Google is that you're then syndicated onto other sites and search engines all over the Internet. Facebook ads can be even more targeted.

These pay-per-click ads are good for generating traffic to your site and great for testing what keywords and keyword phrases generate a lot of traffic and what percentage of that traffic converts to potential customers and actual customers.

Just be careful: make sure you're tracking all of your efforts through Google Analytics or within Facebook. You really need to know what you're doing since you're paying for the ads. If you don't convert the ads into sign-ups and paying clients, you run the risk of spending a lot of money and not getting any real return on the investment. Keep in mind that a website is useless if you can't sell something immediately or secure the email addresses of visitors to your site along with their permission to follow up with them. You'd hate to pay for traffic to your site and not convert any of it. That's like driving a station wagon packed with cash and throwing it out the windows as you aimlessly drive around town. However, if you do convert a good percentage of that traffic to potential clients and a percentage of them become actual clients, well, now you've invested wisely. In fact, if you run the numbers, you can see your exact return on investment.

4.15.12 Booked Solid Action Step: Go to https://google.com/ads and set up an account. Then create a test ad campaign for one of your products or services. Make sure that you cap your daily spending at a low amount so that you learn how to profit from pay-per-click before you rack up significant fees. Google.com has great tutorials and help pages that can answer your questions. Track your conversion so you know what kind of return on your investment you are getting.

The Two Essential Principles of Visitor Conversion

You want to attract visitors to your website and turn them into friends, then potential clients, and finally current clients. You can generate all the traffic you want, but if that traffic does not want to stay or come back and get more information, advice, or resources from you in the future, it's not doing much good.

There are two essential principles of visitor conversion: enticement and consumption. Understand them, implement them, and profit from them, but never abuse them.

Enticement

Your website is like your home. What's the first thing you do when someone comes to visit? You offer a drink and a bite to eat. You ask, "Are you hungry? Can I get you something to eat? How about a glass of water or some iced tea?" If you know your visitors well, you can offer them their *favorite* snack and beverage. In fact, when family or close friends come to visit, you make an extra trip to the supermarket to get all their favorites.

This is the principle of *enticement*. You offer something of value to your website visitors as soon as they land on your site in exchange for their email address and permission to follow up. They give it to you because they're interested in your enticement, and they believe you'll deliver more good stuff in the days and months to come.

Be careful not to hide your enticing offers in the crevices of your website. When you have a dinner party, do you hide the food around the house in strange places or set it just out of reach? Of course you don't. You put the hors d'oeuvres and munchies in the most obvious, accessible places possible. And sure enough, the places you put the hors d'oeuvres are exactly where everybody ends up hanging out! Have you ever been to a party where the host skimped on the hors d'oeuvres? Did you find that everybody started hanging around the kitchen as they got hungrier and hungrier? We're always searching for what we want and need, and your website needs to speak to your visitors' needs and desires. So please, put your opt-in form in the most obvious place possible. We suggest you place it above the fold (the part of your home page that is visible without having to scroll down).

> **4.15.13 Booked Solid Action Step:** Reflect on what would be an irresistible offer for your potential clients that naturally leads them toward your services. Consider something that addresses their immediate needs or concerns, such as a guide on "5 Essential Steps to Take Before Redesigning Your Website" or "15 Pose Ideas to Make the Most Out of Your Personal Brand Shoot." Once you've identified this enticing offer, ensure it is prominently displayed on your website, ideally above the fold, where it's easily accessible to your visitors.

Consumption

The principle of consumption follows the principle of enticement. When your visitors have been enticed and have given you their email address in exchange for a mini-course, white paper, special report, e-book, article, audio recording, coupon, or other free offer, you must follow up to help them consume the valuable information or experience they just received. Most people don't take advantage of all the opportunities available to them. It would probably be impossible to do so. An even smaller number of people follow up on all of the opportunities available to them through the Internet and email, even the ones they've asked for. When someone does opt in to receive your free offer, he or she may not really consume it – really use it, learn from it, and benefit from it. It's your responsibility to help them do so by following up with an email.

Does it sound like it would be a lot of work? Oh, no, it's not. You can use an automatic email responder system to set up a series of email messages that are automatically sent to a new contact at any frequency you specify. You can send one a day, one a week, or one a month for a year – it's up to you. Your messages will check in with your new friend and begin to deliver the services you provide or other helpful resources.

The principle of consumption should follow the principle of enticement. It's just as you would ask your guest, the one you generously supplied with her favorite snack and beverage, "How is the tea? Is it cold enough? Would you like more ice? Is it helping quench your thirst?" Maybe you'd offer a suggestion, "You know . . . if you squeeze the lemon like so, it tastes even better." You'll ask your new friends how they're doing with the information you gave them and you'll help them consume it. If you do this well, you'll increase your likeability, and you'll create a more meaningful and lasting connection with your new friends, turning them from new friends into potential clients or maybe even into current clients.

4.15.14 Booked Solid Action Step: If you don't already have an autoresponder system to help potential clients consume your offer, set one up using MailChimp.com or ConstantContact.com.

Okay, take a break. Take a walk. Take it easy. Then, come on back as we move into Part 3 of the Book Yourself Solid Web Strategy, Building Your Social Media Platform.

PART 3

BUILDING YOUR SOCIAL MEDIA PLATFORM

---

*Social media is not a media. The key is to listen,
engage, and build relationships.*
—David Alston

Social media platforms come and go. Two decades ago, when Michael wrote the first edition of *Book Yourself Solid,* Ryze was one of the most popular business networking sites on the Internet. You've probably never even heard of Ryze. Why? Because it got wrecked, never to rise again. So, it's important to understand the principles that support successful social networking and personal platform building (how well you're known) before you focus on any particular platform.

There is so much conflicting noise about the necessity of social media and the latest trends and strategies promising overnight success, whether it's carousels, talking head videos, or dancing reels. By the time this book is in your hands, there will probably be a new trend, and these will be dated. With key social media players constantly rolling out shiny new features, it can be hard to keep up. More important, however, is to tie your web strategy back to Module Two — establishing yourself as a category authority, building trust and credibility, leading back into the sales cycle process and keep-in-touch strategy.

What most folks miss in the midst of all the noise is that social media (and the Internet) is just a tool. Many people obsess over getting lots of likes, followers, and views. But it's not about the numbers — what good are 50 000 followers if all you need are 25 clients a year? Social media should serve as a bridge to deeper engagement, enticing people to visit your website where you can further develop relationships and build trust. It's also about keeping top of mind, staying in touch, and further cementing your expertise. By focusing on building real connections and trust, you can create a genuine community and get the traction you want and deserve.

In previous editions of *Book Yourself Solid,* Michael attempted to detail all the ins and outs of how to use Facebook, LinkedIn, and X (formerly Twitter). Like the latter, however, they just change too quickly to keep the information current. So, for this edition of the book, we're going to focus on the big picture. If you understand what makes someone popular on any of these sites, you can transfer and apply that understanding to any other social media site so you can play to your heart's delight.

Like all relationship and platform development, when your focus comes to social media or online social networking, you must be willing to make a long-term commitment to the cause if you want to see long-term positive results. And, contrary to some expert advice, we don't believe in outsourcing your social media marketing to an assistant or firm — especially when you're just starting out. Sure, get help with the technical aspects of organizing a Facebook page or LinkedIn profile, if you need it, but if you really want to build your social network online, you've got to show up to do it. I mean *social* is the operative word here. And really . . . how hard can that be? You don't even have to leave your house. You just need to make the time for it. And, as you know, we need to make the time to do our marketing to earn clients. *Earn* is the operative word.

When you do build a large platform of followers on Instagram or Facebook or whatever other social media platform is the site du jour while you're reading this, over time, you'll be able to turn your networking efforts into marketing initiatives that drive sales. And, if you're interested in increasing your search engine ranking, your social media platform will help with that, too. Your return on investment (ROI) in social media networking is both quantitative and qualitative. You are likely to see more leads for new clients and increased profit and, at the same time, enhance your brand identity through positive, professional, and valuable interaction with and service to your community, industry, or field.

For this section of the chapter, we assume two things: first, that you have already done the work on building your Book Yourself Solid foundation; and second, we are assuming that you have a basic knowledge of social media. You're probably active on one or all of these platforms: Facebook, LinkedIn, X, Instagram, Snapchat, and YouTube.

Social media allows a small business person to create awareness about their services within a very short time. Social media makes it possible for you to reach out to the most prominent figures in your field. It can accelerate the process of gaining credibility and trust — all for little or no cost.

Most of these platforms integrate seamlessly with your website, blog, and other social media channels. For example, your blog posts can be automatically shared on your LinkedIn or Facebook page, and your Instagram posts can be cross-posted to Instagram and Facebook Stories. This interconnectedness ensures that your content reaches a wider audience without extra effort on your part.

All of this is great but . . . yes, there's a but . . . you may actually be spending too much time on social media platforms for very little return on your time investment. Generally, we don't need to encourage people to use social media more. On the contrary; in fact, we very often encourage folks to pull back. Spending a little time on each of five different platforms takes up a lot of time in total but often disperses your efforts and waters down any chance of building a real presence. However, focusing your efforts on one platform — one that you enjoy and is filled with your target audience — is often a better and faster way to build an audience when you're starting out.

As teachers and coaches, we attempt to help our students understand how to behave in a given situation, culture, or environment and how things fit together (context). Identifying (and then learning to master) the important details is pretty easy once you know what you're looking for. How to do something becomes pretty easy once you know the rules, how it works, and how the pieces fit together. You can see the pieces more easily if you know what you're looking for.

We encourage you to focus on the big picture of social media and how you're going to use it before getting worried about all the clever little marketing hacks you think you're supposed to be doing on these platforms.

Optimizing Your Social Media Strategy with the Book Yourself Solid System

Social media can be a powerful tool in your Book Yourself Solid arsenal, but like any tool, it must be used wisely. With countless platforms and ever-changing trends, it's easy to feel overwhelmed. The key is to integrate social media into your overall strategy, focusing on quality interactions rather than sheer quantity. By doing so, you can build a strong online presence that complements your other marketing efforts.

Before diving into the specifics, it's crucial to understand what you aim to achieve with your social media efforts. Social media can serve many purposes for your business:

- Finding clients
- Finding networking partners
- Cross-promoting with strategic alliance partners
- Earning credibility
- Creating visibility
- Announcing events
- Promoting your products and services
- Driving traffic to your site
- Driving traffic to your blog
- Building your email list
- Having sales conversations
- Creating a base of raving fans

Now, let's dive into how you can apply the Book Yourself Solid System on social media to achieve these goals. Almost every aspect of the Book Yourself Solid System can be used on social media once you have done the work on your foundation.

1. *Who knows what you know, and do they like you?* One of the most powerful uses of social media is to showcase your expertise in your field. You are able to list your qualifications in your profiles. By making frequent valuable posts to the sites, people get to know what you know. All the social media platforms have the ability to accelerate

the process of gaining credibility. As a creative service provider, addressing your target markets' burning questions and providing loads of value through social media posts is a tremendous way to quickly spread awareness and build credibility.

2. *Book Yourself Solid Sales Cycle process:* By being actively engaged with prospective and active clients on social media, they know that they can find you there and what you can do for them. Since you know who is online among your friends or followers, you can connect through a real-time conversation. By having information that is salient to your target market, you can make your profiles "sticky" through content-rich, informative, interesting posts that invite interaction. Social media can also provide the platform for sales conversations (when the time is right) for those who are following you. You can also announce your "always-have-something-to-invite-people-to" event on your platform of choice. The key is to motivate people to go to your website and subscribe to your mailing list. If you can do that, you can market to them appropriately, moving them through your sales cycle process.

3. *Super simple selling:* Facebook allows you to have many interactions with people and gives them easy access to you when they want to reach you. Because you can connect, you are able to have real-time sales conversations right when it counts.

4. *Networking strategy:* All of the platforms make it easy to share your network, knowledge, and compassion with others.

5. *Direct outreach:* Because social media enables so many connections, it can be easier through social media to meet people you want to get to know. However, it is important to note that when you do reach out, do it with a message that introduces yourself and recognizes the person for his or her accomplishments. Never send a message to someone you do not know asking him or her to do something for you. We know we've said this before.

6. *Referral strategy:* Social media makes it easy to not only give referrals to others, but to promote others' efforts. One of the best ways to get others to help you promote your business is for you to promote their business.

7. *Keeping in touch:* All social platforms make it easy to stay in touch. You can easily send messages, or engage in a chat. It is very easy to make it personal on social.

8. *Speaking and demonstrating:* You can hold Facebook Live streaming events and you can promote your webinars or live events. Your podcast or YouTube channel can make your name as a speaker and thought leader.

9. *Writing:* Facebook and LinkedIn, especially, give you a phenomenal platform for writing. Not only can you write short posts that inform your audience of what you do, but you can also provide information of value and write posts that encourage interaction. Facebook and LinkedIn give you many avenues for your writing, which will enhance your credibility and help position you as an expert in your field.

10. *Web strategy:* All the social platforms easily interface with your website for generating and converting traffic.

The 10, 30, 60 Rule

As we mentioned earlier, it's easy to end up spending too much time on social media with little return on your investment. Instead of spreading yourself thin across multiple platforms, it's more effective to focus on one that you enjoy and where your target audience spends their time. But even on your chosen platform, it's crucial to manage your time wisely.

That's where the 10, 30, 60 rule comes in. Whether you've decided to dedicate one, two, or five hours per week on social media, this rule helps you maximize your efforts by allocating your time effectively:

- **10% of your time:** Spend this portion of your time *actively* scrolling through your feed and engaging with others. Comment on posts, share articles, and interact with the content of people you want to stay connected with (like your Network of 90). This keeps you visible and engaged in your community, showing genuine interest in others' work. Please note we highlighted the word *actively*. Passively swiping through stories doesn't count.

- **30% of your time:** Dedicate this time to creating and posting your own content. Whether it's writing posts, creating videos, or sharing valuable insights, focus on delivering high-quality content that positions you as an expert in your field. This helps attract and retain your audience's attention. We'll get more into this later.

- **60% of your time:** This is where the gold lies. Use the majority of your time for direct messages (DMs). Reach out to potential referral partners, prospective clients, and current and past clients. This is where you can nurture connections, check in, offer assistance, and generate business opportunities.

When reaching out cold to someone she believes would be a great addition to her network, Joana sometimes prefers to reach out through social media. She leverages the power of features like leaving a video or voice note, adding more personality and trust to her message. The recipient can then check out her profile and get to know her better before deciding whether to reply. Doing so often accelerates the connection and rapport, making it easier to establish meaningful relationships.

By following the 10, 30, 60 rule, you ensure that your social media efforts are balanced and effective. This approach emphasizes meaningful interactions over mindless scrolling, helping you build a genuine community and achieve the traction you want and deserve without getting overwhelmed by the noise.

Remember, social media is not just about broadcasting your message; it's about engaging with people, building trust, and creating lasting connections that can drive your business forward.

Capture, Edit, and Amplify

While there are many different types of formats you can use to create content for social media, none is more powerful or receive more reach than videos. Social media platforms like Facebook, Instagram, TikTok, and YouTube tend to favor video content over all other types and will distribute video content to a wider audience than content containing only text or photos. With that in mind, here are three tips to help you create video content that will get you the best results.

1. *Capture:* It may seem obvious, but the first thing you'll need to do is capture the video content you want to share. Don't overthink this step. You don't need a fancy camera or studio setup to record video

content for social media. In fact, you can simply use the smartphone you have in your pocket. Recording video on a smartphone can actually be advantageous as it creates a more spontaneous and authentic look and feel, which often works well on social media. Just remember to shoot in a vertical format if you are creating video content for Instagram, TikTok, YouTube Shorts, or any other social media platform that is optimized for use on smartphones. The mantra "done is better than perfect" applies here.

2. *Edit:* Sticking with the theme of creating a spontaneous and authentic look and feel with your videos, you don't need to do any over-the-top editing before posting your video. However, we do recommend that you add captions to your video. Studies have shown that around 85% of people consuming video content on social media do so without any audio. This means that videos with good captions have better retention, which in turn sends signals to the social media platforms to distribute those videos to a wider audience, meaning more views for you.

3. *Amplify:* When you post a piece of content on social media that performs well with your target market organically, we recommend you amplify that piece of content. While paid options like Facebook's "Boost" button can be effective, we recommend starting with more personal and organic methods. Share the content with your email newsletter subscribers, ask clients or partners to share it on their networks, and encourage clients to comment on it to help increase its reach. These strategies can help your content gain wider visibility and engagement without immediately resorting to paid promotion.

Consider Joana's experience: one of her carousel Instagram posts on branding went viral, reaching more than 10 000 people organically compared to her usual reach of around 800. Recognizing its potential, she submitted it as a guest post to a larger Instagram account, confident that it would perform even better with their broader audience. The result? The post reached 300 000 people, and Joana gained slightly more than 10 000 followers organically within 48 hours, along with a surge of inquiries for her agency's branding services.

25 Creative Content Ideas to Overcome Posting Block

Use these prompts to help you get started with content.

1. *Answer FAQs*

    Think of questions you get asked on discovery sales calls or when potential clients enquire about a project. Answer each of them in a separate video.

2. *Before and Afters*

    Who doesn't love a good before and after? This is a great way to show what you can bring to the table with your craft. Bonus points if you then walk your audience through your decision-making.

3. *Client Testimonials*

    Post written client testimonials or, even better, video testimonials. If collecting these is a challenge, suggest hopping on a call with the client to interview them about their experience. Edit together the best clips and grab the transcript to add a written version to your website too. And don't forget to refer to Chapter 5 for the best questions to ask when getting a testimonial.

4. *Highlight common mistakes you see other service providers make*

    Highlight common mistakes you see other service providers make (without naming names). Explain why these mistakes are detrimental to your audience's business and provide practical solutions to help avoid them. This can be both educational for your clients and effective in positioning you as the expert.

5. *Industry News and Trends*

    Share the latest trends and news in your industry, along with insights on how your potential clients can make the most of them.

6. *Client Pain Points*

    Identify and discuss the main pain points of your target clients before they hire you and how you address them when they do.

7. *Client Objections*

    Similarly, review common objections encountered during sales calls and describe how you effectively address them.

8. *Process Walk-through*

    Walk through a client project and the creative process from start to finish. You can also break it down into smaller parts, such as a post focused solely on the client onboarding process, another on the research phase, and so on.

9. *Tool Showcase*

    Highlight the tools and software you use in your work. If you're a photographer, showcase your studio setup or create a "what's in my camera bag" video. If you're a copywriter, discuss your top recommendations for proofreading software and other essential tools.

10. *Your Workspace*

    People are naturally curious. Invite your audience into your workspace and share a behind-the-scenes look at your setup. Highlight the equipment you use and any special touches that make your environment unique, such as working with your pet or using a custom keyboard. This personal insight can build a deeper connection with your audience.

11. *Your Favorites Lists*

    Create lists of your favorites, like top books in your field, inspiring artists to follow on Instagram, or the best coffee spots to work from. Although these may not directly relate to your services, they provide value to potential clients and can ignite spontaneous conversations with those who share your interests.

12. *Your Story*

    While most of your content should focus on serving your potential clients and adding value to their business, it's important to share a bit about yourself as well. When hiring you, clients want to connect with your story and background. Create a post that shares your professional journey, highlighting experiences that showcase your expertise and credibility. Emphasize key moments that reflect your passion and dedication to your field.

13. *Client Success Story*

    Share a detailed case study of a client project from start to finish, showcasing the initial challenges, your strategic approach, and the successful outcome. Include metrics and testimonials to enhance credibility and provide a comprehensive view of your impact.

14. *Creative Challenges*

    Discuss specific creative challenges you've faced in your projects and how you've successfully overcome them.

15. *Seasonal Tips*

    Provide tips relevant to the current season or upcoming holidays. This could include marketing strategies for peak seasons, creative ideas for seasonal campaigns, or relevant industry-specific advice tailored to the time of year.

16. *Creative Inspiration*

    Share what inspires you creatively, whether it's books, movies, other artists, or places you visit. Explain how these sources of inspiration influence your work and how they can spark creativity in others.

17. *Services Packages*

    Detail the various service packages you offer, breaking down what each package includes, the benefits, and any customizable options available.

18. *Weekly Roundups*

    Create a weekly roundup of valuable content for your audience, including industry news, useful articles, tips, and resources. This keeps your audience informed and positions you as a go-to source for relevant information.

19. *Your Values*

    Discuss the core values that drive your business. Explain why these values are important to you and how they influence your work and relationships with clients.

20. *Highlight a Complimentary Service Provider*

    Highlight a complimentary service provider that your clients might benefit from. Explain how their services enhance yours and why you recommend them.

21. *Tips on What to Ask in a Discovery Call*

    Offer potential clients tips on what questions to ask during a discovery call. This helps them prepare and ensures they gain the most from the conversation.

22. *How to Know If You're Ready for (Service You Offer)*

    Explain the signs that indicate a potential client is ready for the services you offer. Describe common challenges or situations they might be facing that your services can address. Highlight specific milestones or readiness indicators that suggest they could benefit from your expertise. This helps potential clients recognize their own needs and see how your services can provide valuable solutions.

23. *Success Metrics*

    Discuss how you measure the success of your projects and the strategies you implement to ensure their success. Share specific metrics and KPIs you track, and explain their significance. Highlight the importance of these indicators in evaluating performance and achieving project goals.

24. *Upcoming Events or Workshops*

    Promote any upcoming events, workshops, or webinars you are hosting or participating in. Provide details about the event, including dates, times, locations, and topics covered. Highlight the benefits of attending, such as gaining valuable insights, networking opportunities, and actionable takeaways. Share any special features or guest speakers that will be present. Encourage your audience to register or attend, emphasizing how these events can enhance their knowledge and skills.

25. *Live Q&A Sessions*

    Host live Q&A sessions on social media or your website where potential clients can ask you questions in real time. Promote these sessions in advance to build anticipation and ensure maximum participation. During the Q&A, provide thoughtful and thorough answers, addressing common concerns and specific inquiries. Use this opportunity to showcase your expertise, build trust, and engage directly with your audience. Follow up with a summary of key points and insights shared during the session to keep the conversation going.

Social Media: Pulling It All Together

If you are serious about adding social media to your self-promotion strategy, consider starting with a plan and schedule time in your day to devote to each of these platforms. Effective use of social media requires consistency and commitment. Results are not always apparent right away. Give your social media plan three to six months to start working.

Social media expert Nancy Marmelejo suggests that the ROI for social media is threefold:

1. Return on interaction.
2. Return on involvement.
3. Return on investment.

Return on interaction and involvement speak directly to the time you put into finding ideally matched followers and turning them into raving fans. These fans are the ones who gladly and voluntarily do your marketing for you. ROI starts coming in when your loyal legion of followers also become email subscribers and start responding to your offers at different stages of your sales cycle. Your interactions and involvement transform followers into folks who are ready to buy.

Start using social media by developing your own daily, weekly, and monthly routines.

Daily

- Post your updates a minimum of two or three times a day.
- Schedule 15–20 minutes of time in your calendar each day to post and monitor your social networks.
- Get involved in relevant discussions and conversations, and respond to direct messages and invitations.
- Scan your streams for new, relevant information and share it with your social network three times a day.

Twice a Week

- If you blog or podcast, write and post a new blog entry once or twice a week. If you are using article writing to promote your business or doing an e-newsletter, simply reuse the same article in your blog. Blog content can also be used for your business-related posts and updates.
- Visit other industry-related blogs and add to the conversations.

Ongoing

- Add new photos and links to videos you've produced and posted on YouTube, audio from radio or podcast interviews, and so on.

Getting the Most Out of Your Social Media Content

If the idea of creating videos, writing blog posts, and regularly posting to all the various social media sites sounds overwhelming, just remember that there are often ways you can get a lot of mileage out of a single piece of content.

For example, let's say you create a video showcasing five design tips for small business websites. You can have this video transcribed and post it on your website as a blog post. Additionally, you can break the original video into five short-form videos, each highlighting a single tip, and share them on Instagram Reels, TikTok, and YouTube Shorts. You can also send an email to your current and prospective clients featuring the original video. This strategy allows you to transform a single piece of content into multiple formats, maximizing its reach and saving you significant time in the process.

Facebook, LinkedIn, X, and videos – sometimes it can all sound so exhausting. "Do I have to?" a little voice in your head continues to protest. No, you don't, as we said at the outset of this chapter. Perhaps you have the kind of business that can flourish without social media. Great. But, for many of us, an online strategy is important and effective, and using a social media platform to its fullest helps us reach our goals more quickly; plus, maybe it's not nearly as daunting as it might seem at first. Why? Because being social about what you love to do (that is, your business) is not that hard. In fact, it can be downright inspiring to connect with others and share what you know. After all, if you love to serve your target audience, what could be better than serving them better, faster, and more easily? The Internet is your friend. Use it to make more friends. And more money.

Final Thoughts

This is not the end. It is not even the beginning of the end.
It is, perhaps, the end of the beginning.
—Sir Winston Churchill

Wow. You just read more than 87 000 words. We imagine it took considerable time and effort. That demonstrates commitment and the pursuit of mastery. The Book Yourself Solid system is provoking, challenging, sometimes scary, often exciting, and always powerful. The rewards you reap as a result of all your hard work will be well worth the time and effort you've devoted to this process. We hope you'll take the time now to acknowledge all that you've done because it's no small task. In fact, it's really big. We've covered a lot of ground, and you stuck with us, step-by-step, from beginning to end. Not everyone can say that.

You now know who your ideal clients are and how to ensure that you're working only with those who most inspire and energize you. You've identified the target market you feel passionate about serving, as well as what their most urgent needs and compelling desires are, and what investable opportunities to offer to them. You've developed a personal brand that is memorable, has meaning for you, and is uniquely yours, and you know how to articulate whom you serve and how you serve them in a way that is intriguing rather than boring and bland.

You've begun thinking of yourself as the expert you are. You're continuing to enhance your knowledge to better serve your market, and you understand the importance of your likeability factor. You know how to develop a complete sales cycle that will allow you to build trust with those you want to serve. You've learned how to begin developing the brand-building creative services that are a key part of that sales cycle, how to price your services, and how to have sincere and successful sales conversations with your potential clients.

You are networking with others in a way that is genuine and comfortable. You've learned how to build a website that will get results and how to reach out to others in a personal and effective way. You've learned how to generate a wealth of referrals and how to use speaking and writing to reach more of your potential clients. And then how to keep in touch with the multitude of potential clients you'll connect with when implementing all of the Book Yourself Solid core self-promotion strategies.

Everything you've learned is important, but even more important is to remember the philosophy that underlies the entire Book Yourself Solid system: There are people you are *meant* to serve, and they are out there waiting for you. When you find them, remember to give so much value that you think you've given too much, and then be sure to give them more.

We mentioned at the beginning of our journey that the people who don't book themselves solid either don't know what to do or do know what to do but aren't doing it. You now know exactly what to do. There are no more excuses and no more reasons to procrastinate, drag your feet, or hide in your office.

The question now is what are you going to do with what you've learned? Throughout the course of this book we've given you written exercises and Booked Solid Action Steps that can earn you more clients than you can handle. Have you been doing them throughout the book? If you have, fantastic, keep going. If you haven't, are you going to start doing them right now? Your success hinges on your continued action.

To that end, at BookYourselfSolid.com, you can continue to get support and advice about all of the concepts we've laid out in this book. If you want more help, if you want to have your own Certified Book Yourself Solid coach, and if you want to work in a structured environment that will inspire you to action and keep you accountable so that you do book yourself solid, then send us an email at support@bookyourselfsolid.com for more information.

This may be the end of this book, but that doesn't have to mean the end of our work together. Your business is a generative and iterative process. You will be changing and evolving as you adapt to the ebb and flow of your growing booked-solid business, and we look forward to continuing to serve you in the best and most effective ways we can.

We sincerely thank you for spending this time with us by learning the Book Yourself Solid system. It means so much to us that you've taken the time out of your busy schedule to read this book. It's not really ours anymore. It's yours now. We are simply honored to serve you. We hope these principles, strategies, techniques, and tips make a true difference in your life and in the lives of those you serve.

We hope the Book Yourself Solid path helps you to look in the mirror every morning and have a mad, passionate love affair with yourself, do the work that you love to do, and book yourself solid while standing in the service of others and making a difference in their lives.

We love you very much (and not in a weird way).

Think big,

Michael Port

Joana Galvão

References

Brewer, Robert Lee. 2021. *Writer's Market 100.* Cincinnati: Writer's Digest Books.

Godin, Seth. 1999. *Permission Marketing.* New York: Simon & Schuster.

Godin, Seth. 2004. *Free Prize Inside! The Next Big Marketing Idea.* New York: Penguin Group.

Mayeroff, Milton. 1990. *On Caring.* New York: William Morrow.

Peters, Thomas. 2006. *In Search of Excellence: Lessons from America's Best-Run Companies.* New York: Harper Business.

Sanders, Tim. 2002. *Love Is the Killer App: How to Win Business and Influence Friends.* New York: Crown Publishers.

Sanders, Tim. 2005. *The Likeability Factor: How to Boost Your L-Factor and Achieve Your Life's Dreams.* New York: Crown Publishers.

Younger, Ben. (Director). 2000. *Boiler Room* [Film]. New Line Cinema.

Ready to Be Fully Booked?

Get on the Fast Track to Insane Growth by Letting Three Renowned Business Experts Take YOU Under Their Wings with the Book Yourself Solid Network

It's like having three business partners who will start your engine roaring and send you out the door with a complete system you can use to propel your business, your income, and your life.

Learn more at BookYourselfSolidChallenge.com/BYS.

Join the Book Yourself Solid Network on Facebook at facebook.com/groups/bookyourselfsolidnetwork.

Email our team at questions@bookyourseflsolid.com.

Never hesitate to be in touch. We're here to serve you. And it's an honor to do so.

Fulfill Your Destiny

Thousands of others have turned their passion for what they do into an abundant career that profoundly affects others. You can too.

About the Authors

Michael Port is an American entrepreneur, author, and angel investor. A *New York Times* and *Wall Street Journal* best-selling author, Michael's nine books have been translated into 29 languages. After spending a decade delivering thousands of paid speeches on the world's biggest stages, Michael sold his first company, Book Yourself Solid Worldwide, and founded Heroic Public Speaking with his wife, Amy Port. Heroic Public Speaking develops and nurtures the next generation of thought leaders, as well as CEOs and founders, best-selling authors, business owners, and movement leaders. For more, visit HeroicPublicSpeaking.com.

At the end of the day, his most significant accomplishment and responsibility is probably just like yours: the job of being a devoted parent, son, friend, and citizen.

Please direct questions to questions@heroicpublicspeaking.com.

Joana Galvão is the cofounder of award-winning design agency Gif Design Studios. Based in Porto, Portugal, her agency specializes in brand identities and conversion-led web design and serves industry leaders in 17 countries on five continents. Additionally, in 2021, she founded the Ambitious Creatives, an online education company helping creative freelancers get booked solid with dream projects, to six-figures and beyond, without burnout. For more, visit theambitiouscreatives.com.

Joana speaks internationally on entrepreneurship and creativity, and her work and has been featured in many of the top publications and podcasts of the creative freelance industry. She is recognized for her expertise in guiding freelancers to build, manage, and scale successful creative businesses without compromising their values. Above all, Joana's proudest achievement is being a mother to her wonderful son and daughter.

Please direct questions to joana@gifdesignstudios.com.

Index

10, 30, 60 rule, 259–260

A

Accomplishment, feeling, 31
Administrative details, inclusion, 184
Adobe community, contact, 148
Affiliate fees, impact, 186–187
Agency name, operation, 36–37
All-about-me form, usage, 98
Always be communicating (A, B, C), 33
Always-have-something-to-invite-people-
    to-offer, usage, 123
American Institute of Graphic Arts (AIGA),
    contact, 148
Anticipated permission marketing, 93
Anxiety, freedom, 31
Article, writing/publication, 220–228
Artificial intelligence (AI), emergence, 98
Ask.com, press release placement, 248
Asset, indispensability, 166
Attention-grabbing title, creation,
    219–220
Audiences
   contributions, reward, 204
   education level, determination, 218
   evaluation forms/follow-up forms,
      usage, 199
   finding, process, 196
   knowledge, 198–199
   pre-questionnaire, creation, 199
   target audience, 215, 218–219

Authors, resource box (writing), 223
Automated email sequences (creation),
    CRM system (usage), 103

B

Back-end, retainer (combination), 111–112
Back-of-room sales, permission, 200
Baer, Jay, 142
Behar, Howard, 211
Blocks, release, 37–41
Blogs, usage, 225, 238–239, 257
Booked Solid Action Steps, 58, 144–145
Booking
   levels, 194–196
   presentation contents, 198
   usage/potential, 194–196
Book Yourself Solid 50/50 Networking
    Rule, 135–136
Book Yourself Solid Always-Have-
    Something-to-Invite-People-to-
    Offer, 87, 89
Book Yourself Solid Dialogue, 191
   adaptation, 54–55
   development, 52–53
   entry, ease, 58–59
   formula, 53–57
   long version, 55–57
   mid-length version, 54–55
   short version, 54
Book Yourself Solid Direct Outreach
    Strategy, 130, 155, 157

Book Yourself Solid Four-Part Sales
    Formula, 124–126
Book Yourself Solid Keep-in-Touch
    Strategy, 92
  automation, 101–103
  content, 94–96
  cool keep-in-touch, 94
  follow-up, 101, 103
  keep-in-touch tools, selection, 98–101
  product/service offerings, 94, 96–98
  special announcements, 94
  strategies/tips/techniques, 94, 95
Book Yourself Solid List of 20,
    172–173, 176, 193
Book Yourself Solid Networking Strategy,
    130, 133, 134
Book Yourself Solid Network of 90,
    145–147, 192–193
Book Yourself Solid Online Strategy, 130
Book Yourself Solid paradigm, perspective
    (shift), 122
Book Yourself Solid Referral
    Strategy, 130, 177
Book Yourself Solid Sales Cycle
  function, knowledge, 77
  no-barrier-to-entry offers, 82
  phases, sequence, 82
  process, 75, 81–87, 258
  stages, 83–87
  usage, 90–91
Book Yourself Solid Self-Promotion
    Strategy, 213
Book Yourself Solid Six Core
    Self-Promotion Strategies, 129,
    189, 238–239
Book Yourself Solid Six Keys, 77–81
Book Yourself Solid Speaking Strategy,
    130, 188, 212
Book Yourself Solid Super Simple Selling
    System, usage, 127–128
Book Yourself Solid System, 197
  design, 132
  steps, 123–124
  usage, 257–259
Book Yourself Solid Way, shift, 134–135
Book Yourself Solid Web Strategy,
    230, 253

Book Yourself Solid Writing Strategy, 130,
    213, 215–228
Brand identity, 30, 232
Branding, 27, 35–41
Built to Sell (Warrillow), 142
Bundle pricing, 112
Business
  branding/marketing materials, usage, 27
  cards, requests, 151
  resources, list, 142

C
Case studies, usage, 100
Category authority, 67–72
Chamber of Commerce meetings, 148
Claims, credibility (addition), 100
Clients
  absence, reaction, 9
  achievement, 53, 124
  assistance, need, 124
  benefits, identification, 179
  consultation session, booking, 116–117
  contact, 61
  creative services, past experiences
      (learning), 184
  desires, 27–28
  dud clients, dumping, 5–7
  experience, core benefits, 53
  experiences, creation, 192
  feelings, 125
  filtering, 233, 236
  finding, 257
  free product/service, partner
      contribution, 246
  gaining, 69
  goal, 124–125
  help, need, 32–33
  ideal clients, 14–15, 157
  importance, 66–67
  increase, absence (reasons), 131
  interaction, 124, 126, 184
  investable opportunities, presentation, 53
  knowledge, 269
  list, pruning, 9–11
  needs, understanding (development), 19
  pain points/objections, 262
  pinpointing, 19

pre-qualification, Book Yourself Solid
  Super Simple Selling System
  (usage), 127–128
pruning, continuation, 15–16
purpose/spirit, connection
  (assistance), 108
referral, reasons (identification), 179–180
relationship, 184, 194
resource, creation, 107
results, determination, 28–29
safety, feeling, 76
sales conversation request, 106
serving, Book Yourself Solid Sales Cycle
  (usage), 90–91
success story, 263
testimonials, usage, 262
thoughts, 76
urgent needs, 27, 33
Common interests, identification, 165
Communication channels, target market
  activity, 19
Communities
  online communities, leverage, 244
  power, leverage, 89
Compassion, 136, 145
Competition
  crushing, method, 134
  identification, 165
  reduction, 243
Complimentary service provider,
  highlighting, 264
Conduct, success, 170–171
Confidence, increase, 69
Connection
  creation, Book Yourself Solid Six Keys
    (usage), 77–82
  increase, knowledge (impact), 165–166
  numbers, factorial math, 139–140
Consultation sessions, booking, 116–117
Consumption (visitor conversion
  principle), 252–253
Contact
  accomplishments, identification, 165
  case, making, 173–176
  introduction, flexibility, 146
  knowledge/interaction, excitement, 166
  number, management, 146

outreach, 172
peers, identification, 165
possibilities, beliefs, 166
sharing, 137–140
usage, 134
Content, delivery, 99
Conversations, 134, 150
Cool keep-in-touch, 94, 97
Coolness, perspective, 89
Copy, colleague/client review, 100
Core benefits, uncovering/revealing,
  33, 53
CreativeMornings, contact, 148
Creative service providers, online
  mistakes, 233–234
Creative services, client past experiences
  (learning), 184
Credibility
  builders, 64–66, 123
  building, 61, 124, 127, 235
  creation, 69
  earning, 257
Cross-promotion, marketing partners
  (usage), 245–246

D
Database
  building, 101–103, 233
  management, 101–103
  program, selection, 101–102
Data, entry, 102–103
Decision maker, contact, 157
Decisive Respectful Engaged Adaptable
  Motivated (DREAM), 12
Delayed gratification, learning, 229
Demonstrations, client contact
  opportunity, 190–192
Destiny, chain link (handling), 169–170
Dialogue, usage, 52–53
Diligence, usage, 171
*Directory of Association Meeting Planners and
  Conference/Convention Directors,*
  usage, 196
Direct outreach, 258
  activity, 173
  execution, 167–169
  plan, 175–176

Direct outreach (*Continued*)
    problems, 157–164
    strategy, 238
Discount
    lowering, timing, 114–117
    strategies, usage, 115–116
    types, 115–117
Discovery call, advice, 264
Diversity, equity, and inclusion (DEI), 100
Do What statement, 43, 45, 54
Duct Tape Marketing (Jantsch), 142
Dud clients, dumping, 5–7

E
Economic conditions, impact, 117
Economy pricing, 113
Editors, assistance, 228–229
Educational events, client contact
        opportunity, 190–192
Email newsletters
    article publication, 225
    focus, 99
    keep-in-touch tool, 98
    layout, 99–100
Emails
    address, usage, 64
    example, problems, 161–163
    frequency, factors, 100–101
    list, building, 257
    preparation, 226
    public email address, contact, 159
    sequences, creation. *See* Automated
        email sequences.
    signature, leverage, 244
    version, alternatives, 161
    writing, 146
Encyclopedia of Associations, usage, 196
Energy, maximization, 127
Enns, Blair, 142
Enticement (visitor conversion
        principle), 251–252
Entrepreneur, transitioning, 28
Essence, recognition, 36
Events, 257, 265. *See also*
        Networking events
Expertise, 61, 63
    establishment, 61
    perception, 270

Q&A offerings, 190
    scope, determination, 215
Eye contact, making, 150

F
Facebook
    activity, 256
    article publication, 225
    keep-in-touch tool, 98
    Stories, usage, 256
Facebook Live, usage, 259
Fascinate (Hogshead), 142
Fear, business mentality, 134
Feedback, usage, 190
Feeling, sharing, 137, 143–145
Financial, emotional, physical, and spiritual
        (FEPS) return on investment, 107
Five-Part Book Yourself Solid Writing
        Strategy, 215–228
Flat-fee pricing, 110
Flexible pricing, 112
Formal networking opportunities, 148
Freelancers Union, contact, 148
Frequently Asked Questions (FAQs),
        answering, 262
Friends, client status, 76–77
Fun/enjoyment, 32

G
Generosity, expression, 134
Ghostwriter, hiring, 214
Giving, focus, 149
Global marketplace, website (impact), 233
Godin, Seth, 93, 156
Goleman, Daniel, 170–171
Google Analytics, usage, 250
Google Keyword Planner, 243
Google News, press release placement, 248

H
Handwritten note, sending, 146
Headlines, writing, 100
Hogshead, Sally, 142
Hug Your Haters (Baer), 142

I
Ideal clients, 14–15, 157, 182
Ideas, focus, 221

Improvement, commitment, 171
Income (creation), services (impact), 107
Industry information, 94
Industry-specific conferences, attendance/
     contacts, 148
Informal networking
     opportunities, 148–149
Instagram, usage, 98, 256
Intangibles, identification, 136
Interviews, chances (strengthening), 229
Investable opportunities, benefits
     (uncovering/demonstrating), 29–33

J
Jantsch, John, 142
Joint venture (JV), perspective, 163

K
Keep-in-touch content, 100
Keep-in-touch strategy. *See* Book Yourself
     Solid Keep-in-Touch Strategy
Keep-in-touch tools, selection,
     98–101
Keywords/keyword phrases, selection, 226
Knowledge, 22–25
     networking intangible, 136
     sharing, 137, 140–143, 145

L
Lead-generating information products,
     usage, 123
Lean In (Sandberg), 142
Level-setting statements, deletion, 127
Licensing deals, 110–111
Life experience, sharing, 217
Life lessons, learning, 215
Likeability, 72–74, 89
Limiting beliefs, release, 121–122
LinkedIn
     activity, 256
     article publication, 225
     keep-in-touch tool, 98
     recommendations, 158
Live copy critiques, provision, 190
Live demo, hosting, 191
Live Q&A sessions, usage, 265
Long-term profits, maximization, 113
Loss-leader pricing, 112–113

Love Is the Killer App (Sanders), 136
Low-cost morning retreat, hosting, 191

M
Mailers (keep-in-touch tool), 98
Mailing list, building, 99
Markdown discounts, 115
Marketing
     materials, usage, 27
     ongoing campaigns, creation, 99
     paradigm shift, 30
     purpose, 20
     social media, usage, 153
     viral campaign, creation, 99
Marketplace, domination (process), 134
Market share, gaining, 114
Marmelejo, Nancy, 265
Mayeroff, Milton, 136
Medium, article publication, 225
Mental shift, 71–72
Message, impact, 69
Michalowicz, Mike, 142
Motivation, content, 165

N
Name, usage/operation, 36–37
Natural talents, importance, 22–25
Needs, identification, 27–28
Networking
     Book Yourself Solid 50/50 Networking
          Rule, 135–136
     Book Yourself Solid Networking
          Strategy, 130, 133, 134
     continuation, 154
     formal networking opportunities, 148
     groups, contact, 148
     informal networking
          opportunities, 148–149
     online networking, social media
          (usage), 152–154
     opportunities, 147–148
     partners, finding, 257
     problems, 154
     requirement, 136
     ROI, 255
     social media, usage, 153
     strategy, 238, 258
     success, intangibles, 136
     usage, 133–134, 270

Networking events
actions/responsibilities, 149–152
business cards, requests, 151
complaining, avoidance, 152
conversations (initiation), questions
(asking), 150
eye contact, making, 150
handshake, offering, 151
host, introduction (importance), 149
inclusivity, 151
introverts, actions, 151
meeting, offerings, 150
preparation, 149
Network, sharing, 144, 172
Never Split the Difference (Voss), 142
Newsletter, writing (publication), 214
Niche club, initiation, 191
Niche websites/blogs, article
publication, 225
No-barrier-to-entry offer, 82, 123
No-cost morning retreat, hosting, 191
*NTPA: National Trade and Professional
Associations of the United States,*
usage, 196

O
Offering, awareness (creation), 106, 123
Offer specials, lowering (timing),
114–117
On Caring (Mayeroff), 136
Ongoing marketing campaigns, creation, 99
Online communities, participation, 244
Online magazines, article publication, 225
Online meetings, client contact
opportunity, 190
Online networking, social media
(usage), 152–154
Online presence, cultivation, 27
Online press releases, usage, 248–249
Online publication, 225
Online reviews, power (leverage), 247–248
Online sessions, real-time audit
offerings, 190
Online workshop, offering, 190
Open house, hosting, 191
Opportunities, benefits (uncovering/
demonstrating), 29–33

P
Package pricing, 110
Packaging, 30, 118
Pain, relieving, 1107
Passions, 22–25, 215
Patience, importance, 176
Pay-in-full discounts, 115
Pay-per-click advertising,
profitability, 249–250
Perfect pricing, 105, 107
Performance, 203–212
Permission Marketing (Godin), 93, 156
Permission marketing, types, 93
Persistence, importance, 176
Personal brand
building, challenge, 46–48
components, 36, 43
development, 34, 36
identity, development, 123
Personal permission marketing, 93
Physical/emotional stress, freedom, 31
Piece of mind, creation, 108
Pitches, deletion, 127
Playfulness, 32
Pleasure, creation, 107
Podcasts, usage, 98, 192–193
Portfolio website, 233–234
Postcards, usage, 98, 146
Posting block (overcoming), content ideas
(usage), 262–265
Poverty mindset, avoidance, 108–109
Praise, offering, 161
Prestige pricing, 113
Prices, conditions/timing, 114–119
Pricing
models, 110–114
objectives, 113–114
strategies, perfecting, 105
types, 110–113
Pride, feeling, 31
Printed newsletters (keep-in-touch
tool), 98
Print publication, opportunity, 227
Print publications, writing submissions, 214
Private consultations, scheduling, 184
PRNewswire, press release placement, 248
Process walk-through, 262–263

Product
    awareness (creation), Six Core Self-
        Promotion Strategies (usage), 106
    offerings, 94, 96–98
    promotion, 163, 257
    purchases, understanding, 123
    sales, purchases (reasons), 17
Professional opportunities,
        follow-up, 101, 103
Professional photographs, usage, 64
Profit First (Michalowicz), 142
Promotion, 163
    contrast, 160
    others, impact, 193
    usage, 159–160
Promotional content, 100
Proposal, client consideration, 173–174
Prospects, follow-up, 101, 103
PRWeb.com, press release placement, 248
Publication contents, analysis, 228
Public calendar, usage, 116
Public email address, contact, 159
Public speaking, performance tips, 203–211
Purpose, spiritual connection, 31

Q
Quantity discounts, 115
Query letter, writing, 228
Quick referral analysis, 178
Quote inquiry form, usage, 236

R
Readers
    assistance, 218
    education/teaching, 217
    interest, headlines (writing), 100
    point of view, writing approach, 100
Recommendation, supply, 158
Red Velvet Rope Policy, 3, 11–14, 123, 127
Referable Speaker, The (Port/Davis), 189
Referral
    connection, facilitation, 183
    conversation, opportunity (creation), 182
    follow-up, 183–184
    making, clarification/communication, 181
    meeting, places (identification), 180–181
    opportunities, finding, 178–179

partners, contact, 61
presentation, practice, 184–187
process, initiation, 179–184
quick referral analysis, 178
reference, identification, 179–180
requests, 182–183, 185
source, alternatives, 185–186
strategy, 238, 258
types, identification, 180
Referrers, 181, 183–184
Reflection, usage, 171
Relationship management, 171
Relaxation, 32
Relevant permission marketing, 93
Reputation, building, 89
Resource, creation, 107
Response, absence, 173
Responsiveness, importance, 66
Retainer, back-end (combination), 111–112
Reward programs, impact, 186–187
Royalty deals, 110–111

S
Sales
    conversations, 257
    cycle, 82–83, 123. *See also* Book Yourself
        Solid Sales Cycle.
    increase, 69
    purpose, 20
Sample work portfolio, client
        appreciation, 76
Sandberg, Sheryl, 142
Sanders, Tim, 136
Scarcity, business mentality, 134
Search engine optimization
        (SEO), 242–243
Seasonal discounts, 115
Self-attention, continuation, 134
Self-awareness, 171
Self-confidence, increase, 31
Self-expression, 27, 134, 233
Self-management, 171
Self-promotion, 189–193
Selling, 122–123, 126–127
Service
    awareness (creation), Six Core Self-
        Promotion Strategies (usage), 106

Service (*Continued*)
    client awareness, 123
    creative service providers, online
        mistakes, 233–234
    financial, emotional, physical, and
        spiritual (FEPS) return on
        investment, 107
    free services, 115–116
    income creation, 107
    offerings, 94, 96–98
    packages, offering, 264
    promotion, 257
    providers, 262, 264
    quality, 66
    selling, 99
    standards, 66–67
Short-term profits, maximization, 113
Simple selling, 105
Sincerity, expression, 134
Six Core Self-Promotion
        Strategies, 106, 123
Skill development, 117
Slim, Pam, 142
Snapchat, activity, 256
Social Intelligence (Goleman), 170
Socially successful conduct, 170–171
Social media
    Book Yourself Solid System,
        application, 257–259
    content, exploitation, 267
    keep-in-touch tool, 98
    networking, ROI, 255
    platform, 231, 239–240, 254
    profiles, representation, 64
    purposes, 257
    ROI, 265–266
    sites, article publication, 225
    strategy (optimization), Book Yourself
        Solid System (usage), 257–259
    usage, 152–154
Soul, presence, 136
Speaking engagements, 259
    acronyms, avoidance, 207
    audience, relationship, 104, 206
    big moments, center stage (usage), 208
    booking, 197–200
    conclusion/follow-up, importance, 202–203
    decision, 212

    embellishment, usage, 207
    end goal, 200
    excitement/attention, contrast/extremes
        (usage), 205
    ideas, unpacking, 204
    idioms, usage (caution), 207
    impression, making, 201–203
    introduction, development, 201–202
    invitation, 198
    jokes, usage (caution), 207, 210
    material, knowledge, 202
    open hands, usage, 204
    preparation, 199–200
    presentation, setup/breakdown time
        (allowance), 200
    props, usage, 205
    public speaking, performance tips, 203–211
    rehearsal, learning, 208
    self-proclaimed experts, enlisting, 206
    speech length, reduction, 203–204
    stage blocking, understanding, 208
    stand and land, 205
    stand-up comedy, study, 207
    storyteller voice, avoidance, 210
    storytelling, 206
    video, presentation, 209
    voice/speech training, importance, 209
    yelling, avoidance, 210–211
Speaking strategy, 238
Speaking venue, knowledge/
        understanding, 200
Special announcements, 94, 97–98
Spelling/grammar, checking, 226
Sponsorship, 194
Steal the Show (Port), 189, 211
Strangers, friendship, 76–77
Strategic alliance partners,
        cross-promotion, 257
Subject-matter expert, collaboration, 214
Success metrics, discussion, 264–265
Super simple selling, 120, 258

T

Tagline, identification, 44–46
Target audience, 225–226
    learning interest, 215
    relationship, 218
    understanding, 218–219

Target client/customer, 77–81
Target market
  activity, 19
  challenge, 25–26
  desires, identification, 27–28
  identification, 18–26
  introduction, 53
  problems, identification/summarization, 53
  selection, 19, 33
Teaser title, usage, 219
Tell-a-friend forms, usage, 246–247
Testimonials
  obtaining/showcasing, 64–65
  usage, 100
Text
  message, sending, 146
  outloud reading, 100
Time
  leverage, 89
  maximization, 127
  money trade, 110–111
  open-ended amount, fee
    (recurrence), 111
Time-sensitive discounts, 115
Tool showcase, 263
Topic, defining, 216
Trade shows, attendance/contacts, 148
Training, completion, 117
Trust
  building, 61, 124
  creation, 69
  earning, 123
  relationships, building, 61, 75–76

U
Uniqueness, 41–43
Urgent needs, identification, 27–28

V
Value
  addition, 99
  providing, 134
Values, highlighting, 264
Video
  amplification, 261
  capture, 260–261
  content, creation, 260–261
  edit, 261

Viral marketing campaign, creation, 99
Visibility
  creation, 257
  gaining, 69
Visitor conversion, principles, 242, 251–253
Voice/speech training, importance, 209
Voss, Chris, 142

W
Warrillow, John, 142
Webinars, client contact opportunity, 190
Website
  24/7 passive-revenue profit machine,
    creation, 233
  benefits, 232–233
  budget, consideration, 239–240
  building, 64, 240–241
  call to action, clarity, 235
  case studies, display, 235
  client filtering, 233, 236
  contest, usage, 246
  credibility (building), social proof
    (usage), 235
  cross-promotion, marketing partners
    (usage), 245–246
  database, building, 233
  design, 30, 231, 232
  development, offerings, 30
  elements, 234–237
  email signature, leverage, 244
  global marketplace reach, 233
  offerings, communication
    (clarity), 234–235
  online press releases, usage, 248–249
  online reviews, power
    (leverage), 247–248
  optimization, 242–250
  pay-per-click advertising,
    profitability, 249–250
  platform, selection, 239–240
  portfolio website, 233–234
  potential, maximization, 237–239
  purpose, 232–233
  self-expression, opportunity, 233
  special promotions, co-production, 246
  strategy, 259
  targeted traffic, attraction, 243
  tell-a-friend forms, usage, 246–247

Website (*Continued*)
  traffic, 248, 257
  visitors, attraction, 231, 242
Weekly creative challenge, offering, 191
Weekly roundups, usage, 264
Whatever-It-Takes-Direct
    Outreach, 174–175
What You Do, discussion process, 49
Who Statement, 43, 45, 54
"Why E-Mail No Longer Rules,"
    152–153
Why You Do It statement, 44–46
Win Without Pitching Manifesto, The
    (Enns), 142
Word count, listing, 226
Work, familiarity (demonstration), 161
Workshops, promotion, 265
Workspace, invitation, 263
Writing. *See* Book Yourself Solid
    Writing Strategy
  article, 220–228
  attention-grabbing title,
    creation, 219–220
  body, 221–222
  conclusion, 222–223
  editors, usage, 228–229
  exit process, 214–215
  focus, 216–217
  guidelines, request, 227
  introduction, creation, 220–221

  keywords/keyword phrases,
    selection, 226
  layout, consistency, 221–222
  lists, usage, 221
  main points, restatement, 223
  objective, determination, 217
  online publication, 225
  positive note, 223
  proofreading, 224
  query letter, 228
  resource box, usage, 223
  social media platform, 259
  spelling/grammar, checking, 226
  strategy, 239
  subheadings, usage, 221
  subject, decision, 215–216
  teaser title, usage, 219
  title, optimization, 220
  topic, selection, 216–219
  word count, listing, 226

X
X (formerly Twitter)
  activity, 256
  keep-in-touch tool, 98

Y
Yahoo! News, press release placement, 248
Your Body of Work (Slim), 142
YouTube, activity, 256